For the Birds

For the Birds

AMERICAN ORNITHOLOGIST
MARGARET MORSE NICE

Marilyn Bailey Ogilvie

UNIVERSITY OF OKLAHOMA PRESS : NORMAN

Also by Marilyn Bailey Ogilvie

Women in Science: Antiquity through the Nineteenth Century; A Biographical Dictionary with Annotated Bibliography (Cambridge, Mass., 1986)

(with Kerry Lynne Meek) *Women in Science: An Annotated Bibliography* (New York, 1996)

(and Clifford J. Choquette) *A Dame Full of Vim and Vigor: A Biography of Alice Middleton Boring, Biologist in China* (Amsterdam, 1999)

(and Joy Harvey, eds.) *Biographical Dictionary of Women in Science: Pioneering Lives from Ancient Times to the Mid-20th Century* (New York, 2000)

Marie Curie: A Biography (Westport, Conn., 2004)

Searching the Stars: The Story of Caroline Herschel (Stroud, Gloucestershire, 2008)

This book is published with the generous assistance of the Wallace C. Thompson Endowment Fund, University of Oklahoma Foundation.

LIBRARY OF CONGRESS CATALOGING-IN-PUBLICATION DATA

Name: Ogilvie, Marilyn Bailey, author.

Title: For the birds : American ornithologist Margaret Morse Nice / Marilyn Bailey Ogilvie.

Description: Norman : University of Oklahoma Press, 2018 | Includes bibliographical references and index.

Identifiers: LCCN 2018002703 | ISBN 978-0-8061-6069-6 (hardcover : alk. paper)

Subjects: LCSH: Nice, Margaret Morse, 1883– | Ornithologists—United States—Biography.

Classification: LCC QL31.N5 O35 2018 | DDC 598.092 [B] —dc23

LC record available at https://lccn.loc.gov/2018002703

To my good friend
and esteemed colleague
Joy Harvey

CONTENTS

ILLUSTRATIONS

PREFACE

I have been publishing biographies of women scientists since 1986, when MIT Press published my 186-entry bio/bibliographic dictionary.[1] I then coedited a two-volume 2,500-person biographical dictionary with Joy Harvey, published by Routledge in 2000.[2] Harvey and I were inspired, as were others working on women scientists, by Margaret Rossiter's triad of books on women in science in America (1982, 1998, 2012). Many new short biographies, encyclopedia articles, and full-length biographies of women scientists began to appear after Rossiter's initial book. Thematic studies of women in science soon appeared in multiple collections. I, along with other historians of women in science, contributed brief biographical articles to many of these compilations. Although an interested reader can acquire information through articles about important women scientists, a more profound understanding can be gained through a longer, deeper, and more analytical look at a complete life within the context of the culture. A full-length biography provides the reader with an in-depth view of the education, professional experiences, cultural interactions, and hurdles experienced by a single woman scientist. After I had researched the short biographies, I felt encouraged to attempt comprehensive accounts of the lives of individual women scientists.[3]

My new full-length biography of Margaret Morse Nice discusses her research, her work in conservation and preservation, her productivity, her activities after the Second World War, and her social and political views. In addition to delivering a glimpse into early- and mid-twentieth-century scientific life, it discusses the special problems and opportunities facing a woman scientist. An understanding of Nice's international connections provides a broader view of the role of scientists in the period surrounding the Second World War.

I became interested in Margaret Morse Nice when I was curator of the History of Science Collections at the University of Oklahoma. At that time, Joy Harvey and I were working on our two-volume biographical dictionary, and Nice was one of our subjects. A manuscript written in pencil became available, detailing the early language acquisition by her three-year-old daughter. When I purchased it for the collections I realized that Nice, initially unable to continue research in ornithology because of domestic duties, had turned to considering the development of her five daughters. As her daughters became older, her domestic situation became more manageable, and she returned to ornithology. The more I read about Nice and her importance to both ornithology and ethology, the more convinced I became that she deserved a full-length biography.

The choice of Nice was fortunate; the material on her life and work turned out to be extraordinarily rich. Her many published works and extensive archival information have made this project not only possible but exciting. Multiple archives reveal the range of her scientific work. Amherst College holds a collection of the papers of Nice's father, Anson Morse, professor of history. The Mount Holyoke College archives include material relating to her college life as well as a nearly complete bibliography of her works. Two special collections at the University of Oklahoma, the Western History Collections and the History of Science Collections, preserve important materials, including correspondence between Nice and the ornithologist and renowned painter of birds George M. Sutton. In Ohio, the Columbus Historical Society has letters from her later life. Cornell University holds the largest collection of materials, consisting of eighteen boxes of Nice's correspondence with American and European scientists and a major collection of her papers. The evolutionary biologist and ornithologist Ernst Mayr corresponded frequently with Nice; his papers are held by Harvard University, and the number of letters between them indicates her extensive contacts with a major scientific figure. Nice herself published an autobiography that described the participation of her family in her scientific work. Many years later, her daughter Barbara added her somewhat different recollections of life in the Nice household. I have had occasion to correspond with Nice's grandsons, who have been extremely helpful in providing details about this remarkable woman.

As Nice managed her multitude of professional responsibilities, her role as mother to five little girls and as wife to her physiologist husband,

Blaine, remained central to her life. As I delved more deeply into her life, I realized that Nice's ornithological research, integrated with her complicated family life, her political and social ideas, and her relationship with European behavioral scientists before, during, and after World War II, make her one of the more interesting women scientists during the first half of the twentieth century.

ACKNOWLEDGMENTS

I am indebted to the many people who have encouraged me and provided much-needed help on this project. I am especially grateful for the support of Margaret Nice's grandsons—Barbara Nice Thompson's sons Bruce, Michael, and Dr. Steven Thompson; and Marjorie Nice Boyer's sons Drs. Hugh, Timothy, Russell, and Kenneth Boyer. Both Kenneth and Michael have graciously provided some firsthand recollections of their grandparents and have been generous in allowing me to use their photographs. Michael provided me with the autobiography of his mother, which was very important in understanding the family dynamics.

My conversations with colleagues have been very helpful, especially my many discussions with Dr. Joy Harvey. When I was working in the Harvard and Mount Holyoke archives, she invited me to stay at her house, and we had many long conversations about Nice and about how Nice both differed from and was similar to other women scientists. Joy's daughter, Katherine Harvey, often joined us in these conversations. Patricia Manville hosted me in Columbus and drove me to the Columbus Historical Society as well as the area around the Olentangy River, the area that Nice called the Interpont, where she did her Song Sparrow research. In the midst of a busy semester, Professor Sally Kohlstedt took the time to read two of the more problematic chapters and made appropriate suggestions. I am especially grateful for her help. Special thanks are due to Dr. Sheila Dean for her patient reading and excellent comments on the manuscript. Aja Tolman provided some much-needed technical advice. I especially appreciate the part that my editor, Kathleen Kelly of the University of Oklahoma Press, played in the publication of this work.

The four talks that I gave at professional meetings about Nice helped me organize the materials. I am indebted to Professor Pnina Abir-Am for inviting me to give a talk at Brandeis very early in this project and another very late in the project in Prague in 2015. Hosted by Professor Kathleen Sheppard, I gave an address on Nice at the Midwest Junto for the History of Science at the Missouri University of Science and Technology in Rolla, Missouri, in 2012. Dr. Van Herd and Dr. Angela Smith invited me to give a talk on Nice at a seminar at the University of Texas at Austin in 2013.

I am indebted to Professor Emeritus Douglas W. Mock at the University of Oklahoma for his help in sorting out modern trends in animal behavior and evolutionary biology. Our considerable e-mail correspondence encouraged me when I was on the right track and made useful suggestions when I missed some important details. My colleagues at the History of Science Collections and the History of Science Department at the University of Oklahoma, including especially Professor Kerry Magruder and Professor Emeritus Kenneth Taylor, have been very helpful.

The archivists at Cornell, Harvard, Mount Holyoke, the Columbus Historical Society, and the Western History Collections at the University of Oklahoma have all been very helpful in locating appropriate materials and in granting permission for their use. I am especially grateful to Lily Birkhimer of the Ohio History Connection; Virginia Hunt and Juliana Kuipers from the Harvard University Archives; Eisha Leigh Neely from the Carl A. Kroch Library, Division of Rare and Manuscript Collections, Cornell University; and Jacquelyn Slater Reese from the University of Oklahoma's Western History Collections.

For the Birds

INTRODUCTION

Blessed is he who has gained knowledge in nature . . .
who observes the ageless order of immortal nature.
How it is constituted and when and why:
To such the practice of base deeds never cleaves.

EURIPIDES *(quoted by Margaret Morse Nice*
in a letter to Doris Huestis Speirs)

Ornithologist Margaret Morse Nice (1883–1974) changed the course of American behavioral science through her two pioneering field studies in 1937 and 1943 on the Song Sparrow, *Melospiza melodia.* Although students of bird behavior understand her importance, few general readers recognize her name, much less her significance. There are many reasons this omission should be remedied: her outstanding professional accomplishments, her ability to balance family and career, her management of gender issues, and her work in conservation, preservation, and the popularization of science.

Professional Contributions

The European ethologists and Nobel Prize recipients (1973) Konrad Lorenz (1903–1989) and Nikolaas Tinbergen (1907–1988) praised Nice's two Song Sparrow works. Lorenz described them as the "first long-term field investigation[s] of the individual life of any free-living wild animal."[1] On Nice's seventieth birthday, in 1953, Tinbergen commended her research: "Through your works you have become known to ornithologists throughout the entire world as the one who laid the foundation for the population studies you so zealously persecuted [*sic*]."[2] Ornithologist and evolutionary biologist Ernst Mayr (1904–2005) also applauded Nice's work: "I have always felt that she, almost single-handedly, initiated a new era in American ornithology and [presented] the only effective counter-movement against the list chasing movement. She early recognized the importance of a study of bird *individuals* because this is the only method to get reliable life history data."[3] Nice's research methods were appropriated by subsequent behaviorists and ornithologists and served as models for their studies.

Although there is little doubt that Nice's two monographs on the Song Sparrow are her most important publications, they represent only a fraction of her lifetime contributions to ornithology and behavioral science. Her bibliography includes more than 244 papers, articles, and published letters; seven books and book-length monographs; and 3,000 reviews. She also presented a multitude of talks on her research at conferences all over the United States and in Europe. Her early publications, produced while she lived in Norman, Oklahoma, centered on the geographic distributions of various bird groups. Nice's first major work, her publication with her husband, Blaine, *The Birds of Oklahoma* (1924), was based on both the scant available literature and her extensive travels throughout the state. Although this work received good reviews, Nice realized that she had only scratched the surface and immediately began to prepare a second, updated version, which was finally published in 1931. In the interval between the publication of these two works, the Nice family moved from Oklahoma to Columbus, Ohio. Nice continued publishing her observations on various birds during this time, presenting papers at meetings, and writing reviews, but, most importantly, she began a new project that became her signature accomplishment. In March 1928 she banded her first Song Sparrow; Nice eventually wrote a series of articles in the 1930s on these birds, launching the research that established her scientific reputation.

Undoubtedly, another of Nice's important contributions to the field was her role in introducing European and American researchers to one another, resulting in contributions that would not have been possible without this mutual awareness of the other's research. These introductions became possible only because of her friendship with the German-born ornithologist and evolutionary biologist Ernst Mayr, whom she had first met at the 1931 meeting of the American Ornithologists' Union (AOU) in Detroit. The two got along well from the beginning. They agreed on the importance of intercontinental cooperation among scientists, and Mayr, impressed by Nice's facility with languages, introduced her to his European colleagues. Once introduced, she initiated a correspondence with many of them. Mayr also suggested a literature exchange.

Nice obligingly requested reprints from her European correspondents and became familiar with this literature, which was generally unknown to Americans. It was she who introduced her friend the American behaviorist Wallace Craig (1876–1954) to the Austrian ethologist Konrad Lorenz; the resulting interaction benefited both men. She also arranged for American behaviorist Francis H. Herrick (1858–1940) and Lorenz to correspond. This correspondence resulted in Herrick convincing Lorenz to prepare an English summary of his seminal *Kumpan* work (see chapter 13) for the ornithological journal *The Auk*. Along with Mayr, she organized Dutch ethologist Niko Tinbergen's trip to the United States in 1938, during which he met herpetologist G. K. Noble (1894–1940). His meeting with a skeptical Noble offered Tinbergen an opportunity to make a successful case for European ethology. International cooperation has been important in the development of most sciences, but it had been lacking in the field of animal behavior until Nice provided a conduit for collaboration.

One of the thankless tasks that cost Nice innumerable hours of work during her career was producing reviews and critical abstracts for the journal *Bird-Banding*, resulting from her interest in international cooperation. For most of her working life, Nice considered the reviews an important contribution. This journal's agreeable editor concurred with her plan to reorganize *Bird-Banding*'s reviews to include papers by European ornithologists and behaviorists. Since the other American ornithological journals initially refused to include European works, *Bird-Banding* provided a unique function, one in which Nice took pride. Toward the end of her career the reviews became burdensome, but when the journal could not find a similarly dedicated individual, she agreed to continue and was still writing reviews the year before her death.

A break because of health problems resulted in a shift in her research interests that included a broader incorporation of the historical understanding of bird behavior. After many years of pushing herself to the limit, in 1943 Nice's sixty-year-old body rebelled and she was temporarily unable to do research that involved physical labor. After the second Song Sparrow volume was published in the same year, her research underwent a period of drought during which she published mostly notes and reviews. Once her health returned in 1946, she again became engaged in several projects.

One of her major late-in-life efforts was a paper published in the *Transactions of the Linnaean Society* (1962), "Development of Behavior in Precocial Birds."[4] A second and slightly earlier project was on a subject new to Nice, the history of ornithology. This research, including quotations from Aristotle to Arthur Cleveland Bent (1866–1954), resulted in two papers, one in *The Condor*, "Problems of Incubation Period in North American Birds,"[5] and the second in *Centaurus*, "Incubation Periods throughout the Ages."[6] The latter paper represents an entirely different aspect of Nice's work. Just as her early research involved detective work regarding bird habits, so did her attempt to understand the historical source of errors in the research on incubation periods. The answers to the earliest problems she investigated involved personal observation, whereas the second involved extensive library research, with the latter enriching and correcting some of the errors that had been perpetuated over many years.

Family and Career

Although this biography situates Nice within her professional scientific culture, it also stresses her accomplishments as a woman who carefully managed her personal life while successfully diluting the prejudice that often hampered women's scientific achievements. Nice was both an ordinary and an extraordinary woman for her time. As an ordinary woman, she was a loving daughter, a wife who followed her husband around the country, a mother of five children, and a loyal friend. What makes her extraordinary is the passion she felt for her research in natural history. It dominated her life and colored everything she did.

The life of a scientist, like that of any person, is multidimensional and involves both personal and professional demands. However, the way in which scientists manage their lives is complicated by the requirements of their disciplines. In order to be successful, they must devote many hours to professional duties, and this sometimes leads them to neglect personal responsibilities. In the case of a female scientist, this relationship is complicated by the societal expectation that she should consider her family first, and then engage in her career only if it does not interfere with the former. The conundrum posed by these two aspects of Nice's life followed her throughout her career in science. The title of her autobiography, *Research Is a Passion with Me*, indicates her unwillingness to subordinate her research to other needs. However, she was devoted to her husband and children. In her own mind, she not only wanted to have it all—a family and a career—she actually had it, a conclusion one of her daughters would later question.

Even as a child, Nice was very much her own person—often on the cusp of rebellion but never totally willing to defy early-twentieth-century cultural norms. Once she had decided on a career and was able to convince her reluctant parents to allow her to attend graduate school, professional success became possible. However, she was never entirely free of societal and familial expectations. When she was well on her way to earning her PhD degree, she married, thus changing the trajectory of her life.

Nice's positive relationship with her husband, Blaine, and his willingness to help with their children and housework made it possible for her to conduct her research. A husband who helped with domestic duties was unusual in early-twentieth-century culture, but Blaine recognized the nature of the woman he had married and accepted her absolute need to do her scientific work. The result for the girls was a kind of forced self-reliance that worked better for some than for others. During the Oklahoma days when the children were small, the family often enjoyed outings that combined camping and birding. Having parents in Massachusetts who were willing to babysit when the need arose allowed Nice to attend meetings and work on research away from home. When the press of publication totally absorbed her, Blaine and the children were more on their own than might have been desirable, but from Margaret's perspective it was absolutely necessary.

The title of Nice's autobiography, *Research Is a Passion with Me*, is appropriate when we consider the diverse topics that make up her lifetime research corpus. Beginning with her work on the acquisition of language by her own children and ending with a problem in the history of ornithology, Nice exhibited great flexibility and a pragmatic approach to satisfy this "passion." Early in her career, she developed strategies to overcome what, for many, would have been impossible handicaps. Apparently destined to be an amateur ornithologist because she lacked a PhD degree, she used the resources she had on hand to achieve unprecedented success. While her children were young and she was more confined to home, she published papers on available subjects—her own children, especially their acquisition of language.

The purchase of a car in 1920 permitted her to collect data on the birds of Oklahoma, allowing her to recover her previous love of birds. While acquiring this material, Nice recognized that ornithological research involved more than mere species identification and the reporting of geographic distributions. She set about acquiring a personal ornithological library and began to rely on these printed resources to learn of the field's scholarly research. Nice also recognized the importance of developing a network of associates who could critique her work and whose research she could draw upon. As time passed, she continued to expand her knowledge and friendships so that she could overcome many of the obstacles that would have otherwise hindered her achievements. As her children grew older, the family required less of Nice, and research became even more central to her life.

At least one daughter, Barbara, did not think the arrangement worked out so well for the children. In the "Prelude" to her own autobiography, Barbara wrote that if she could write history differently she of course would have had Eleanor (the daughter who died as a child) survive. She added, "My sister Constance [the oldest daughter] would be an able, aware, productive woman. Janet [the youngest daughter] would be living a normal, productive life. Marjorie [the second daughter] would be gentler, warmer, responsive." Barbara believed her family lacked "the warmth" she wished she had experienced. There is no evidence that Constance, Janet, or Marjorie shared Barbara's assessment.[7]

Gender Issues

Neither of Margaret's parents believed that their daughters should prepare themselves for a profession. Margaret chafed under the "ideal" of becoming a "perfect housekeeper and homemaker." Probably because the Morse family was well off but not wealthy and always had servants, she never imagined that as an adult she would have to do much housework. Throughout her life, she did the bare minimum necessary and relied on her husband and children to take over the chores whenever possible. Keeping a spotless house, cooking tantalizing meals, and dressing smartly never appealed to Nice, and she seldom succumbed to the desirability of these "feminine" duties so touted by her parents. However, Nice was never completely free from cultural expectations. When she left Clark University to get married, she made a traditional choice that suited her family and compromised her dedication to research; she assured herself that she could do both. She and Blaine were deeply committed to each other, and he was willing to make compromises to keep his wife happy. Nevertheless, societal strictures meant that it was Blaine who would finish his advanced degree and have a paying job, and Margaret who had to be satisfied with following him and squeezing her research in between family obligations.

Gender affected every aspect of Nice's career, including her membership in professional organizations, her relationships with her male peers, her publications, and her rapport with other women ornithologists. Nice never quite forgave the Wheaton Club in Columbus, Ohio, for excluding women (see chapter 6). Undeterred in her early attempts to become a professional, she joined organizations such as the Audubon Society and the Wilson Ornithological Club that catered to amateurs. Although by the time she became involved in ornithology most professional organizations accepted women as members, during the early stages of her career a tiered membership structure meant that women were seldom able to meet the qualifications for the higher ranks. Only later in life, after Nice had gained respect because of her publications, was she finally able to reach the exalted status of "fellow" (1937) in the prestigious American Ornithologists' Union (AOU). In 1942 she received the AOU's Brewster Medal for an exceptional body of work on birds of the Western Hemisphere. The society membership that seemed to make her most happy was her election to the prestigious Deutsche Ornithologen-Gesellschaft in 1934.

Nice's publication success and accumulated respect helped other women ornithologists break through the glass ceiling of the ornithological societies. She had many friends, both male and female, in the ornithology community. For her women colleagues, Nice's achievements were inspirational, convincing them that they too might be successful. Her own role models included her friend and amateur ornithologist Althea Sherman; they first became acquainted when Sherman was sixty-eight and Nice thirty-nine. Then, as Nice became more accomplished and more certain of herself, their roles reversed. Although Sherman had collected reams of observational data, she published very little of it. Nice tried unsuccessfully to convince Sherman to publish and vowed never to get into a similar situation. She promised herself that she would publish whenever the opportunity presented itself. In various amateur bird societies, Nice met other women birders who became friends and correspondents. One of these women, Canadian amateur birder Doris Huestis Speirs, was so impressed by Nice that she founded the Margaret Nice Ornithological Club in 1952, open only to women.

Gender was important for Nice in her relations with her male as well as her female colleagues. Her strategy, whether conscious or unconscious, was to position herself as a student who had much to learn from those whose work she respected; these scientists included Ernst Mayr, Konrad Lorenz, Nikolaas Tinbergen, and Erwin Stresemann (1889–1972). In her relationship with these colleagues, Nice struck a critical balance. While presenting herself as a student willing to learn from their knowledge, she also had definite ideas of her own that were valuable to them. The relationship between Nice and these men was symbiotic. By introducing her to other important European scientists, they helped her publish in prestigious journals. For her part, Nice was very familiar with the American ornithological literature and informed her European counterparts of research that positively influenced the direction of their studies. Through her own work she convinced male colleagues on both sides of the Atlantic that a woman could accomplish excellent work on bird behavior.

Nice crafted her relationships with some male scientists very carefully, approaching them as a seeker after knowledge willing to share her ideas. She worked extraordinarily hard to maintain a correspondence with ornithologists and animal psychologists from all backgrounds throughout the world. This strategy netted her support, especially from her admired European experts. She was less popular among her American colleagues because she was not shy in her criticism of her own country's scientists who studied animal behavior, and she often disagreed with their approach based on human psychological behavior.

Earlier successful female scientists had often developed strategies to gain support from male scientists. These strategies may or may not have been deliberate. Depending on their personalities, some female scientists appeared self-effacing when interacting with male colleagues. The eighteenth-century British astronomer Caroline Herschel (1750–1848) denigrated her own accomplishments through humor as she chuckled over her reputation as a savant in a letter to her nephew, astronomer John Herschel (1792–1871). Because Caroline Herschel's observations did not threaten their reputations, many contemporary astronomers were willing to recognize her achievements.[8] The mid-nineteenth-century physical scientist Mary Somerville (1780–1872) also deprecated herself and received praise from her male colleagues when she reported that as a woman she had little originality.[9] On the other hand, French scientist Clémence Royer

(1830–1902) exemplified another personality type, and she did not hesitate to step on male toes, including Darwin's, when she felt it warranted. Royer was often criticized for her views.[10] Nice's personality lay somewhere between these examples. She managed to acquire support when it was needed, but without appearing self-effacing.

Conservation, Preservation, and the Popularization of Science

Nice's interest in the conservation and preservation of bird species formed a significant part of her life. Her early surroundings in rural Massachusetts encouraged conserving and preserving nature. As a child, however, she did not apply these principles to all plants and animals. She was convinced that some animals (birds) were good and others (reptiles and cats) bad. Recalling her early biases, she later modified her views to allow predators their place, but her love for birds never allowed her to completely overcome these attitudes.

In order to prevent people from making uninformed or misinformed decisions about wild areas, Nice engaged in education programs. Convinced that with the proper education people would see the importance of protecting their environment, she wrote and published articles in popular venues that would interest a wide variety of readers. Her advocacy took the form of letters to the editor, articles in magazines, a radio program, and a book for general audiences.

Nice sought to inform the public about the importance of conservation, beginning with her early days in Oklahoma. When she heard that hunters had requested a change in the game laws to allow an earlier season on doves, she undertook a study of dove nests, concluding that many unfledged birds remained in the nest during the proposed earlier season; Nice argued that it would be a dreadful mistake to make the change. Later, she was indignant when a portion of her overgrown Song Sparrow research area, the Interpont, was plowed up in order to make room for a community garden.

With the same goal of educating the public, Nice hosted an informational radio show in Columbus. However, her most ambitious undertaking was the popular book published in 1939, *The Watcher at the Nest*. This was based on two articles she had published in *Bird-Lore* in 1936, "The Way of a Song Sparrow" and "The Nest in the Rose Hedge," and she hoped the book would whet the appetite of the public for more information. Throughout her life, Nice remained a conscientious steward of the environment.

Humanitarianism and Political Involvement

Just as Nice's love for animals did not extend to the domestic cat because it was deadly to her beloved birds, her expansive compassion for people did not include those whose ideas she deemed harmful to humanity in general. After the Second World War, she was a potent force behind the relief effort to assist European scientists who were victims of the conflict. She helped friends, strangers, allies, and former enemies of the United States. She spent her own scarce funds to send clothing, food, and research materials to Europe. She was unable to tolerate the jingoistic, the bigoted, and the ignorant, and her letters to editors were scathing indictments of these people.

Most of Nice's political concerns involved conservation and humanitarian issues, but after the war she became a candid, liberal spokesperson against McCarthyism, despising its excesses. Her many letters to newspapers and magazines made it apparent that she considered much of the postwar anti-Communist rhetoric to be anti-American.

Need for Biography

Although historians of biology have recognized the importance of Nice's contributions to ornithology and animal behavior, and historians of gender and of women in science have noted her ability to manage a complex juggling of family and work when few women had a career, until now Margaret Morse Nice has never been the subject of a full biography. This work will remedy this omission. It relies heavily on Nice's own descriptions of her life as relayed in her correspondence, her autobiography and that of one daughter, and the words of her colleagues and family members. It also includes the perspectives of her fellow scientists to indicate how she fit into the scientific community.

Although many books and papers provide context for Nice's works, and some will be discussed later, two outstanding books explicitly discuss her work: historian of ornithology Mark V. Barrow Jr.'s *A Passion for Birds: American Ornithology after Audubon* (1998), and historian of behavior Richard W. Burkardt Jr.'s *Patterns of Behavior: Konrad Lorenz, Niko Tinbergen, and the Founding of Ethology* (2005).

Barrow describes the intellectual, cultural, and social climate in which Nice worked. He considers Mayr one of the first scientific ornithologists to appreciate and champion Nice's work; together the two of them were crucial to introducing the new field of ethology to the United States. Barrow credits Nice with providing a vital link between the American and European ornithological communities, noting that Mayr believed Nice was responsible for initiating a new era in American ornithology. Burkhardt also stresses Nice's importance to the development of ethology in the United States. He places her research within the broader European geographic context and clearly discusses her relationship to ethologists Konrad Lorenz and Niko Tinbergen. His description of the scientific theories of the animal behaviorists and his discussion of the effect of the Second World War on science were invaluable.[11]

Another excellent source is Gregg Mitman's and Richard W. Burkhardt Jr.'s chapter "Struggling for Identity: The Study of Animal Behavior in America 1930–1945" in *The Expansion of American Biology* (1991).[12] Although Sally Gregory Kohlstedt's *Teaching Children Science: Hands-On Nature Study in North America, 1890–1930* (2010) does not mention Nice by name, it provides perspectives on the nature study movement that influenced the future course of her life.[13] Bruno J. Straser's "Collecting Nature: Practices, Styles, and Narratives" provides a new and different theoretical perspective on the relationship between natural history and experimental science.[14] After Nice's death, the obituaries reflected the respect her colleagues had for her. One especially complete reflection was an eleven-page tribute to her accomplishments by her former colleague Milton Trautman in the journal *The Auk*.[15]

It is impossible to look at Nice's life and not conclude that gender played an essential role in her career. Historian of science Margaret Rossiter gave her a prominent place in *Women Scientists in America: Struggles and Strategies to 1940* (1982). Nice's importance as a woman scientist was recognized by Ann Elizabeth Dahlberg, who wrote a Harvard University BA thesis on Nice titled "Strong Sympathy and Fellowship: Margaret Morse Nice's Alternative Scientific Framework" (1995). Canadian historian of ornithology and ornithologist Marianne Gosztonyi Ainley discussed Nice's gendered life in an essay, "Field Work and Family: North American Women Ornithologists, 1900–1950," in the essay collection *Uneasy Careers and Intimate Lives: Women in Science, 1789–1979* (1987). Marcia Myers Bonta devoted a chapter to Nice in her book *Women in the Field: America's Pioneering Women Naturalists* (1991). On the popular front, Julie Dunlap wrote a biography of Nice for children, *Birds in the Bushes* (1996). Popular books on ornithology, such as *Neighbors to the Birds* by Felton Gibbons and Deborah Strom (1988) and *A World of Watchers* by Joseph Kastner (1986), include extensive discussion of Nice and her work.[16]

Through sampling some of the secondary literature, I will show that Margaret Nice was important to varied constituencies. Her rich variety of interests, plus her incredible energy in accomplishing so many tasks well, makes this early-twentieth-century woman an ideal subject for a biography that ties together the themes making up her life.

Chapter 1

FAMILY BACKGROUND
AND CHILDHOOD

O n September 26, 1883, the American Ornithologists' Union (AOU), an offshoot of the Nuttall Ornithological Club of Cambridge, Massachusetts, had its first meeting in New York City. Later that same year, on December 6, Margaret Duncan Ely Morse and Anson Daniel Morse became parents for the fourth time when their daughter Margaret was born. Margaret later commented in jest that 1883 was an important year for ornithologists! Her birth kept the family's boy-girl, boy-girl ratio alive, as she joined Anson Ely, Sarah Duncan, and William Northrop. The family continued to expand with the advent of three more children after Margaret: Harold Ely, Katharine Duncan, and Edward Stiles.[1]

Although there were no ornithologists in her background, the character of Margaret's ancestors influenced her future path, both positively and negatively. Both of her parents had long-standing roots in the New World. Her father was descended from an early settler, John Moss, who moved to New Haven Colony, Connecticut, in the early seventeenth century. The family name remained Moss until Margaret's grandfather Harmon changed it to Morse in the nineteenth century. Education was important to both her proximate and more distant relatives. Her father, Anson Daniel Morse, was an academic who spent forty years on the faculty of his alma mater Amherst College, where he was a professor of political science and history. He is best known for his participation in the nineteenth-century movement that emphasized political parties as the most effective tool for expressing the will of the people. As Calvin Coolidge's professor, he is credited with influencing the future president's political writings. More important for this biography, however, was his ability to stimulate his children's interest in books and nature. An avid gardener and a devoted explorer of the nearby wilderness, he encouraged his children in these pursuits.[2]

The first recorded ancestor of Margaret's mother, Margaret Duncan Ely Morse, was Richard Ely, who emigrated from Plymouth in Devonshire, England, between 1660 and 1663. Although the Elys for the most part were farmers, several were involved in missionary work. Margaret's grandfather Zebulon Stiles Ely had a sister who traveled with her husband to India as a missionary. Zebulon's brother, who was an excellent scholar and linguist and a graduate of Yale University and the Princeton Theological Seminary, also had missionary leanings but died before he could accomplish his goal. Zebulon Ely himself was greatly attracted by missionary enterprises but also loved the outdoors. Margaret never knew her grandmother Sarah Duncan Ely, who had died of tuberculosis before she was born. The grandmother Margaret knew was "Aunty Stiles," Zebulon's second wife, Mary Post.[3] Unlike her daughter Margaret, who showed little interest in organized religion, Margaret Duncan Ely Morse took to heart the religion of her relatives.

Margaret's mother, a humorless woman preoccupied with family, church, and community responsibilities, instilled a sense of duty in her children. As a typical Victorian woman, she engaged in domestic pursuits and expected her husband to play his role as a wage earner in the male public sphere. Apparently, she had no regrets that as a Mount Holyoke Seminary graduate she had no opportunity to use her education outside the home. As an adult Margaret began to appreciate her mother, but as a child and young woman she often resented her mother's acceptance of Victorian gender expectations. When her children were away from home, she wrote them innumerable "almost undecipherable" letters. Margaret absorbed some of her mother's characteristics as she grew into an adult, reading her letters aloud at the dinner table, and, as daughter Barbara noted, "We listened, though not alertly, for each letter contained only a recital of events attended, a lecture, a visit to an old family friend, a drive with some of her grandchildren. There was no portion of herself in her letters, no indication of her feelings."[4]

Writing about her grandmother, Barbara gave an example of her lack of expressed emotion:

> Once, when I suddenly realized that my grandmother had lived in
> the same town with Emily Dickinson, whose existence had become
> a matter of utmost excitement, I asked her somewhat tentatively
> what it had been like then. My grandmother was casual. "I used to

send a cake to Lavinia now and then. She was such a dear woman. Of course nobody ever saw her sister [Emily]." I waited hoping for more, a crumb for my adolescent devotion. My grandmother picked up her mending. That was all.[5]

Margaret seems to have had a much closer relationship with her maternal grandparents than with her father's parents.[6] Her grandfather Zebulon had a country home in Lyme, Connecticut, where Margaret and her siblings were free to roam during the summers. These summers, as Margaret noted in her autobiography, were filled by wandering with her siblings, cousins, and her aunt's dogs through fields and pastures, "sometime with pails for blackberries, but usually just for fun." However, even though she did not realize it at the time, she was learning to appreciate the outdoors. "The wide spaces, uninhabited by man, and our own freedom to explore, made of Lyme a magic place. All our expeditions were on foot or with horses. Thus, we gained an intimacy with our surroundings that is impossible nowadays with our incredibly speeded-up transportation that reduces one's impressions to a blur."[7]

Nice and the Nature-Study Movement

Nice's early interest in nature mirrored changes in attitudes toward natural history during the late nineteenth and early twentieth centuries. As historian Mark Barrow points out, a backlash occurred in the generations after the Civil War, largely because of the transformative social, economic, and technological modifications that shifted the United States from a rural, agricultural nation into more of an industrial, urban behemoth. A similar reaction had begun earlier in late-eighteenth-century Europe in the form of romanticism as a protest against the extreme rationalism and mechanism of the Enlightenment. The transcendentalism of Ralph Waldo Emerson (1803–1882), Henry David Thoreau (1817–1862), and Bronson Alcott (1799–1888) represented the unique American iteration of romanticism. The philosophical basis of transcendentalism translated into the "back-to-nature" movement in the United States and a new interest in conservation, collecting, taxidermy, and the formation of societies to further these interests.[8]

Children as well as adults were the beneficiaries of the new romanticism. The literature of the back-to-nature movement took many directions.

The idea that the glory of God was reflected in nature spawned quasi-religious writings that were deemed suitable for children. Others wrote of nature as a teacher who provided ethical lessons to teach children. Some authors, however, inspired children to observe the habits of animals while providing excellent information. Even stories that did not appear to have a didactic function but stimulated a child's imagination were common.

As historian of science Sally Kohlstedt reports in her research on the nature-study movement from 1890 to 1932, the idea that even very young children could and should learn about the natural world through hands-on experience with their local environment was pervasive in the early decades of this period.[9] Advocates also agreed that books that encouraged a child's imagination about nature were acceptable. Margaret and her siblings unconsciously participated in the goals of this movement.

Books on Nature

Both Margaret's mother and father stressed the importance of reading as an important activity for their children. Books on nature were an important part of Margaret's childhood. Charles Kingsley's *Water Babies* was one of her favorites, but the "most cherished Christmas present" of her life was Mabel Osgood Wright's *Bird-Craft* (1895).[10] Wright was the author of twenty-five works of fiction and nonfiction, the associate editor of *Bird-Lore* magazine (now *Audubon*), an avid conservationist, and an accomplished landscape photographer. She was also the force behind the establishment of an early privately owned bird sanctuary in the United States. Although Wright's life unfolded in a very different way from that of Nice, they both found ways to navigate society's expectations for a young ambitious woman.

Mabel Wright (1859–1934), the youngest daughter of Samuel Osgood and Ellen Haswell Murdoch, was born in New York City. Her father, a Unitarian pastor who later became an Episcopalian priest, was a major figure in his daughter's life. Although considered liberal for his time, he held traditional Victorian beliefs about the proper role of women. He influenced Mabel in her choice of career, marriage partner, and place of residence. She had originally planned to study medicine at Cornell University but succumbed to and accepted her father's views as to the proper sphere of women. Samuel Osgood wrote, "If young women wish to be lawyers, preachers, physicians, or merchants we would put no harsher obstacles before them than our honest opinion that such is not their providential career, whilst we would do everything in our power to throw open to their pursuit those spheres of action most congenial with their nature."[11]

Not only did Wright give up any desire to become a physician, she was almost viciously critical of women who made that choice. Late in life she wrote a novel, *The Woman Errant: Being Some Chapters from the Wonder Book of Barbara, the Commuter's Wife*, in which she wrote a thinly disguised and supposedly fictional account of the life of a woman physician, excoriating this woman's choices. The physician described in her book so closely resembled Mary Putnam Jacobi (1842–1906) that there was little doubt she was the model.[12]

Mabel's British husband, James Osborne Wright, a rare book dealer, commuted to work in New York City, and Mabel often found herself alone during the summers in their house in Fairfield, Connecticut. She spent much of her time roaming the byways of the Fairfield area. Her love affair with nature began at that time, connecting her to the back-to-nature movement. She began to write books on nature and specifically on birds, first anonymously for the *New York Times* and the *New York Evening Post*, combining an almost sentimental view of nature with notably accurate observations. She collected these articles into what became her first book, *Friendship of Nature* (1894). This volume combined poetic language with an accurate representation of the local landscape and its inhabitants. From this beginning she continued publishing and in 1895 produced a field guide, *Birdcraft*, which included descriptions of two hundred native birds and won her praise from ornithologists. The ornithologist Frank M. Chapman (1864–1945) admired her writing style and encouraged her to contribute to the magazine *Bird-Lore*. Wright's writing career blossomed, and she wrote numerous nonfiction books and children's books (including the popular Tommy-Anne books) and even tried her hand at fiction (not very successfully). Her work in nature education, including the founding of the Connecticut Audubon Society, was well received.[13]

Birdcraft's colored bird drawings caught Margaret's imagination, and she credited it with being the "first great step in my ornithological education." Another book, of an entirely different kind, equally influenced her development as a naturalist. She explained that while playing in the attic she had found a tattered, coverless pamphlet missing the information usually found on a title page. The pamphlet announced on the first page that it was to be "An Artificial Key to the Birds of Amherst." It was a three-part work: "Birds of Regular and Certain Appearance in Amherst at the Proper Season," "Birds of Irregular and Uncertain Appearance in Amherst," and "Birds Extremely Rare or Accidental in the Country." Margaret later found the missing publication information. The entire pamphlet was titled *An Artificial Key to the Birds of Amherst and Vicinity* (1887), written by Hubert L. Clark when he was only seventeen years old. These two books plus John B. Grant's *Our Common Birds and How to Know Them* (1891) formed the basis of Margaret's childhood study of birds. From *Birdcraft* she gained general information on birds and then applied this information to Clark's list. She corrected Clark on the economic importance of various birds, physically dismantled his book, interleaved her own observations, and reassembled it with a cover she had made.[14]

Margaret and her favorite brother, Harold, explored the areas around their home. He was her companion in her outdoor adventures and also enjoyed discovering and identifying birds. However, this companionship came to an abrupt end with Harold's drowning death in a stream near Amherst in August 1896, when Margaret was twelve years old. The entire family grieved after this tragedy, but it affected each family member in different ways. Literal religious beliefs comforted Margaret's mother and brought a kind of resignation, while her father blamed himself for being too busy to play with his son—"earthly opportunities forever missed." It was a family custom to sing hymns each Sunday night, and Anson Morse established a tradition to close the songfest with "Now the Day Is Over" in memory of Harold.[15] In contrast to her parents and grandparents, ten-year-old Margaret found religion to be of little consolation. Her sorrow was especially poignant, and she turned "to birds with a passion that was not to be matched for many years." This fervor resulted in her second surviving diary, from October 25 to December 6, 1896.[16]

Four or five months later, time had tempered some of Margaret's grief. For Christmas, she asked for any book by another of her favorite nature authors, Olive Thorne Miller.[17] Olive Thorne Miller was the pen name of Harriet Mann Miller (1831–1918), who wrote a series of children's stories that were mostly about animals. Although much of her children's fiction did not remain popular over the years, her nature sketches for children and adults are still read. After Miller's four children grew up, she became an avid bird watcher; this period lasted from 1880 until her death in 1918. Her treatment of birds was often anthropomorphic, but most of her facts

were accurate, reflecting a close observation of their habits. Miller's publications were important in stimulating popular interest in natural history.[18]

The Christmas of 1896 did not bring Margaret the book by Miller that
she really wanted. Rather than the desired essays on birds, her mother had
purchased Miller's *Four-Handed Folk* (1896), a book about monkeys. Her
resourceful mother found a way to alleviate Margaret's disappointment by
suggesting that she trade books with her sister Katharine, who had received
a book by Margaret's other beloved author, Mabel Osgood Wright. The
book she received in trade, *Tommy-Anne and the Three Hearts* (1896), made
up for her disappointment. This book was very different from the one that
had whetted her enthusiasm for birds. Still, she found *Tommy-Anne* fascinating, because the heroine was a nature-loving girl who had been given
magic spectacles that allowed her to talk with wild creatures in their own
languages. Enjoyable as this book was, she later realized that it had led her
away from serious ornithology.

Leaving talking animals behind, Margaret returned to the accurate
observations she had recorded in her notes written on *Birds of Amherst*. She
also produced a small booklet titled *The Fates and Fortunes of Fruit-Acre Birds*.
In this little book, thirteen-year-old Margaret recorded her observations of
twelve nests of Robins, Chipping Sparrows, and Least Flycatchers on the
family's land. She reported that out of forty-five eggs laid, six produced
fledglings.[19]

School

School offered few challenges for Margaret. She and her siblings attended
kindergarten for two years, followed by five years of a private elementary
school. Even though nature study was integrated into many schools by the
time Margaret was in elementary school, her teachers were more old-fashioned. "Miss Perkins and gentle, gray-haired Miss Hills" were neither aware
nor interested in becoming aware of the new nature-study movement. In
the seventh grade, Margaret entered public school, where she continued
through high school. The ninth grade, although not academically challenging, allowed her to be more creative and follow her own interests. In
Margaret's case, this meant observing and writing about birds. When bored
with school she amused herself by producing a newspaper and writing a
book. She attributed the book's authorship to a bird named Hermit Peck-
wood, a "conceited Hairy Woodpecker." Although she regretted it later, the

villains in her stories were predators, a prejudice she had absorbed from *Birdcraft* and *Tommy-Anne*.[20]

School had some pleasant moments. Margaret recalled writing a Thanksgiving story about the plight of two chickadees that mourned when the trees grew covered with ice and celebrated when the ice melted. Her teacher appreciated her story and asked her to write a paper on "winter birds." She proudly read the paper to the class and did not seem unduly upset when the boys teased her about Yellow-bellied Sapsuckers. They would ask if she had seen any Yellow-bellied Sapsuckers recently, and she would "gravely answer 'Yes' or 'No.'"[21]

After the ninth grade, Margaret found school more challenging. But for a person with her interests, the college preparatory curriculum at Amherst High School left something to be desired. In addition to Latin, Greek, French, German, mathematics, English, and history, courses in physics and chemistry were offered. But to Margaret's dismay, there were no courses in the biological sciences. Consequently, she had to pursue her interest in birds outside of school.

The school building itself captured Margaret's attention, not because of the Greek and Latin recitations carried on inside, but because of the colony of pigeons that lived in the attic. She climbed to the attic, brought home some squabs, and established them in the barn at her home. Margaret also enjoyed the walk home from school, for it gave her the opportunity to note the presence (or absence) of various birds.[22]

Pecking Order

In 1897, Margaret's father, Anson Morse, spent several months in California for his health, and Margaret's letters to him are filled with clues as to her future vocation. In her autobiography, the adult Margaret was able to more accurately understand what the child Margaret had been thinking with the help of these letters. Not only was the fourteen-year-old girl still fascinated by wild birds and their habits, but she was becoming a meticulous observer of animal behavior in domestic species. With her older sister, Sarah, she used the family's Brown Leghorn hens as experimental subjects. The two girls kept careful records of the hens' laying abilities and other behavioral characteristics. To their Christian parents' chagrin, the girls informed them that they had learned much from the hens about human psychology. Margaret and Sarah recognized the hierarchical system of social organization in animals, known as "pecking order," long before Thorleif Schjelderup-Ebbe (1894–1976) described the behavior of poultry in 1921. In her autobiography, Margaret reported that she started a notebook on the behavior of the hens, recording that "Rexie bossed Prexie, Prexie bossed Queerie but, amusingly enough, Querrie pecked Rexie." Unfortunately, after she had noted characteristics of about six hens, she became bored, assuring herself that she did not need to record all the details: "I'll remember these things all my life." To her disappointment, she later found she did not remember the details. When Margaret did read Schjelderup-Ebbe's doctoral dissertation, she reported, "It seemed too absurd to be reading ponderous statements in German of what we had known so well in our teens." Many years later, she told University of Chicago ecologist and animal behaviorist W. Clyde Allee of her teenage work and he replied, "That would have been a first [to understand pecking order]."[23]

Good Animals, Bad Animals

When a snake threatened her beloved chickens, Margaret took a stick and "beat him to death." Many years later she deplored her "behavior in killing that poor snake," blaming her "hatred of predators" on Mabel Wright's books. Perhaps her attitude toward stereotypes of animals and plants began to change after she attended two lectures on weeds given by John Tyler, professor of zoology at Amherst College. He explained that it was a great compliment to call a plant a weed, because it showed that it was hardy and successful in the struggle for existence. She later wrote in her autobiography, "This was a new viewpoint for me who had been taught to hate weeds as pests; who had pulled them up in the family garden at the stipend of three cents an hour, and under the spur of my Grandfather Ely's detestation of the graceful Queen Anne's lace had uprooted 'lace weeds' at the rate of one cent for fifty."[24]

Margaret had learned many things from her hens, including practical husbandry, keeping accurate records, and saving the money she earned from selling the eggs. Neither of her parents was happy with this hobby, which continued until her graduation from high school; her father disliked paying for the chickens' expensive "tomato-tonic" and did not appreciate their scratching in his beloved garden, and her mother resented the time Margaret spent with the chickens.[25]

Parents and Frustrations

Margaret's childhood provided her with the foundation that would serve her well in the future. It was just as proponents of the nature-study movement would have prophesied. Her unfocused experiences with nature as a child provided her with the tools she would use in "real" science. She also had a good deal of freedom to roam through the countryside, although she resented the strictures (real or imagined) her family placed on her activities. Margaret was encouraged to love the classics; had congenial brothers and sisters, and two maids to do the housework; and enjoyed the advantages of the proximity of Amherst College. All these factors contributed in different ways to the development of her interest in ornithology.

However, by the time she reached her teens, Margaret was much less content. She dwelled on the fact that her parents were old-fashioned and overprotective and did not believe that their daughters should prepare themselves for a profession. They clearly subscribed to the "separate spheres" ideology, insisting that being a perfect housekeeper and homemaker was the desirable ideal for a young woman. Whereas Margaret was definitely a free spirit, often rebelling against the mores of her family and the expectations of society, her mother was "a woman who rebelled in no way from the spirit of her time." Although Margaret's mother (also named Margaret) had planned to be a "daughter-at-home" and care for her parents, a life that she would have found totally acceptable for her own daughter Margaret, she married at age twenty-three and moved to Amherst, where her husband taught history for forty years. She was uninterested in intellectual pursuits, found solace in religion, was a good manager, and supported worthy causes. Her insistence on conformity from her children went against the grain for daughter Margaret. Although Margaret unwillingly conformed to her parents' requirements, she resented following their demands. These rules represented common views that "liberal" early-twentieth-century parents required of their daughters.

In 1918 Paul Popenoe and Roswell Johnson published *Applied Eugenics*, a eugenics textbook that may have epitomized the views of Margaret's parents, especially those of her mother, about rearing a female child. Equality, according to Popenoe and Johnson, meant that even though they could accept women's enfranchisement and access to higher education, they still denied their biological equality. To them, equality meant that "woman is as well adapted to her own particular kind of work as is man to his." A liberally educated woman's work should provide her with a general education but gear her toward her role as a mother.[26]

Margaret's thinking independently of her parents was buttressed by a lecture at Amherst by G. Stanley Hall (1844–1924), president of Clark University in Worcester, Massachusetts, when she was fifteen years old. She took notes in her diary and included quotations on his topic, "Love and Study of Nature." The part of the lecture she quoted indicated her state of mind regarding nature and religion. "Science, art, literature, religion (except Christianity) originate in love of Nature. Nature is the backbone of all education. Love is the great principle of nature and life."[27]

Margaret was incensed by the restrictions placed on women. She later told a story about Union Civil War nurse and surgeon Dr. Mary Walker, a visitor to her father's class, who rebelled against the acceptable women's clothing, including tight corsets and long, heavy skirts. According to the story Margaret recounted, Mary was continually being jailed for wearing men's garb. Although Margaret and her sisters still wore long skirts, they led "active, out-of-doors lives," took long walks, and rode bicycles. They also rode their "intelligent but rather temperamental horse Rex." For this last enterprise they wore divided skirts, as they always used a "man's saddle."[28]

Nevertheless, she wrote in her late teens that "we three girls all wished we had been boys, since boys had far more freedom than girls did to explore the world and to choose exciting careers." When her brother Will asked her what she wanted to do in the future, she replied, "I wish I could help Nature, make people love Nature more."[29]

Chapter 2

ADVENTURES IN SELF-RELIANCE
Mount Holyoke College and Clark University

College allowed Margaret to leave her sheltered home environment and spread her wings. Mount Holyoke College in South Hadley, Massachusetts, was an excellent choice for a young woman with Margaret's interests. From its beginnings in 1837 as Mount Holyoke Seminary, the institution emphasized the natural sciences. When Mary Lyon (1797–1849) first founded the seminary, her idealistic goal was to change the world for the better through educating young women. Holyoke's primary mission, educating teachers "with certified Christian character," expanded to preparing highly qualified women to work within many scientific disciplines.[1] By the latter half of the nineteenth century, competition with other colleges and research institutions had become acute. However, the niche Holyoke had carved out in the sciences and the connections it had formed within the evangelical community, and later within Protestant academic circles, made possible its transformation from a seminary to a college in 1888.[2]

By September 1901 when Margaret matriculated, Mount Holyoke had revised its biology curriculum to follow the pattern suggested by Charles Otis Whitman (1842–1910), founder of the Marine Biological Laboratory in Woods Hole, Massachusetts, and the American Morphological Society. Margaret's future teacher at Mount Holyoke, Cornelia Clapp (1849–1934), heard Whitman propose a restructuring of American science in a lecture at the Marine Biological Laboratory in 1890. In his lecture, "Specialization and Organization, Companion Principles of all Progress," he proposed a gender-neutral ideal for organizing not only the scientific research community but all of American society. With the scientific community taking the lead, he envisioned a social web emerging from the way that scientists ideally should structure their own research and teaching. In his scheme, research would revolve around mutually supportive individuals and institutions, including colleges and universities as well as governmental and industrial organizations. Duplication of effort would be avoided through division of labor. As Miriam Levin noted, his ideas would allow institutions to "integrate their smaller scientific enterprise[s] into a rationally organized system," and intellectual competence, not gender, would determine how research activities could serve society.[3]

From its origin, Holyoke had specialized in the natural sciences—but the college emphasized teaching rather than research. When Clapp heard Whitman's lecture, she already understood the importance of defining a niche for Mount Holyoke in order to ensure its survival and to secure its position as one of the best New England colleges. By adding research skills and preparation for graduate study to the natural science curriculum, Holyoke defined its place in the complex web of scientific pursuits. Through this expansion of the college's mission, faculty members (both male and female) were able to gain parity with the all-male college faculty in other institutions. The women's colleges such as Holyoke developed curricula that provided a certain amount of specialization as well as an introduction to research methods and theoretical development for the more advanced students. With the restructuring that followed Whitman's scheme, Mount Holyoke College changed from a strictly preparatory school for training teachers to one that prepared students for graduate school and ultimately a scientific career.[4]

Although the other women's colleges—Vassar (1865), Smith (1875), Wellesley (1875), Radcliffe (1879), Bryn Mawr (1885), and Barnard (1889)—had later starts than Mount Holyoke (seminary 1837; college 1893), they also benefited from Whitman's ideas. For example, Vassar College produced the astronomer Maria Mitchell (1818–1889), who not only became this college's first professor of astronomy and advanced the knowledge of her discipline, but, most importantly, trained a new generation of women astronomers. Bryn Mawr College also produced notable women scientists, such as the cytogeneticist Nettie Maria Stevens (1861–1912), who produced new data and new theories, yet beyond these accomplishments passed along her expertise to a new generation.

When Margaret entered Mount Holyoke in September 1901, she found a freedom that she did not have at home. The parental constraints on her actions and behavior that she found so onerous were no longer present. Her complaints about her parents were typical of those of teenagers of all times:

they were old-fashioned and overprotective. They probably insisted that she go to bed at certain times, not take long hikes by herself in the woods, or engage in any activities that they, not she, thought were dangerous. Most important to Margaret, they did not take her seriously when she proposed to prepare herself for a profession. When she was away from home these small annoyances were blunted. This is not to say that the college had no rules, but the strict discipline of the old seminary had been softened considerably. A ten o'clock bedtime was acceptable, and "not walking alone outside the village limits" could be liberally interpreted. Taken literally, riding her horse Rex was "neither walking nor alone." For the first time, she was able to organize her life in ways that suited her. From its inception as Mount Holyoke Seminary, Wednesday had been an all-day holiday, and with her friend Ruth Cutter from Brooklyn, New York, Margaret often explored the countryside on that day. The "organization" of her life included not *wasting* Wednesday in studying, and confining her academic work to "the five other weekdays and to the evenings from seven to nine-thirty."[5]

Margaret's academic work must have interfered with the more enjoyable activities of hiking and exploring. From a list of the rigorous courses she took during her first year at Mount Holyoke, it seems that she *must* have spent a good deal of her time studying. During the 1901–1902 semester, she took two French courses, two Latin courses, two mathematics courses, and one English course. Her second semester was also difficult; she studied medieval history, general history, and biblical history and literature, in addition to two English courses and two more French courses.[6] Still, during this first year Margaret and Ruth found time to explore the areas near South Hadley. Unlike her hikes around her Amherst home, these adventures did not include keeping notes on observations but instead just enjoying the beauty of the countryside. Margaret found another ardent hiker in English professor Jeanette Marks. A rivalry grew between Marks and the students, and in an attempt to impress their professor Margaret and Ruth attempted a forty-mile hike. Exhausted, they finally caught a train back to South Hadley. Margaret recalled that walking long distances just to say she had done so left much to be desired.[7]

During her summer vacation in June 1902 at an Amherst College tenth reunion celebration at her family's home, Margaret met Hubert Lyman Clark (1870–1947), whose book *Birds of Amherst* had inspired her as a child. She informed Clark that she had collected records of the first appearance of some summer birds that were even earlier than he had reported. She was elated that he did not consider her presumptuous but, to the contrary, promised to include her additions in his second edition of *Birds of Amherst*. She received the new edition in 1906. It credited her observations by reporting, "Additional notes on other species, particularly in reference to spring arrivals, have been very kindly furnished me by Miss Margaret Morse."[8]

Instead of returning to Mount Holyoke for her sophomore year (1902–1903), Margaret took advantage of an opportunity to visit Europe with her step-grandmother, "Aunty Stiles," and Aunty's friend Ella Higgins, along with one of Aunty's nieces, Mabel Coulter. During this trip she experienced a culture whose antiquity she had encountered only through reading. For once, birds took the back seat in her diary while history, art, scenery, and architecture occupied the foreground. The traveling party spent the winter in Italy, giving Margaret the opportunity to study the Italian language. This concentrated experience of being in an environment where Italian was spoken led her to a love of language, second only to her love of birds.[9]

Returning to Mount Holyoke for her sophomore year (1903–1904), Margaret found that her good friend and exploring companion Ruth Cutter had graduated. Fortunately, she found another like-minded individual, Lucy Day. This friendship provided her with a new Wednesday exploration comrade. Both girls traveled through the country on horseback and railed at the prohibition against girls walking in the woods and fields without a brother or other male family member. In a letter to her father during her sophomore year, Margaret retorted that if her parents were so worried about her adventures she would purchase a .22 rifle for protection. Her father strongly objected, replying that "1. it is exceedingly dangerous; 2. it brings upon a young woman who is addicted to it [shooting] the name of being eccentric."[10] In spite of her father's objections, Margaret bought the rifle. She and Lucy reenacted the Russo-Japanese War by shooting at paper targets on tree stumps. Her mother was not amused. She wrote to her daughter, "I cannot smile, I fear, on your rifle practice; it seems to me dangerous, and not an appropriate pastime for young women." Although Margaret confessed that she had disobeyed her parents in purchasing the rifle, she did not admit that she had also bought a revolver. Margaret's parents also disapproved of the canoe that she wanted for her explorations. They finally consented to allow the boat if it had "air-chambers" on each side for safety. Thus, Margaret and Lucy had more equipment for their adventures.[11]

Margaret continued with a rigorous schedule in the academic year of 1904–1905 that included philosophy and psychology, English, German, art and archaeology, zoology and physiology, biblical history and literature, Italian, and botany. During 1905–1906, she concentrated on science and language courses, studying geology, comparative anatomy, embryology, cellular biology, general botany, floriculture, and astronomy. In addition, she took both French and German courses, history of painting, and special studies in the life of Christ. Although she actually received her degree with a French major in June 1906, she chose to remain affiliated with her original class of 1905.[12]

Looking back on the academic courses that best prepared her to become an ornithologist, Margaret rated those in French, German, and Italian as especially important. These languages gave her the tools she needed to translate foreign papers and enabled her to communicate with European ornithologists. She also praised the courses given by excellent teachers in the natural sciences—geology, botany, and especially zoology.[13]

Margaret's geology teacher and friend Mignon Talbot (1869–1950) was one of a new breed of professional science professors. Born in Iowa City, Talbot did her undergraduate work at The Ohio State University; she then attended Yale University, where she earned a doctorate. She spent her entire career at Mount Holyoke College, rapidly progressing up the academic ladder. When she was Margaret's teacher, she was an instructor and a newly minted PhD. She quickly moved from instructor to assistant professor, associate professor, and professor and chair of the department (1908). When the geology and geography departments merged, Talbot became chair of the joint department, a position she retained until her retirement in 1935. Her research interests were in both vertebrate and invertebrate paleontology. Talbot's discovery of the approximately eighteen-centimeter dinosaur *Podokesaurus holyokensis* in the Triassic sandstone near Mount Holyoke in 1910 established her reputation in vertebrate paleontology. Postulating that this small dinosaur was a bipedal carnivore, she described it herself and became the first woman to name a nonavian dinosaur. During her thirty-one years at Mount Holyoke, she had gathered a large collection of invertebrate fossils, Triassic footprints, and minerals for the Holyoke College museum. Unfortunately, the building burned down in the 1920s and her specimens were destroyed, including the only extant skeleton of *Podokesaurus*.[14]

Zoology was Margaret's favorite subject, and she was fortunate to have three excellent teachers who provided her with both a practical and theoretical foundation. Louise Baird Wallace (1867–1968), a graduate of Mount Holyoke, earned both a master's (1904) and a doctorate (1908) from the University of Pennsylvania. After earning her AB degree (1898), Wallace remained at Mount Holyoke until 1912, although she took time off to work on her advanced degrees. She was an associate professor when Margaret took her classes. After leaving Mount Holyoke, Wallace accepted a position at Constantinople College, where she remained for thirteen years before returning to Mount Holyoke in 1927 as a professor. This time she remained at Holyoke for only one year, leaving to take a position at a historically black women's college, Spelman College in Atlanta, Georgia, in 1928. Wallace's research subjects were toadfish and spiders.[15]

Abby Howe Turner (1875–1957), another graduate of Mount Holyoke, later earned a PhD at Radcliffe College (1926) and then remained at her alma mater to teach. She taught Margaret physiology early in her career. Turner later became head of the physiology department and worked in close association with Cornelia Clapp to build up the science program at the college. Her research was on blood circulation, and interestingly, she made scientific observations on generations of undergraduates; she added these to materials she had used for her PhD dissertation, "Respiratory and Circulatory Tests of Physical Fitness in Healthy Young Women" (1926).[16]

Cornelia Clapp is probably the best known of Holyoke's trio of zoologists. Although she published little, she devoted much of her time to research. An alumna of Mount Holyoke Seminary (she had completed the three-year course in 1871), Clapp attended Louis Agassiz's Anderson School of Natural History on Penikese Island in Buzzards Bay, Massachusetts, during the summer of 1874. After this experience, she devoted herself to promoting the observation-centered method of studying natural history. As Kohlstedt has noted, the Agassiz school was important in training teachers and students in the methods of nature study and in bringing European ideas to the United States.[17] Although Clapp did not neglect theory, she was interested primarily in fieldwork. After spending a year teaching Latin at a boys' school in Andalusia, Pennsylvania, she joined the staff at Mount Holyoke Seminary in 1872, where she taught gymnastics and mathematics.

Having qualified by examination, Clapp received a PhB degree in 1888 and a PhD degree from Syracuse University in 1889. During the period of Mount Holyoke's transformation from a seminary to a college, Clapp took a three-year leave of absence for graduate study at the University of Chicago, where she received a doctorate in 1896. Upon her return to Holyoke, Clapp became professor of zoology (1896–1916). Much of her research centered on the newly established (1888) Marine Biological Laboratory at Woods Hole, Massachusetts.[18]

Although Nice studied ornithology in one portion of her first-year zoology course, she was neither impressed nor inspired. The students kept lists of spring bird arrivals, but Nice was unaware of any appealing problems left to be solved. She reported that she could see "very little connection between the courses in college and the wild things" she loved: "I benefited from the knowledge acquired of varied forms of life, but the approach seemed to me a dead one. I did not like to cut up animals."[19] Nevertheless, she found the four years at Mount Holyoke College productive and happy. One of the most important lessons Margaret learned at Holyoke was that she was not the only woman interested in matters of the mind. She singled out Mary Young of the Romance Language Department, Mignon Talbot, and Cornelia Clapp as especially inspiring.

Graduation! What to Do?

After graduation, Margaret was at loose ends. She did not want to teach, was uninterested in laboratory zoology, and did not consider herself an expert in any of the foreign languages she had studied. Her only choice seemed to be to return home to Amherst to become a "daughter-at-home" as her parents wished.

First, however, Margaret spent six weeks studying at the biological station at Woods Hole, where she found a new congenial friend, Emma Longfellow. Inevitably, the pleasant summer ended and she returned home. During the fall, she attended her father's American history classes, cared for his greenhouse, rode horseback, and generally did nothing she considered important. Although she went by train with her mother to California in February to attend her brother's wedding and was fascinated by the geological formations and fauna of the West, her interest in birds was not strengthened by observations on this trip. However, while she was in California she attended two lectures by William E. Ritter in a course on bird study at the University of California, Berkeley, and for the first time learned about the life-zones concept proposed by C. Hart Merriam (1855–1942). Through studying the indigenous plants of the San Francisco Peaks in Arizona and areas in northwestern North America, Merriam had observed that the changes in plant communities as latitude increased and elevation remained constant were similar to the changes seen when elevation increased and latitude was constant. Although Merriam attempted to apply his concept throughout the North American continent, it clearly worked best in the West. After learning of this theory, Margaret expanded her interests beyond the observational and into the theoretical.

The western trip included a visit to Mexico. Margaret was the only one of her party with a smattering of Spanish, although she complained that her Spanish was "deplorable." Commenting on the "strange trees and flowers and wondrous great fireflies," she said that the only birds she recalled seeing were the "superabundant vultures."[20]

Although the trip was interesting, when she returned home in May, Margaret had no more idea of what she wanted to do with her life than she did when she left. Frustrated with living at home, she did not consider any of the alternatives appealing, either. She found social work mildly interesting, but her only qualifications were a "smattering of languages and a kind heart." In spite of her previous antipathy to teaching in general, she decided that teaching nature study might be enjoyable. However, she complained that there were no jobs in this one tempting career. Although Kohlstedt indicated that nature study was becoming important in many schools and that well-qualified teachers were difficult to find, Nice did not find such an opportunity. She was also unaware that in addition to teaching, new opportunities were becoming available for writing curricula for schools, organizations such as the Boy and Girl Scouts, and even popular conservation organizations.

As a stopgap measure, Nice enrolled in summer courses given by the Massachusetts Agricultural College. Although she was unimpressed by the nature and gardening courses, she was greatly influenced by a guest lecturer, Dr. Clifton F. Hodge of Clark University, who introduced the class to the study of animal behavior. After hearing the lectures, Margaret talked to Hodge about studying the subject at Clark. He was enthusiastic and even suggested a project for her, studying farm-raised Bobwhites. At last, Margaret declared, she knew what she wanted to do. Her parents, however, were less than supportive, and she claimed that they "were full of doubts."[21] Fortunately, just before she and her brother were about to embark on a camping trip, she found the following note from her father on the breakfast table: "I am verging to the conclusion that in view of all your talents, proclivities, likings and dislikings and accomplishments, it may be advisable for you to specialize in the field of Biology with the purpose of teaching and writing."[22]

With the approval of her father, Margaret and her fifteen-year-old brother, Ted, embarked on a two-week camping trip in mid-August 1907. After taking a train to Hinsdale, New Hampshire, they "headed for the primeval forest," which Margaret had once visited on horseback. They carried all their "worldly goods" on their backs, and Margaret reported that all they needed "for a night's lodging were two trees to support our silk tent, and a source of water near-by." They trudged through beautiful country and walked ninety miles in all. Along the way, they met her teacher Mignon Talbot and were "entertained in her tent and the cottage of her friends." During their climb up Mount Monadnock, they became so thoroughly soaked by a continuous rain that Ted could not start a fire, "so our rice stayed in its bag." She also confessed that they had miscalculated on provisions, and on their final day all they had left was a "few crackers and a pittance of brown sugar." She later considered this experience a "parable of life; a journey, stripped down to essentials and involving struggle and hardship," which enabled her "to see and to love some of the wonders of the world."[23] This trip was the prelude to Margaret's graduate school experience at Clark University in Worcester, Massachusetts.

Clark University

Clark University's successful businessman founder, Jonas Gilman Clark (1815–1900), was born in Hubbardston, Massachusetts, about twenty miles northwest of Worcester, Massachusetts. Although his formal education ended after he completed common school, his mother inspired in him a love of reading, collecting books as objects, and libraries. After apprenticing himself to a carriage maker, he opened his own carriage shop and soon expanded it to include the making and marketing of chairs. He amassed a considerable fortune in the retail furniture business but, seeking a higher return, transferred his capital from furniture to tin. During these early years, Clark married his childhood companion, became an avid abolitionist, and supported the common school movement.

In the 1850s, Clark sold his interest in the hardware business, moved to the West Coast, where he manufactured high-quality furniture, and became the largest furniture wholesaler west of the Rockies. In 1860, he liquidated his businesses and reinvested much of the capital in real estate in the San Francisco area. After the outbreak of the Civil War, he became active in many Union-related causes and became an investor in the then high-risk and later high-yield bonds that financed the war.

In 1868 Clark returned to the East, bought a mansion in New York City, collected rare books, and continued to invest in real estate and securities. The Clarks moved to Worcester in 1878; Jonas had a new project in mind. His love for books combined with his lack of formal learning led him to accumulate a parcel of land in Worcester with the idea of establishing a university. In 1887 he petitioned the legislature for an act of incorporation for an institution of higher learning to be established on his property. He planned to model the new university after Cornell, Johns Hopkins, and the proposed plans for Stanford. He planned to first hire a president and faculty and then build up the library and undergraduate program. His rationale for starting with the undergraduates was that by the time the first seniors graduated, additional facilities would be available to house the graduate and professional programs. Although Clark pledged a large amount of money to this end, he recognized that for the institution to be a success, community members must also donate.

Clark and the other trustees hired psychologist G. Stanley Hall to be the university's first president. From the beginning, Hall's vision of the institution differed from Clark's. Whereas Clark wanted the undergraduate programs to be established first, Hall insisted that it was most important to begin with the graduate programs and add the undergraduate offerings later. He tried to convinced Clark that it was prudent to begin with the graduate university so that once the first students graduated they could teach the undergraduate courses. Reluctantly, Clark agreed to accept Hall's plan. However, as time passed, it became obvious that Hall had no interest in the undergraduate college. On October 2, 1889, Clark University opened as the first all-graduate university in the United States.

Even after Clark donated a large amount of his own money to the new institution and encouraged others to contribute by promising to match their donations, the community failed to respond sufficiently. Clark blamed Hall for many of the financial problems. From the beginning, Hall had made extravagant promises to the faculty that he could not fulfill. The donors blamed Clark for Hall's broken promises. Hall also misled Clark about the financial situation at the university. The final blow to their relationship came after it became clear to Clark that Hall, who had continually pushed the creation of the undergraduate division into a nebulous future, had no intention of initiating the program.

The financial situation at the university became increasingly dire. When Clark's admonitions to cut expenses until there was more public support were ignored, he resigned as treasurer, although he remained president of the board of trustees. After his resignation as treasurer, Clark spent little time in Worcester and cut his annual pledge. Hall and his supporters remained adamant in their refusal to establish Clark's proposed undergraduate college. They even asked Clark to add to his current gift. He agreed to give an additional amount for the academic year of 1892–1893 but refused to make a long-term financial commitment. Clark again proposed an undergraduate program that would attract donors and increase tuition revenues. Once more, Hall and the board rejected Clark's offer, claiming that scientists who had come to Clark for research opportunities and to teach graduate students would leave if they had to teach undergraduates, thus essentially dismantling the university. Clark's pledge for 1892–1893 was the last money he gave to the university during his lifetime.

When Clark's will was probated, he finally got his retribution. The university would receive a good deal of money if it fulfilled the will's requirements. The will established a new division that would function independently of Hall under a separate president who would also be responsible directly to the board of trustees. When the contents of the will became available, the trustees realized the necessity of creating an undergraduate college or losing the remainder of Clark's fortune.[24]

Margaret was unaware of the dissension between the university's founder and its president. When she matriculated in 1907, Clark University was a unique institution dedicated entirely to graduate students. Perfect for her needs, Clark was small (sixteen faculty members and sixty-four students) and had few rules to inconvenience the independent Margaret. The atmosphere was egalitarian. She claimed that all were on the same social level, from the president, G. Stanley Hall, to "Henry the furnace man." Especially important to her was the gender equality: "There existed a companionship very welcome to me" between the men and women students.[25]

Her chief companion was Edith Wallace (1881–1964), the only other female student in the biology department.

Hall's vision of Clark as a research institution appealed to Margaret. Two professors—Hall, professor of psychology; and Clifton Hodge (1859–1919), assistant professor of biology—provided Nice with the educational tools she would need for her future research. Nice claimed that Hodge and Hall resembled each other, for each possessed a brilliant, original mind but lacked the patience to verify his intuition. A German-trained psychologist, Hall was recruited from Johns Hopkins and was interested in child development. Regretting the increasing urbanization of America, he was attracted to the idea of nature study.[26] Hodge, however, most directly influenced Nice. A graduate of Johns Hopkins and a former fellow at Clark, he not only inspired her to come to the university but also directed her research. Hodge was very active in the burgeoning nature-study movement and published a popular textbook, *Nature Study and Life* (1903). As the movement grew, Hodge's particular views on the nature-study curriculum became somewhat contentious, but at the beginning of his career when Margaret encountered him, he impressed her with his zeal to both save the native fauna and flora and exterminate pests—"flies, mosquitoes, House Sparrows, and cats."[27]

Exposed to the "dynamic duo" of Hall and Hodge, Margaret was convinced that she had finally found her purpose in life. Her professors and fellow students demonstrated to her that the world was full of challenges waiting for solutions, and that "nature [was] waiting to be studied and understood."[28]

Hodge suggested Margaret's first research problem, the food of the Bobwhite. The original studies on this subject were done by Sylvester D. Judd, an economic ornithologist with the U.S. Bureau of Biological Survey, who examined the crops and gizzards of 918 specimens of Bobwhites collected in twenty-one states, Canada, and Mexico. Margaret's task was to add species of both weeds and insects to Judd's list and to observe how many of each the birds ate in a day.[29] She spent much of her research time hunting weed seeds, catching grasshoppers, and feeding them to the Bobwhites.

Her formal academic activities during this year involved attending lectures, seminars, and journal club meetings as well as taking informal courses in bacteriology, histology, and neurology. During the summer, Hodge went on a lecture tour, leaving Margaret in charge of the birds at his farm. She diligently performed feeding tests on the adults and chicks. One hen was a prodigious consumer. Her daily record consumption was 1,532 insects, of which 1,000 were tiny grasshoppers. As was her wont, Margaret made a pet out of one Bobwhite, which was the only survivor of its brood. When she left for the summer, she took the pet bird, Loti, with her, and convinced her sister Katharine to take care of him while she and her brother Ted took a canoe trip up the Deerfield and Connecticut Rivers.[30]

When Margaret returned to Clark with Loti in September, she found that several of her friends had left to teach at other universities. The departure of one of these, biology instructor O. P. Dellinger (1877–1957), made a profound difference in her future life. Dellinger was replaced by Leonard Blaine Nice (1882–1974), also a Hodge graduate student and an instructor in physiology. Nice was born in the year Republican James G. Blaine made his unsuccessful run for the U.S. presidency—hence his name, Leonard Blaine. He always went by the name Blaine.[31] When she met Blaine Nice, Margaret planned to work on an MA thesis titled "The Food of the Bobwhite" and to expand the subject for a PhD dissertation. Her family objected strongly to this plan and urged her "unceasingly to return and again be a daughter-at-home."[32]

Academic Degree on Hold

In her second year at Clark, Margaret continued her feeding observations on Loti, but her plans to both carry out a large series of such tests with baby Bobwhites at the nearby state hatchery in Sutton and go on another canoe trip with Ted never materialized. Instead she married Blaine Nice in 1909. A newspaper of August 17, 1909, reported that the Morse-Nice wedding took place at Grey Rocks, "Prof. Morse's summer home at West Pelham [Massachusets]." The ceremony was quite traditional, with Margaret "prettily dressed in white lace and net" and carrying "white sweet peas and maiden-hair ferns." Her sister Katharine was maid of honor; she walked in to the "Lohengrin wedding march" and walked out to "Mendelssohn's wedding march." One of the two ministers who performed the ceremony, the Reverend Austin Bradley Bassett, was the husband of Margaret's aunt. Since Reverend Bassett had come from Connecticut, where he was a professor at the Hartford Theological Seminary, the family thought it prudent to "kill two birds with one stone" and hold a christening after the

Portrait of a young Margaret Morse   Portrait of a young Leonard Blaine Nice.
Nice. *Courtesy Kenneth Boyer Collection.*   *Courtesy Michael Thompson Collection.*

wedding for William Duncan Morse, the grandson of Anson and Margaret Duncan Morse.[33]

Leonard Blaine Nice

After the wedding, the couple traveled to Blaine's farm home in southeastern Ohio. Here Margaret met her new in-laws. Blaine had grown up in a family even larger than Margaret's. He had eight siblings and was the second oldest of five boys and four girls. His great-grandfather Philip Nice had emigrated from Germany. Philip's son, also named Philip, married a Scotch-Irish girl, Rebecca Meek, and they had eighteen children. The sixteenth child, Fred, married Romina Adams, and they farmed on 167 acres in Athens County, Ohio. It was on this farm that Blaine and his siblings grew up, working hard, living frugally, and gaining practical experience in farming while learning about wildlife. Blaine's early education was sporadic. After attending an ungraded country school (a school that did not arrange students according to age-based grade levels) off and on, he spent only one year at New Marshfield High School. After this year, he got a teaching job at the same country school he had attended and where six of his siblings were pupils. With his savings from teaching, he was able to afford the preparatory school for The Ohio State University. Needing money beyond his savings, he convinced county officials to establish a new rural route and hire him as a mail carrier. At Ohio State, he helped pay for his board by waiting tables. Planning to become a physician, Blaine majored in zoology and graduated in 1908 with a bachelor's degree. He then went to Clark University, where he met Margaret, because one of his teachers, Frank Copeland, who had received his PhD degree from Clark, recommended him for an assistantship in physiology.[34]

Early Married Life

Marriage did not change Margaret's values. Apparently, Blaine did not mind sharing the couple's flat with Loti, Margaret's beloved pet Bobwhite. Loti was constantly underfoot and Blaine trod carefully, fearing he would step on him. Although Margaret never liked housekeeping or cooking, she did find that she enjoyed experimenting with the necessary tasks, while leaving time "for activities of more lasting value." As for cooking, she took a weekly class and learned from Blaine, who had cooked for his father's lumber camps. Eschewing meals that required time to prepare, she explained that her cooking was confined to "good and simple meals." By sending out the washing and ironing and doing the necessary cleaning chores quickly, she could save precious time.[35]

The project that Margaret was saving time to work on was a paper using her Bobwhite feeding data. Her mentor, Dr. Hodge, wrote in an introduction to the paper that it "presented the most complete and convincing statement of the food of any bird." He sent the paper to the prestigious ornithological journal *The Auk*. The editor returned it, concluding that it was too long but might be accepted if abbreviated. However, before she modified the paper she learned that the editor of the *Journal of Economic Entomology* was willing to publish the paper in its entirety. After "The Food of the Bobwhite" appeared in 1910, it received a scathing critical review from W. L. McAtee (1883–1962), economic entomologist of the U.S. Biological Survey, who claimed that Hodge had praised the paper too highly. It was fallacious, he complained, to draw conclusions about the food of a wild species by learning what a captive individual would eat. He went on to heap scorn on the idea that it was important to discover that a Bobwhite would eat clothes moths, mosquitoes, and houseflies. Finally, he found that "the paper fails as a contribution to knowledge of the economic value of the Bobwhite."[36]

Although neither Dr. Hodge nor Margaret replied to the critique, Hodge justified Margaret's work by insisting that he hoped to have the Bobwhite in semidomestication everywhere, "so that household pests *could* be eaten by such birds." Although Margaret agreed with much of McAtee's analysis, she objected to his statement that the experiments on the quantity of food consumed were "even more disappointing" than those on the objects eaten. She explained that her data were very similar to those of an earlier study by Sylvester D. Judd on the specimens collected in crops and gizzards. Nevertheless, Margaret was later relieved that bird enthusiasts seldom read this rather obscure journal. She, on the other hand, purchased three hundred reprints and sent them to friends, relatives, and state and government game departments. In spite of McAtee, she received good publicity from the article and was quoted in several popular books and journals.[37]

In a letter to her 1905 classmates at Mount Holyoke, Margaret described her early life with Blaine:

> In 1908 I was studying biology at Clark University, intending to go on for a Ph.D. But instead I married a fellow student, Leonard Blaine Nice, a graduate of Ohio University. We kept house in Worcester for two years; I like cooking but don't care to spend too much time on it. Most of my energies were spent in university work, both on my own problems and those of my husband's [*sic*]. A year and a half ago we came to Cambridge, Mr. Nice having an instructorship in physiology in the Harvard Medical School. We find Cambridge and Boston intensely interesting; perhaps I appreciate more than anything else the Harvard library. We have two lovely little girls, two and a half years and three months old. They are our joy and pride.[38]

In September 1913, Margaret and Blaine left the East to take a position in Norman, Oklahoma, where Blaine had been appointed professor of physiology and pharmacology at the University of Oklahoma.

Chapter 3

MOVE TO OKLAHOMA

Margaret must have had mixed feelings about marriage. Although she and Blaine clearly loved one another and he seemed willing to make concessions in order to make the marriage work, she was still concerned that her professional dreams would be compromised. Her parents were elated that their unorthodox daughter finally appeared to be embarking on a more traditional life trajectory. In spite of her and Blaine's apparent compatibility, Margaret soon regretted that she had not continued to work for her PhD degree.

Tradition required that the man should be the wage earner, and for that to happen it was vital for Blaine to finish his doctorate. To enable him to do this, the couple stayed in Worcester for two additional years. These two years should have presented the opportunity for Margaret to finish her own doctorate, but she later explained, "No one had ever encouraged me to study for a doctor's degree; all the propaganda had been against it. My parents were more than happy to have me give up thoughts of a career and take up home-making, and in every way they helped us in the new venture."[1]

Because Margaret failed to get her degree when she had the opportunity, her intellectual endeavors were always subordinate to Blaine's, even after she became better known in her field than he was in his. When his career caused him to move, she followed. Life did not become easier with the birth of the couple's first child, Constance Ely, who was born in 1910 while Blaine was still finishing his degree. After Blaine earned his PhD degree, his first job was as a temporary instructor at Harvard Medical School. The move and the birth of the baby meant that Margaret stayed at home with baby Constance in Cambridge, Massachusetts, rather than pursuing her own intellectual interests.

Since Blaine's position at the medical school was temporary, when a position as professor of physiology and pharmacology opened at the recently established University of Oklahoma in Norman, he accepted it gladly. By this time, the young couple had a second daughter, Marjorie Duncan, who was born in 1912. With a three-year-old and an almost two-year-old, in September 1913 the family packed up, left the East, and took a train across the country.

A New Venue

It would be hard to imagine a more stark contrast between the lush hills the Nices left behind in the East and the bleak prairie that became their new home. But instead of being distressed by the new environment with its endless sky and limited trees, Margaret took to her new surroundings almost immediately.

"We were enchanted with the new, open country, the clear air, the prairie wild flowers, the Scissor-tailed Flycatchers, Mockingbirds and Cardinals, with the friendliness of the people and the mild winter weather. At that time there was no gas in town; the streets were largely unpaved and only two members of the faculty possessed automobiles."[2]

When the Nices moved to Oklahoma, both the town of Norman and the university were very new. In the 1870s the federal government had

Main Street, Norman, Oklahoma, in the 1920s. *Western History Collections, University of Oklahoma Libraries.*

commissioned a survey of the land that was later to become Norman. This survey, designed to provide a mechanism whereby white settlers could occupy the land, had originally been intended to house relocated Indian tribes. The head of the surveying party was Abner Ernest Norman. A member of the survey group carved a sign on an elm tree growing in their campsite that read "Norman's Camp" in order to honor their leader. Abner Norman returned to his home in Kentucky and never again visited the town named for him.[3]

As the territory (Oklahoma did not become a state until November 16, 1907) grew, party politics and individual greed were evident in the decision to establish a university in the growing town of Norman. Determinations had to be made by the territorial legislature on many items, among them the locations of the capitol, the normal school, the agricultural and mechanical college, and, of course, the state university. Coalition building was important in determining the location of the two "plums," the capitol and the university. Realizing that Guthrie and Oklahoma City were more suitable locations for the capitol, Norman lobbied for the university. In October 1890 a compromise was reached that allowed Norman to "locate and establish the University of Oklahoma." After the legislation was massaged until it was acceptable to all parties, the bill establishing the university passed and was signed by the governor on December 19, 1890.[4]

Campus of the University of Oklahoma in the 1920s. *Western History Collections, University of Oklahoma Libraries.*

Vacant prairie land half a mile south of the Norman townsite was selected for the location of the university. Faculty members were recruited, buildings constructed (although they often burned down in the dry, windy climate of a town without a fire department), and trees planted. The formerly treeless town benefited from the ministrations of the first president of the university, David Ross Boyd (1853–1936).

Although Boyd was only one of several people responsible for the "forestation" of Norman, he recalled the plantings to Margaret Nice many years later. "When we set out the first trees [in 1893], there were no woodpeckers to get the insect enemies and they could hardly survive the borers. . . . Finally I thought of the plan to haul a number of large dead trunks of cottonwood trees—beginning to decay and full of insects, and I 'planted' them in different locations. It was not long till the woodpeckers and other birds discovered them and made cavities for nests and inside of a year several nested; they soon settled the borers and other insect enemies."[5]

Birding in Norman

By the time the Nices moved to Norman, the small prairie university town had grown considerably. The Nice family also grew. Constance and Marjorie were joined by three additional children: Barbara Stewart in 1915, Eleanor Margaret in 1918, and Janet Duncan in 1923. It took all of Margaret's ingenuity and Blaine's patience for her to continue with her research interests. One of their immediate needs was a reliable babysitter. Fortunately, they met Gladys Hilsmeyer, who became a close friend and not only helped with the housework but stayed with the girls while their parents explored the countryside. As for the birds of the new region, Margaret had obtained a copy of a volume by Frederick S. Barde (1869–1916) titled Field, Forest and Stream in Oklahoma, published by the State Game and Fish Department as its 1912 Annual Report. This book included a list of 244 species and three subspecies of birds recorded for Oklahoma. This list was known as "Barde's List," and most of the records were supplied by Professor George W. Stevens (1868–1936) of the Northwestern Normal School at Alva, Oklahoma.

Unfortunately for Margaret, the descriptions seldom included the area in the state where the birds had been seen. She also complained that "some of the statements were clearly erroneous, so the list offered small help in telling us what to look for in central Oklahoma." Stevens was not the only contributor to the list, for twenty-three bird names were followed by the initials "G. S.," indicating that they had been reported by the Oklahoma Geological Survey. A zoology professor warned Margaret against using these "G. S." records, claiming that they were supplied by "ignorant students" who "misidentified many birds." It turned out that it was the zoology professor who was "ignorant," not the students who worked for the Geological Survey. "G. S." had stated that the Song Sparrow occurred in Oklahoma—a blatant falsehood according to the professor (who was indeed wrong), and one that Nice was able to correct after she had observed these birds herself. Nice later identified the offending zoology professor as Henry H. Lane, professor of zoology at the University of Oklahoma from 1906 to 1920. He sometimes taught an ornithology class, but "he was not too interested in birds."

Nice regretted that she had initially accepted the professor's evalua- tion of the value of Barde's list. "Instead of opening my eyes and finding Song Sparrows wintering in the thickets from October to April, I felt it was impossible to know what birds were supposed to be here. I gave up trying to find out what to expect and contented myself with enjoying the most conspicuous species."[6]

Margaret and Her Young Children: Speech Development

Since Margaret's experience with Oklahoma birds was less than satisfac- tory, because of both the time it required her to be away from her children and the inadequate information available, she turned to the education of her children. In order to give Constance (Marjorie was then just a baby) companionship, Margaret organized a Montessori nature-study school for six small local children from January through May 1914. Updating her Mount Holyoke class of 1905, she wrote, "My greatest interests now are the education of children and the study of children."[7] In June 1914 Nice traveled to Alva in northern Oklahoma to observe a "proper Montessori School." However, she also used this trip to visit the normal school in Alva and talk with George Stevens, who was the authority for most of the birds in Barde's list.

"I asked him [Stevens] *nothing about birds* here," she reported, but she did request his help in identifying the "glorious" wildflowers. The two of them rode the train back to Oklahoma City together. While at dinner with the Nices, Stevens showed them a pamphlet, *The Oklahoma Bird Day Book*, and explained that he was writing a book on the birds of Oklahoma. This was not to be, for he soon left Oklahoma and spent two years at Harvard working on a doctoral thesis on Oklahoma flora. In a letter from Harvard in 1915, Stevens reported that he still planned to revise and enlarge his book on Oklahoma birds. "I am doing some research work here in Harvard and have had to give only part time to the bird-book revision. The contract for the printing is let, and it is expected not to be very long before the book is ready. It will have 275 illustrations in color, and will discuss over 350 kinds of birds."[8] Stevens never published his Oklahoma bird book.

Children and Language

Although Margaret enjoyed the chance to talk about natural history with Stevens, she sublimated her enthusiasm for ornithological research into an attempt to understand how her daughters learned. In 1913, while the older children were still quite young, Margaret discovered a way to do research that would demand little fieldwork. Frustrated by the difficulty of seriously studying birds while being confined to home with her children for much of the time, she decided to investigate the development of vocabulary using her own children as subjects. As she wrote in her class letter, "I have published four studies on the speech development of children and have many other researches in various stages in [sic] completion."[9]

Nice joined other early-twentieth-century investigators (including the most famous one, Charles Darwin) who drew on their own families to study the emotions of children and how they acquired language. In gathering material for his *Expression of the Emotions in Man and Animals* (1872), Darwin conducted experiments with his own family members and the children of Thomas Henry Huxley. Darwin's oldest child, William, was his father's favorite subject. Darwin made a series of notes on William's development but did not publish the information until he became the doting grandfather of baby Bernard, his son Francis's child. After reading a paper in the new psychology journal *Mind*, in which Hippolyte Taine (1828–1893) described his daughter's early development and emphasized her acquisition of language, Darwin considered publishing his early notes in the same journal.[10] He sent these notes to the editor, George Croom Robertson, remarking, "If you do not think it fit, as is very likely, will you return it to me?"[11] Darwin applied the careful observation and data recording that served him so well in natural history to understanding the origin of children's emerging language skills and intellect.

One of Darwin's female correspondents, Bostonian Emily Talbot (1834–1902), was impressed by his paper in *Mind* and wrote to him asking for a series of questions that might be usefully answered by studying child development. Darwin's reply to Talbot included the requested questions and was circulated by the American Social Science Association, reprinted in a *New York Times* article, and later published by Darwin in *Nature*.[12] Nice used several of these questions in her own publications, including the effect of the education of parents upon the development of their children.

The idea of using one's children as research subjects gained momentum in the last part of the nineteenth and early part of the twentieth centuries. In the same report cited in the *New York Times* article and edited by Emily Talbot, additional cases of the widespread use of children as subjects were described.[13] An additional important source of information on children as subjects was supplied by an influential English-born German-educated physiologist, William Thierry Preyer (1841–1897), who spent much of his career as a professor of physiology and director of the Physiology Institute at the University of Jena. Inspired by Darwin's evolutionary ideas, he was a pioneer in research on human development based on empirical observation and experimentation. His landmark books *Die Seele des Kindes* (The mind of the child) (1882) and *Specielle physiologie des embryo* (Special physiology of the embryo) (1885) were basic to later studies in "scientific" child psychology.[14]

The observational methods described by Preyer were translated into English and widely circulated in the United States. They appealed to women, who joined the rush to study the development of their own children. However, one of the most innovative of these women, Milicent Washburn Shinn (1858–1940), author of *The Biography of a Baby*, never married or had her own children. Shinn worked as an editor at the *Overland Monthly Magazine* for ten years before she resigned to work on her PhD degree at the University of California, Berkeley. She became the first woman to receive a doctorate (1898) and the eleventh PhD overall from Berkeley. Her interest in developmental psychology stemmed from observations of her brother's newborn baby, Ruth. She systematically studied Ruth and meticulously recorded her actions and reactions for two years. For her dissertation she wrote *The Development of a Child*, published by the university in three installments. Her most important work, *The Biography of a Baby* (1900), recognized that although babies are born and grow up in many households, "very little has yet been done in the scientific study of this most important of all possible subjects—the ontogenetic development of the human mind."[15] Convinced that the human mind develops evolutionarily, she saw the need for accurate observational records of young children to support these theories of development. Although she found many of the early works on children lacking, she praised the contributions of Darwin, Joseph LeConte, and Preyer. She suggested that women were more suitable investigators of children's behavior than men, but she still recognized that the work of women who used their own children as subjects was inadequate, possibly because many lacked the needed education.[16]

Another American woman, Kathleen Carter Moore, writing before Shinn, produced her own version of the development of a child, crediting Preyer with inspiring her; she discussed the acquisition of language by children in great detail.[17] The articles and books already mentioned imply that these types of studies were becoming more mainstream during the years Nice studied at Clark.

Nice had no doubt been exposed to these ideas as a Clark graduate student. Although her own research had been on the Bobwhite under Clifton Hodge, she was also influenced by G. Stanley Hall in his role as a psychology professor. Hall was heavily involved in the study of the development of children. After graduating from Williams College, he attended Union Theological Seminary, where his work centered on theology. His interests changed after he read structuralist Wilhelm Wundt's *Principles of Physiological Psychology*. Studying under Harvard psychologists William James and Henry Bowditch, Wundt earned a PhD in experimental psychology from that university; he was the first American to receive a doctorate in this field. His special interests were in evolutionary psychology and child development. After beginning his career as a professor of psychology and pedagogics at Johns Hopkins University in 1882, when Clark University opened in 1889 he became president and, as Nice noted, was always available to students. Nice studied with Hall, who served both as president of the university and as a professor of psychology. In Hall's classes she probably would have been exposed to applications of Darwin's theory of natural selection that house the historical roots of evolutionary psychology. Darwin wrote in *On the Origin of Species*, "In the distant future I see open fields for far more important researches. Psychology will be based on a new foundation, that of the necessary acquirements of each mental power and capacity by gradation."[18] Darwin made his views even clearer in *The Descent of Man, and*

Selection in Relation to Sex (1871) and *The Expression of the Emotions in Man and Animals* (1872).

Evolutionary biology as an academic discipline began with the modern evolutionary synthesis in the 1930s and 1940s. This synthesis sought to merge disparate disciplines, such as population genetics, paleontology, cytology, ecology, morphology, and systematics into a single theoretical structure, evolutionary biology. The structure was further broadened with the work of Nice's friends and colleagues Nikolaas Tinbergen and Konrad Lorenz, who founded the study of animal behavior known as ethology. Edward O. Wilson (b. 1929) in 1975 then built on the works of Lorenz and Tinbergen and combined aspects of their ideas with evolutionary theory to form sociobiology. Adding psychology to the mix, evolutionary psychologists applied natural selection to human psychological adaptations. Thus evolutionary psychology itself became an eclectic discipline made possible only because of twentieth-century advances in evolutionary theory.

Studying with Hall, Nice would have been trained to interpret psychological traits such as memory, perception, and language from an evolutionary perspective. However, applying natural selection to the acquisition of language had become "somewhat of an intellectual orphan" during much of the twentieth century. Linguist Noam Chomsky (b. 1928) reported, "Evolutionary theory is informative about many things, but it has little to say, as of now, of questions of this nature [the evolution of language].[19]

Nice the Psychologist

Back in Oklahoma, studying her own children's development in the area of language acquisition was one way Nice could satisfy her passion for research. Her subjects were close at hand, and she could study the children while either at home or close to home. Child development was clearly popular with her contemporaries, and her own background at Clark University prepared her for this type of research.

In addition to her papers analyzing vocabulary, patterns of speech, formation of sentences, and acquisition of different parts of speech, Nice also published on differential creativity, the significance of "handedness" in the development of speech, and the importance of the outdoors in determining children's vocabulary. When writing about her observations of her own children, Nice did not refer to them by name but designated each one by a letter.

The Nices' oldest daughter, Constance, was Margaret's first subject; she published the result of this research as "The Development of a Child's Vocabulary," the first of eighteen articles she produced on the subject. Like Darwin, she asked a series of questions that she hoped could be answered by her careful observations. Some of Nice's questions were similar to Darwin's, but she was less concerned than he was with the origins of the behavior and more concerned with the effect of the environment on the development of vocabulary: "Where does he [the child] get his words, from indoor or from outdoor surroundings, from personal experiences or wider relations, from real life or from stories? What are the most important factors in his life when he first begins to talk and each succeeding year? Finally, what can we discover about a child's mental development from his vocabulary?"[20]

Margaret's careful records note which words Constance used at what age. She concluded that her first words were derived mainly from personal experiences. The next greatest number came from experiences in the outdoors, followed by those from the indoor environment, people, and stories, in that order. This order changed as Constance grew older. At three years of age, personal experiences still ranked first and outdoor experiences second. At four years, the outdoor environment claimed the largest share of her nouns and personal experiences, whereas the indoor environment and people were both less important than previously. As might have been expected, abstract words increased with each succeeding age. Although at the age of four Constance probably knew more facts about animals and flowers than many adults, she had only about thirty-eight abstract words in her vocabulary. Nice concluded that a very young child was not capable of understanding "much reasoning or religion." She concluded, "One gets into trouble in trying to superimpose too elaborate abstract ideas on a limited foundation."[21]

Nice followed this paper with a second, published in the same journal in 1917. In this publication she expanded the first study to include Constance's five- and six-year-old vocabulary.[22] In 1926, Nice was granted the degree of master of arts from Clark University for her work on her children's vocabulary development. Although the degree was not granted until 1926, it was for the work done in 1915. The actual granting of the degree was delayed until after Nice had established her excellent publication record so that her success would enhance the university's reputation.

Her second child, Marjorie, also became a subject for Nice's vocabulary research. In an extant manuscript, Margaret precisely transcribed Marjorie's answers to Nice's probing questions.[23] The stories in this manuscript illustrate the thought processes of this imaginative young child. At one point Marjorie was obsessed with death, particularly violent death, and she described animals being eaten by other animals. Cats were often the villains eating helpless birds.

When three-year-old Marjorie found her mother writing a letter to a friend, she asked Margaret to tell her friend what she (Marjorie) was thinking: "I love her. I like frogs and toads. I love Barbara [younger sister] very much and I love turtles too. I love butterflies and I love something else, Mother—you and Constance. And the moon. Put in the moon. I love Father, I love the University. I love the house, Mother . . . we found the mouse. I love the mouse. I heard a scratch scratch scratch. It was the mouse. Father killed him with the tools-thing and throwed him away. Did he come back any day?"[24]

Nice found Marjorie's development especially interesting, because this child did not say her first word until she was twenty months old, but then she suddenly acquired words so rapidly that she outpaced her sisters, with the exception of Barbara, who started talking much later. In her paper on this subject, Margaret listed all the words according to parts of speech that Marjorie acquired and when.[25] In a later paper she speculated on the reason for Marjorie's initial delay in acquiring words, followed by a rapid increase. In a study of seven children who were slow in acquiring language skills, Nice eliminated most of the possible causes such as health problems and mental retardation. The only consistent factor shared by these children was ambidexterity. However, she recognized that some children who were ambidextrous did not have delayed speech, and a hypothesis about this relationship would require many more examples.[26]

Barbara, the third child, was the subject of a paper titled "A Child Who Would Not Talk." She was much slower in acquiring words than her sister Marjorie, who after a slow start progressed rapidly. Barbara hardly talked before she was three years old: "Before this she had what practically amounted to a language of her own that was understood by almost nobody." Margaret considered this study to be important, because little work had been done on children who were exceptionally slow in learning to speak. Since parents were often faced with the meaning of this delay, she considered it an important topic. What should the parents do? "Should failure to talk at the conventional time be a cause of parental worry? Should the child receive special training in speech? Need parents feel that delay in the appearance of speech is in itself a sign of inferior intelligence?" When mental retardation was clearly not the case, Nice did not mention withholding "vital" articles such as food and water, as was suggested by a study undertaken by the psychologists Margaret and Smiley Blanton. The Nices did not try anything as drastic with Barbara, "and our practice of trusting to the force of good example was justified by the outcome." She did indicate that if Barbara's refusal to talk had continued much longer they would have tried more direct methods of encouraging correct speech. The Blantons posited that speech would be acquired only when there was a need for it. Nice "emphatically" disagreed with this explanation and substituted her idea that "speech was not primarily for purposes of communication but was largely a matter of self expression."[27]

Nice was also interested in the scientific aspects of delayed speech. She considered possible reasons for this atypical development. She hoped to provide information on the invention of words and languages by young children. But most importantly, she considered the course of language development in a child such as Barbara as providing "an enlargement of the normal process: the prolongation of the learning period [that] may offer opportunities for study of certain phases of development that are run together or omitted in the career of a highly imitative child."[28]

Child number four, Eleanor, had her turn as the subject of her mother's papers. Nice noted, "Every child is a law unto himself in the way in which he learns to talk," and "as examples of children accumulate, one becomes more and more impressed with the diversity shown." She speculated that health might influence when a child begins to speak. Eleanor, she noted, was "the most uniformly sturdy" of all their children, and "she began to speak earlier than Marjorie or Barbara." The structure of this paper was quite similar to that of those published on the older girls, noting which words Eleanor used when, in what order she used various parts of speech, and when and in what context new words appeared.[29]

By the time Nice investigated the development of speech in her fifth daughter, Janet, she had altered the general pattern she had followed for the four older girls. In an earlier paper, she had postulated that the length of sentences served as a criterion of a child's progress in speech.

She proposed four stages in the development of the sentence: single words, early sentences averaging more than one word, short sentences of three to four words, and complete sentences of six to eight words.[30] Through Janet's acquisition of sentences, Nice demonstrated what had previously been purely theoretical.

Nice was interested in imagination and the way it manifested itself in children of different ages. In 1919, she produced a paper, "A Child's Imagination," based on stories that Constance had told her and that she had recorded. She wrote that a child's "imaginations are akin to poetry; they increase the joy of the world." While concluding that children's imaginings were original and creative and contained "a spark of genius and should be cherished accordingly," she lamented that it was unfortunate that almost nothing was known "of the underlying factors that govern creativity or how to utilize them." The fragments that were known only emphasized "our profound ignorance of how really to educate our children and to develop their possibilities."[31]

Whether it was because Constance was the first child or whether it was because her interests corresponded more closely to Margaret's, Constance was the subject of more of the child development papers than the other children. For example, in 1921 Nice wrote a paper titled "A Child and Nature," in which she explored the roles heredity, environment, and training played in developing a child's interest in the natural world. She concluded that Constance was influenced by all three factors. Heredity provided an innate tendency, the environment was favorable, and training (although not "officious" instruction) combined with heredity and environment to produce a child who was fascinated by the natural world of plants, animals, and rocks. However, Margaret recognized that an ardent love of nature did not develop in every child who grew up under what appeared to be the same conditions. "Our younger children under practically the same conditions have shown this characteristic only in a moderate degree."[32]

Among children who were left-handed, through observing those who were forced to use their right hands, those who were allowed to use the dominant hand from the beginning, those who spontaneously changed handedness, and those who were ambidextrous, Nice discovered some interesting patterns in the acquisition of language. For her research on left-handedness, she studied the fourth daughter of a college teacher, a girl who was in her Montessori Nature Study School from the time she was three years and four months old until she was three years and nine months old, and again a year later. This child had been prevented from using her left hand until she was two years old. When Nice first observed her in school, few people could understand her speech. Her family's attempts to improve her pronunciation were hopeless. Although Nice found that her speech remained imperfect, it was decidedly better at the end of her observation period than at the beginning. By the time she was four years and six months old, she spoke English nearly as well as her contemporaries. Nice was convinced that the interference with her left-handedness created a disruption in the speech center that caused her speech to be unintelligible. After she was allowed to use her left hand she began to improve, apparently spontaneously, at three and a half years. Nice postulated that at this age, the right side of the brain "apparently gained the mastery over the left side," and the subsequent improvement was rapid. However, since the experiment did not have a control, it was impossible to say for sure that allowing her to use her left hand caused the improvement, for it could have been just maturation.[33]

In a paper on ambidexterity and delayed speech development, Nice cited several anecdotal accounts from children of friends in Norman. Both of the two Nice children, Marjorie and Barbara, who were slow to talk were ambidextrous at an early age. Nice recorded one entire day's conversation with two-year-old Marjorie in which Marjorie used only seven different words. Comparing Marjorie's meager vocabulary to that reported in the literature of one boy of the same age who used 5,194 words and another who used 10,507 words, Nice jokingly declared that Marjorie appeared "considerably retarded." Marjorie outgrew her ambidexterity, settled on her right hand, and acquired words at a rapid rate. Barbara, the third daughter whose speech was so alarmingly delayed, was also ambidextrous during her first months. By the time she was twenty-seven months, she had become almost entirely right-handed and her speech had improved.[34]

Other women scientists used their children as research subjects. Marie Curie recorded every aspect of her daughter Irène's life in the same way that she meticulously recorded every detail of her laboratory data, carefully recording her weight gain, diet, and the appearance of each tooth. In her description of Irène's activities, she noted that she "plays with the cat and chases him with war cries, . . . is not afraid of strangers any more . . . sings a good deal, . . . and gets up on the table when she is in her chair."[35]

Margaret Mead also took numerous notes on her daughter Mary Catherine's behavior.[36]

Even after her return to ornithology, Nice continued her research in developmental psychology. For thirteen years, she averaged a paper a year on speech development in her own and in other people's children.[37] However, the time she spent on this research decreased as the opportunity to study birds increased.

Family Life in Oklahoma

The rapidly expanding family of girls demanded coping skills that Margaret found challenging. In the journal she kept throughout her life, the Nices' third daughter, Barbara, provided information on family life as seen through her eyes. Barbara was born on August 9, 1915, in Pelham, Massachusetts, near Amherst, where her grandfather Morse had retired. Although the large extended family, consisting of parents, grandparents, and two older sisters as well as other relatives, welcomed her birth, Barbara always felt that as the third daughter she was at a disadvantage. In spite of assurances to the contrary, she was convinced that her parents were disappointed with having another girl. Margaret tried to reassure her by saying that although she had hoped for a son, when each daughter arrived she was delighted. Barbara also was persuaded that her two older sisters were her parents' favorites. Margaret, she believed, preferred Constance because they shared an interest in nature. Blaine, on the other hand, was closer to Marjorie because she shared many of his characteristics, such as being efficient and studious.[38]

There are indications that Barbara may have been a difficult child. As a youngster, she was often ill and probably needed more attention than the other children. It is also possible that Margaret and Blaine were not very tolerant of the demands that this sickly child, who was slow in acquiring language skills, placed on their time.

The first house in Norman that the Nices rented was very small. Their living conditions improved in 1918 when they moved to a bungalow at 445 College Street. Barbara reported that this house and the one next door had been built by Blaine. The two houses were long and narrow and shared a common garage. Although material objects were of little interest to Margaret and Blaine, Barbara resented that "a room of one's own, even less a bed of one's own was an idea that did not merit consideration."[39]

The lack of a car was not unusual in Norman during that time, but it certainly hindered Margaret from exploring the natural areas around the town. Whenever a car appeared, it was a special event. Barbara recalled an incident in which family friends drove up in a new car that was "tall and black," with wheels that seemed to be her height, and a "running board so high and narrow" that she was not sure she could manage it. When Eleanor, daughter number four, was about two years old, she slipped and fell under a visitor's car, and the driver, unfamiliar with the gears, first drove forward and then reversed, driving over Eleanor's leg twice. Although her leg was bruised, she was not otherwise injured.[40]

Family life during this time seemed to be quite pleasant. Barbara recalled her mother taking their picture as Halloween ghosts decked out with pillowcases with slits cut in them so they could see out, "seated on the pedestal flanked by a jack-o-lantern."[41] From this early time, Barbara appeared to resent her parents' lack of interest in material appearances. The house at 445 College had a large closet that contained an assortment of outdoor clothes, shoes, and leggings. The leggings were army surplus from the First World War and were highly practical from Margaret's point of view. However, Barbara recalled that she was mortified when she arrived at school wearing them on a stormy day and "at least one boy in my class pointed and snickered" at her "unorthodox clothing."[42]

The things that were important to Barbara's friends' mothers could not have interested Margaret less. "Housework in our family was considered a necessary evil, an impediment to having time free for accomplishing something 'worthwhile.'"[43] She credited Margaret's lack of kitchen skills to the fact that she had grown up in a house where there was always a cook. On her own, Margaret devised shortcuts and special methods to handle necessary tasks. When Constance and Marjorie became old enough to cook, Margaret gladly allowed them to prepare whatever meals they wanted. She then "took her turn in washing dishes."[44]

Neither Margaret not Blaine had a penchant for order. Barbara's journal provides some information about her father's personality and how he related to the family. His special area in the house was the cellar, which contained a coal-burning furnace and a workbench smothered under a large pile of unorganized tools of all sorts. Although he was competent and confident in the use of the tools, he was the only one who could locate the needed one "amidst the jumble of pliers and wrenches and bolts and pipe fittings, as only he had the skill to use it effectively." The children were not encouraged to become familiar with the use of these tools, and when they tried to help him in a task, "he grew impatient with the ineptness of . . . [their] effort and took over the job himself."[45] Barbara's son, Michael S. Thompson, observed that his mother complained that Blaine "rapped his daughters' knuckles with a ruler as they were learning to type if their fingers didn't move quickly or accurately enough over the keyboard."[46]

During the 1920s, it became more common for homemakers to use tools for minor repairs around the house, mainly because of the expansion of the field of home economics. There was an understanding that a woman who wanted to run her own home should have a basic knowledge of hardware and equipment.[47] In the Nice house, however, the use of tools was still gendered. Blaine was reticent not because he believed that females could not learn to use tools, but because he thought it a waste of time to teach them how to do tasks that he could accomplish quickly. To do so would also have required him to organize his own area. Since Margaret had little interest in general household maintenance activities, she was happy to have Blaine take care of them.

The children's favorite summer activity was visiting their grandparents' house at Grey Rocks, near Amherst. They could play in much the same way that Margaret and her siblings had. This part of the world always had a huge pull on Margaret's life. She returned to her parents' home for all her children's births, except for Janet, who was born in a hospital in Oklahoma City. Margaret's desire to return to her parents' house is somewhat surprising, since her personality and that of her mother often conflicted. In spite of their differences, the younger Margaret loved and respected her mother. As a grandmother, Barbara mused, she "fulfilled a child's image, . . . ever welcoming, ever loving, ever present even though we only saw her once in every three years. Letters from her arrived weekly, full of small events of the day, chronicling the activities of various uncles and aunts and cousins, never gossipy." She was a "small, indomitable figure" who directed the household.[48]

From the different amounts of text that Barbara dedicated to each grandparent, it was obvious that her grandmother Morse was much more influential than her other grandparents. Although she did not visit him very often, her grandfather Nice also made an impression on her. She wrote that he had a fiery temper and was a man of "firm principles and not one to push around."[49]

Frustration

After the summer visits to her parents and occasionally to Blaine's, Margaret was happy to return to her own home in Norman. But even in the larger house she was often frustrated. She described what it was like to have four children aged six months to eight years in what still seemed to be cramped quarters, with "no one enjoying housework, and much of the time without even a college girl to come in an hour a day to wash the dishes." She felt trapped in the house "with no means of transportation" but her "own legs and the baby carriage," and with "no free Sunday afternoon for tramps to the river." She felt that people assumed that "my husband and the children had brains, and I had none. He taught; they studied; I did housework."[50] Even by sending out the washing and ironing and preparing simple meals, Margaret could average only about an hour a day on research on speech development. She lamented, "I decided it would be better to be a bird. Birds are very busy at one period each year caring for babies, but this lasts only a few weeks with many of them, and then their babies are grown and gone. Best of all, they leave their houses forever and take to camping for the rest of the year. No wonder they are happy."[51]

On March 10, 1919, Margaret expressed her dissatisfaction with this period in her life. She felt compelled to do research, whether it was in psychology or natural history. She wrote in her notebook, *"Research is a passion with me; it drives me; it is my relentless master. Ten days ago I finished and sent off 'A Child's Imagination' [1919], and then turned to my mussed-up house and clamoring neglected duties. Many of these odds and ends I have done. Yet now I find myself longing, yea pining, to begin on my paper on Constance and nature."[52]* Luckily, this period was relatively short. She credits three events for pulling her out of her depression: "finding birds again; Eleanor's growing out of babyhood; and in the spring of 1920," the "purchase of an ancient car."[53]

Chapter 4

THE MAKING OF A CAREER

A newspaper article in the *Daily Oklahoman* (Oklahoma City, OK) in August 1919 helped inspire Nice to make the study of birds her career. When she read in the paper that the state game warden advocated an open season on the Mourning Dove beginning in August because "all the young doves are off the nest and strong fliers," she was certain that he had his facts wrong. Thus, on the August evening after the paper came out, "we packed our supper into the carriage with the baby and trundled off to the [Oklahoma University] campus." Nice immediately located three doves on nests and a week later three more.[1] She found a total of fourteen nests in August and twenty-eight new nests in September. In three of these September nests, the young did not fledge until October. Clearly the game warden was not only wrong, but very wrong. Nice wrote letters to both the Oklahoma City and Norman newspapers, titled "Doves Must Not Be Shot in August."[2] In 1917, Margaret and Blaine had already demonstrated their interest in protecting birds when they supported a ten-year closed season on Bobwhites and tried, unsuccessfully, to exert an enlightening influence on the Oklahoma legislature.[3]

During her early years in Oklahoma, Nice continued to be involved in efforts to preserve birds. In 1921, she wrote a letter to state representative Ralph C. Hardie opposing a bounty to be paid on hawks, owls, and crows. The bill had already passed the state senate, and she demanded that Hardie oppose it in the house, writing, "When it comes up in the House, I depend on you to oppose it." She discussed economic reasons why such a bounty was a bad idea.[4]

The dove campaign enthused Margaret to turn again to what she most enjoyed, research in nature. She continued to take long walks, admiring the flowers, insects, and especially the birds. After a particularly inspiring walk on August 20, 1919, she wrote, "The glory of nature possessed me. I saw that for many years I had lost my way. I had been led astray on false trails and had been trying to do things contrary to nature." She promised herself that she would return to her "childhood vision of studying nature and trying to protect the wild things of the earth."[5] Nice found it inconceivable that she had friends who never took walks in Oklahoma because "there was nothing to see." She was "amazed and grieved by their blindness." Nice "longed to open their eyes to the wonders around them; to persuade people to love and cherish nature." Perhaps, she suggested, "I might be a sort of John Burroughs for Oklahoma."[6]

When Nice first saw herself as a potential female John Burroughs (1837–1921), the likelihood that she would reach her professional objectives was dim. Although the number of women scientists had increased between 1920 and 1940, women had to work especially hard to reach their goals if their ambitions included a scientific career. Nice was always willing to work hard. Instead of the confrontational approach they had used in previous years, some women scientists adopted a new conservative tactic in order to obtain and retain career positions. Many tended to accept that inequity in the scientific workplace was something they could not change, and that the best way to achieve success was to work longer hours and to complain less about discriminatory practices. This not very rosy picture showed that the life of a career woman scientist required real dedication. According to statistics from the National Research Council (NRC) of the National Academy of Sciences, the number of women earning doctorates in the sciences increased in the 1930s and 1940s, although the number of men increased more. However, it is more difficult to determine from these data how many women became career scientists. Margaret Rossiter notes that the NRC's data do not include information on the careers of women doctorates. More important for the case of Margaret Nice is the omission from these data of women who never completed a doctorate.[7] Recognizing that she lacked the credential to compete in the career marketplace, Nice turned to a field in which an amateur of either sex could be successful. In this situation, it is appropriate that she chose naturalist John Burroughs as her role model. Even without a doctorate, Burroughs made a great impression through his writings on conservation and natural history.

Nature Study

Whether or not she realized it, Nice's ideas about nature fit neatly into the aesthetics of transcendentalism. Her childhood reading habits and her relative freedom to wander unfettered into the countryside prepared her for the ethos proposed by transcendentalism's high priests Ralph Waldo Emerson and Henry David Thoreau. These men objected to the idea that nature was something to be conquered and controlled by humans.

From her early childhood experiences with nature at Amherst to her later fascination with the lives of birds, Nice fit easily into the natural history movement of the late nineteenth and early twentieth centuries. When she again became interested in birds, the ornithological community was diverse. Since university degrees were not then available in ornithology, amateurs were tolerated. Those interested in bird-watching for aesthetic and conservation reasons represented an important part of this community, as did the collectors, taxidermists, and sport hunters who provided specimens for museums, universities, and private collections. However, unlike in the entomological and botanical communities, women were mostly missing from the amateur ornithological groups during the late nineteenth century. This lack may be partially explained by the emphasis on collecting birds and making study skins. These activities were considered unfeminine, but they provided important tools for studying taxonomic relationships and geographical variation. Collecting birds was potentially hazardous, often involving unladylike activities such as shooting guns, climbing trees, and roaming the countryside. In caring for their young, birds seemed to foster characteristics that paralleled women's activities in the home. Making a study skin out of a nurturing member of the household was considered unacceptable.[8] Although some women might have liked to join their male colleagues in these activities, they were actively discouraged by a culture still in the throes of the two-spheres concept.

Although building collections of bird skins and skulls was vital to the development of ornithology, few women were prepared to participate in the massive collecting and identifying of specimens from all over the world. This activity "depended upon legions of collectors brave—or man— enough to explore the wildest corners of the world for new and rare species."[9] Although this description is accurate for the early collectors, there is evidence that during the late nineteenth and early twentieth centuries a small dent was occurring in the two-spheres concept relating to nature, although not for women in the area of collecting.

Historian of science Carolyn Merchant asserts that during the late nineteenth and early twentieth centuries, some middle-class women as well as men began to enjoy outdoor activities such as hiking and mountaineering. Nice was an example of such a woman. Merchant's discussion appears to challenge the explanation that the lack of female collectors was due to a hesitation to kill animals, as she notes that some kinds of killing, such as sport hunting and fishing, became popular among some women as well as men. The participation of women in these activities was embraced by men who sought to enhance the image of sport hunting as "within the realm of genteel leisure," not as a "lower class, disreputable, and unsportsmanlike" occupation.[10]

Although both men and women were interested in conservation, Merchant notes that many women's societies were formed to participate in local campaigns to improve the environment. However, these were not professional or even amateur scientific organizations. The public perception toward men and women conservationists was different. "Men who saved birds and flowers were subject to potential scorn by those who preserved big game, forests, and mountains."[11] However, the position of women in avian conservation is complex. On one hand, birds were associated with femininity, and beautiful feathers were sought-after treasures to adorn female headgear. The society women who purchased feathered hats were as much to blame as the hunters who supplied them for depleting the avian population. However, other women protested the killing of birds to satisfy a fashion whim. Thoughtful people of both sexes recognized the danger to the environment that this fad represented, and recreational sport hunters of both sexes scorned the hunters who were interested only in financial gain.

Although female collectors were rare, ornithological activities such as bird identification could have been accomplished close to home. It was not necessary to kill birds to study their habits. Birds could be viewed in backyards and local parks. Migration times, fledging dates, feeding habits, courting behavior, and care of young could be observed and recorded. Nice opted for the nonlethal type of ornithology. Learning about birds made her more able to advocate for policies that would promote conservation and preservation. Even without formal training, she was thus able to become an accepted part of the community because of both her knowledge of birds and her ability to promote herself. As ornithology became more professionalized and joined other sciences in establishing standards for the discipline, she evolved with it.

Learning about Birds

The first Oklahoma bird that Nice investigated thoroughly was the same Mourning Dove that she had protected from hunters. She kept accurate records of her observations, noting the kind of tree in which each nest was built, the behavior of the parents, and a description of the juvenile birds. She sent her older children scurrying up the trees to report on the occupants of the nests found on the university campus. The Nices adopted a slightly injured juvenile Mourning Dove, christened Flower by the children, who accompanied family outings perched on the baby carriage. A second dove, Daisy, soon joined the human and avian family.

These two doves had a double purpose, serving as both research subjects and pets. Recalling her studies on the Bobwhite, Nice decided to do a similar project with Flower and Daisy as subjects. She kept careful records and presented a paper on their development and behavior (including the results of feeding tests) before the Oklahoma Academy of Sciences in February 1920; this paper was later published in its *Proceedings*.[12] A later note appeared in *The Auk* in 1929 on the same study, because her results of food consumption derived from night and morning weights of trapped birds did not agree with the results of a bird bander who had made a similar study.[13]

Since preservation and conservation played such a vital part in Nice's ornithological life, she found it important to gather sufficient data to support her contention that an early hunting season on Mourning Doves could adversely affect the dove population. Thus, in addition to her work on food consumption, she published a two-part paper on their nesting habits that corroborated her position. Describing the situation in Oklahoma, she explained that until 1913 there had been an open season on Mourning Doves from August 15 to May 1. For four years after 1913 there was no season, and their numbers increased greatly. However, in 1917, "all protection so far as the State law goes was taken from them. By Federal law the open season extends from September 1 to December 15. Of course, the State should pass a law conforming to this, so that the State game wardens would be responsible for enforcing it."[14]

Although Nice's motive for carrying out this study may have been preservation and conservation, it became a full-blown life-history study of a single species. It dealt not "with intense observation of individual birds, but with statistics on these nests, the numbers of which were large enough to enable us to make averages and draw some general conclusions." The "us" that she alluded to referred to Blaine and to their daughter Constance. She credited them in a footnote: "I wish to acknowledge my indebtedness to my husband Dr. L. B. Nice who went on many searches for Dove nests and to my daughter, Constance, who, with her unquenchable zeal for climbing the trees, was of indispensable assistance to me."[15]

Few things pleased Nice more than walking in a wooded area about a half mile from home. A small stream that she christened "Snail Brook" offered a "woods in miniature." Bordered by large elms, cottonwoods, willows, hackberries, coralberry, poison ivy, and grapevines, this area, she claimed, was the best place close to town to observe birds. With renewed energy after she resolved to study birds as a career, she visited the area whenever the opportunity arose, even if she could slip away for only an hour. Fascinated by the variety of birds she encountered in this area, Nice proposed to do a census of the bird population that would include the half-mile area between West Boyd and Lindsey Streets. Sometimes she was able to study the entire area, but when a long trip was impossible she could survey the area closer to home and add new species to her list. Although she often took the children with her, she confessed that she had greater success when she was able to go by herself.

Nice described a visit sans children on December 19, 1920, when she first met the elusive Song Sparrow, the bird that was to eventually secure her place in the ornithological community. "Today I went birding alone and had much better success than when the small fry were along. Day bright and mild, while a *Song Sparrow*—wonderful sound—sang most of his song! After careful study I discovered that the common, shy brush-hiding Sparrows were my old friends, the Song Sparrows. They are common along Snail Brook wherever there are piles of brush."

There were several reasons she had not observed Song Sparrows previously. Paramount among these was "the zoology professor's conviction of their absence." The bird's shyness and relative silence and the fact that its songs were easily mistaken for those of Bewick's Wren added to the problem.[16] By December 1920, Nice had enough experience with Oklahoma birds to feel sufficiently competent to attempt a Christmas census with Blaine for the journal *Bird-Lore*, an annual project that she continued for many years. On this first successful Christmas bird census, Margaret, Blaine, and Constance reported a total of thirty-three species and 1,120 individuals.[17]

After her "eyes and ears were opened" and she became "really aware of nature" following the bird census, she found it "hard to wait for spring." Nice observed that unlike in the East, plants, not birds, were spring's harbingers. Elms bloomed by February 12, and by the twenty-third she found "chickweed, bluets, spring beauty and anemone in flower." Even a light snow on March 5 did not discourage the early-blooming plants. Nice kept accurate notes on each as it appeared, observing the gradually returning central Oklahoma birds. She described her delight on March 15, 1921:

> Spring is here. Strange frog voices are grunting and wheezing. Robins, Redwings [blackbirds], Savannah Sparrows, and most wonderful of all—four enchanting Green-winged Teal. . . . While looking at some Song Sparrows I heard a rustling, and there were my birds waddling along the brookside, for all the world like tame ducks! I advanced with great care, and when near the bank, crept on hands and knees. At first I could see only the female lying quietly in the water; on creeping closer I saw the three males with the beautiful green on their cheeks and their bright chestnut faces. It was a wonderfully exciting experience seeing these lovely wild ducks within a few yards. I don't understand how anyone could kill anything so beautiful.

Although she missed the waves of warblers that characterized spring in the East, she was entranced by the new, to her, Oklahoma birds. "They came gradually and each one was welcome."[18]

The Nices' knowledge of Oklahoma birds grew through the use of a "Roadside Census" suggested by their daughter Constance. It began as a game. They counted the Dickcissels that were "lustily singing 'jig-jig-jig' along each side of a five mile stretch of road." In a second Dickcissel game that day, they found from six to eight of these birds a mile, on average. Constance then suggested that they should count all the birds they saw on the rest of their trip. At first the task seemed impossible. Nevertheless, they tried it "and found it so worthwhile, that by the middle of July" they had taken 780 miles of Roadside Censuses.[19] Nice explained in a Wilson

Club publication the way this technique worked: "A roadside census is a record of the number of birds on a particular road, on a particular date, between particular hours; that is to be complete, it should tell the time, location, and distance covered besides the temperature and state of the weather."

Although Nice recognized the limited value of this type of study, she saw that it was useful for recording the abundance and distribution of certain birds while revealing the effects of different conditions of time, place, and weather. Nevertheless, she realized it did not give "by any means" a complete list of the birds of any region, nor did it "enable one to say positively that such and such birds do not live in a certain district."[20] Nice's observational knowledge of Oklahoma's birds increased with this study and others.

As her list of Oklahoma birds grew longer, Nice realized that she required additional information. Recognizing that the American Ornithologists' Union (AOU) would be able to help, she asked her friend Dr. Wallace Craig of the University of Maine to nominate her as an associate. The active members, mostly scientific ornithologists, were the voting members and controlled the direction of the organization (see chapter 6 for an additional description). The second tier consisted of a large group of associates and supplied the financial basis for the organization. This two-tiered approach allowed the AOU to claim professional credentials while retaining its important amateur base.[21] Nice joined the large group of associates, which meant she would regularly receive the organization's journal, *The Auk*, and have access to its membership. She also purchased several major works to help her in identification, including *Birds of America*, a three-volume work edited by T. Gilbert Pearson that contained plates colored by the noted bird illustrator and ornithologist Louis Agassiz Fuertes (1874–1927).[22]

One of her greatest problems in identification was attempting to distinguish subspecies in the field.[23] Unfortunately, the field guides of American birds provided little help in identifying elusive subspecies. However, when Nice encountered a problem, she single-mindedly determined to locate the resources that might help her find a solution. In the case of subspecies identification of Oklahoma birds, she sought help from the advisory council listed in the journal *Bird-Lore*. The list included an ornithologist for each state. Nice was referred to Dr. Harry Oberholser (1870–1963) of the U.S. Biological Survey, who answered many of her questions. She soon became a collaborator for the survey herself and kept migration records and a nesting survey of "Snail Brook."[24]

The year 1920 was a happy one for the family. Margaret, having found her vocation, was enjoying the children and family life more. She asked herself why she had not discovered this new career earlier. She noted that it was "curious how all the pleasant, positive stimuli had proved unavailing, and that it was finally the determination to refute error and save the young doves from a lingering death" that had aroused her to action. As she speculated, "no *problem* in regard to wild birds had ever really been posed" to her until then (italics in the original). The "keen interest in the doves" awakened her interest in all birds and made her determined to "fight to preserve some wildness on the earth."[25]

In the late nineteenth and early twentieth centuries, as the nature-study movement gained momentum, interest in preserving and conserving the natural world inspired amateur naturalists toward a more career-oriented approach. Nice joined other like-minded people who began with a romantic interest in the preservation of nature that metamorphosed into a scientific career during the late nineteenth and early twentieth centuries. For example, ornithologist Florence Merriam Bailey (1863–1948), who played a part in Nice's scientific trajectory, had a two-phased career. In the first segment, she was chiefly a nature writer, and in the second, a field naturalist and collaborator with her husband, mammalogist Vernon Bailey (1864–1942). Vernon Bailey became a scientific professional through his homegrown experience with the natural world. As a young Minnesota farm boy, he began collecting specimens and forwarding them to Florence Merriam's brother, C. Hart Merriam (1855–1942), founder of the Bureau of Biological Survey (predecessor to the U.S. Fish and Wildlife Service). Vernon Bailey's knowledge of the natural world led to his appointment as special field agent to the Division of Economic Ornithology and Mammalogy in 1887, and in 1890 he became chief field naturalist, a position he held until his retirement. Florence met Vernon through her brother after she returned to the East from the Southwest, during which time she wrote several popular books on natural history. Florence and Vernon married in 1899. After the marriage, the couple traveled together on many field trips. The case of Florence and Vernon Bailey is an example of one of the many married couples who jointly pursued environmental careers.[26]

Friendship with Another Woman Ornithologist

In 1920 or 1921, thirty-nine-year-old Nice initiated a correspondence with sixty-eight-year-old Althea Sherman (1853–1943), an artist and self-made ornithologist from Iowa. In spite of the age difference, the two women had much in common. Both were well educated and held bachelor's and master's degrees, but neither had completed a PhD. Both of Sherman's Oberlin College degrees were in art. After leaving a position as an art teacher in 1895, she moved back to the family farm in Iowa to care for her infirm parents. Following their death, she became totally immersed in studying birds on the farm, eventually filling sixty notebooks with meticulous observations. She wrote papers for professional journals and was a member of fifteen scientific societies. Her book Birds of an Iowa Dooryard was published in 1943 after her death.[27] Nice admired Sherman's research on the behavior of the Flicker, Chimney Swift, and House Wren, and the two women found they had many things in common. Both were frustrated that their domestic responsibilities intruded on their research, although Nice, with her five daughters, found it even more difficult to carve out time for research. The two women corresponded extensively and exchanged copies of papers.

Sherman responded to a letter from Nice in which Nice had speculated on varying times that baby Mourning Doves left the nest. Nice's interest harked back to her *Oklahoman* article that demonstrated problems with an early hunting season. Sherman noted that "the difference between Oklahoma and Iowa Mourning Doves' ages when leaving the nest" suggested that the warmer Oklahoma climate enabled the birds to stop brooding sooner and allowed the young birds to help their parents collect food.[28]

From 1921 to 1936 the correspondence between Nice and Sherman evolved from professional concerns to friendship. By critiquing each other's works, exchanging papers, and sharing ideas on preserving habitats, they noted the difficulties of being a woman in a man's field. For her part, Sherman was exuberant in her admiration for Nice's work under difficult circumstances. In 1921, she wrote, "When congratulating you upon your work done I do not for a minute forget the greatest task, the rearing of a family of children. That alone seems too great a task for many women."[29] For her part, Nice found a role model in Sherman.

Their different stages in life affected their attitudes toward science. The younger Nice was optimistic about the possibility of overcoming obstacles, while the aging Sherman was beginning to grow weary of the work. Although she had boxes of data, she found that too many tasks got in her way whenever she tried to write a book on the life history of birds, and she complained that she was old and slow.[30] Their friendship was mutually beneficial, however, and they enjoyed meeting in person at the October 1922 AOU meeting in Chicago. In a letter to Nice after the meeting, Sherman wrote, "I am glad to have met you in Chicago and hope for other meetings in the future."[31] After receiving Nice's paper on the Mourning Dove, Sherman praised her: "I am glad that this scholarly work has been done by a woman (yes, I should have said by a woman and her little daughter), for Constance's part [climbing trees and counting eggs and young] must not be overlooked."[32]

Sherman admonished Nice "not to publish piecemeal" but to reserve her studies for a book. She regretted not taking her own advice. Although one of Sherman's major goals was to publish a book on Iowa birds, she never got around to doing it. She wrote to Nice on December 30, 1921, "I am old and am very slow yet within a year I manage to do considerable work. I must keep abreast of the times in world affairs and read the scientific magazines that come to me, so I read while combing my hair, when eating and when resting, but I have written nothing on my bird histories since early last spring."[33] In another letter several years later, on November 23, 1924, Sherman wrote, "You wish for the progress of my bird histories and I wish that your wishes were powerful; not a stroke has been done since last winter." Again, in April 1925 she reported that "the winter went with little writing done," and the last time she mentioned her life histories (March 10, 1926), she wrote to Margaret that instead of concentrating on her book, she sewed.[34] A very abbreviated version of what Sherman had worked on for a lifetime was published posthumously in *Birds of an Iowa Dooryard.*

Margaret absorbed the advice that Sherman did not take herself, resolving that she would not come to the end of her productivity with sixty notebooks, of which comparatively few saw the light of publication. A paragraph that Nice wrote in the journal *Iowa Bird Life* about her correspondence with Sherman indicated the pitfalls that Sherman faced as a woman ornithologist. These obstacles included the "drudgery of housework, illnesses and the infirmities of age, [and] the distractions of visitors (many of them curiosity-seekers)." She added that Sherman's "burning zeal to uphold the truth and to protect 'good birds' from bad . . . made heavy inroads on her time." Sherman was never able to present her findings to her "fellow-students and to posterity in the form she so earnestly desired."[35]

Although it was unsaid, Margaret must have suspected that she herself was a candidate for a similar fate if she did not work hard to avoid it. Writing of Sherman, she noted the following:

> It is a tragic thing that a woman of her intellect, gifts and character should have had to spend so much time in manual labor that she could not give her message to the world. This problem is an increasingly serious one in our civilization. Our highly-educated, gifted women have to be cooks, cleaning women, nurse maids. Men who could do notable research have their time wasted in mere routine. We who cherish things of the mind should face this evil and strive earnestly to give such men and women a chance to make the highest contribution to society of which they are capable.[36]

Nice used Sherman's life as both an inspiration and a warning: "We must follow our path with the courage of our convictions, refusing to be diverted by the clamor and confusion of less important demands."[37] This course was exactly the path she attempted to follow in her research, beginning with a major project that resulted in two monographs on the birds of Oklahoma.

Sources for Birds of Oklahoma

The Nice family purchased a secondhand Dodge in the spring of 1920. The car increased the geographic range of the family explorations and made possible a new project suggested by Charles W. Shannon, director of the Oklahoma Geological Survey (1914–1923). Blaine reported to Margaret that Shannon had asked the two of them to work on the birds of Oklahoma, since they had already begun a roadside census of the birds. Shannon offered to lend them camping equipment and pay their way if they would take on the project. He also provided them with information from two earlier studies on the birds of Oklahoma, one from 1901 to 1902 and the other from 1913 to 1914. The first study had resulted in an unannotated list of 178 birds collected by Charles D. Bunker (collector and taxidermist, 1901–1903) and recorded by A. H. Van Vleet, then head of the botany department at the University of Oklahoma. This list, published in 1901–1902, contained the names of 173 species, all of which were collected. On January 1, 1903, there were 167 mounted birds, but on January 6, a fire destroyed 84 birds as well as Van Vleet's notebooks. According to Nice, this fire was started by a boy "who didn't like to go to school. "He had already burned down the public school house; his next victim was this temporary barracks on the Campus where the collection was housed.[38] To Nice's surprise, Van Vleet's study had been the source of the notes in Barde's list (1914) that were designated "G. S." She found once again that the unnamed zoology professor had given her inaccurate information about Barde's list. Rather than being based on "slight records of untrustworthy students," as she had been told, it was based on actual specimens and Van Vleet's notes. Although many of the specimens and notes had been destroyed by the fire in 1903, some were extant and she was able to verify the accuracy of the data. The incomplete study conducted in 1913 and 1914 by Edward D. Crabb was available in the form of a manuscript on the birds of Oklahoma. It was based on 369 specimens that he had collected in central, eastern, and southwestern Oklahoma. Although it contained useful information, it was incomplete because the money had run out. Many of the specimens and all of the notebooks from this study were destroyed in a fire in the temporary housing where they were stored.[39]

The two incomplete lists and the two specimen collections in the university museum represented the core of available resources. Armed with Florence Merriam Bailey's *Handbook of Birds of the Western United States* (1902); Frank Chapman and Chester A. Reed's *Color Key to North American Birds* (1903); Reed's two *Bird Guides* of 1905 and 1906; heavy, awkward, borrowed camping equipment; and four children (Janet was not yet born), Margaret and Blaine set forth on a trial trip to the Wichita Mountains. They had intended to leave the two- and four-year-old children with a neighbor, but she had a last-minute crisis and was unable to care for them. Undaunted, the entire family set out for these southwestern mountains.[40]

Margaret and Blaine did not allow the presence of the children to detract from the success of their project. They did not hesitate to leave the children in camp when they left before dawn to observe birds, leaving the younger ones in the care of the older. The girls contributed to the venture by serving as wood gatherers and dishwashers. Encouraged by the many birds they identified on this first camping trip, Margaret and Blaine decided that the project was possible and that the entire family could be involved. They looked forward to the next trip. Puzzled, Margaret wrote, "Hardly anyone in Norman but ourselves would *want* to do it."[41]

Margaret, Blaine, and four children—Constance (ten on July 13), Marjorie (seven and a half), Barbara (four in August), and Eleanor (two in May)—piled into the car for a second camping trip, this time to the

Margaret kept a journal of the family birding trips, including drawings by the children. *Western History Collections, University of Oklahoma Libraries.*

Drawing by a Nice child in her mother's journal, showing birds. *Western History Collections, University of Oklahoma Libraries.*

ancient Arbuckle Mountains, sixty miles south of Norman. Margaret's trip notebook includes birds, general daily events, and children's activities. The children drew on pages of her field notebook; Barbara drew a rabbit with a dress on, Marjorie drew generic birds, and Constance drew eagles. At one camp on a creek, the children enjoyed playing in the water. Although baby Eleanor was left out of the fun, she decided that "she would be a spectator . . . no longer." Blaine "slipped off her clothes and let her go in naked and she found it rather cold." She "simply adored the water—jumping up and down in it." When it came time to take her out, "she bellowed lustily." The family celebrated Constance's birthday on the trip. However, the only special treat that was available was her choice of "marshmallows, sweet chocolate and fancy crackers. The poor child was in tears Sunday because we told her we wouldn't get her climbing irons for her birthday."[42]

The birds were quite different from those in both the Wichita Mountains and Norman. Leaving the Arbuckles for an expedition into southern Oklahoma's Pushmataha County, Margaret was impressed not only by the different birds in southern Oklahoma, but also by the different human cultures she encountered. She felt that she had left the West behind and

The secondhand Dodge touring car acquired in 1920 that allowed the Nice family to explore the state of Oklahoma. *Courtesy Kenneth Boyer Collection.*

Marjorie Nice was an expert tree climber and shinnied up trees in search of bird nests. *Courtesy Kenneth Boyer Collection.*

Barbara Nice was not to be outdone by her older sister and also took up climbing trees. *Courtesy Kenneth Boyer Collection.*

The Nice children enjoyed field trips with their parents. *Courtesy Kenneth Boyer Collection.*

had entered an economically challenged rural South. By the end of this trip, the car had given them trouble, rain had poured down and turned the roads into quagmires, and two family members had caught colds. Although they had planned to survey northeastern Oklahoma, they returned home and evaluated their trip.

Summer Birds of Oklahoma

Margaret had intended to write a report on bird distribution, comparing the birds they had encountered on the trip to those of their home in Cleveland County, correlating distribution with "geography, altitude, latitude, longitude, rainfall, and vegetation." However, Charles Shannon had a different plan in mind, one that Margaret thought would strain her competency. He wanted her to write a bulletin on the birds of the entire state of Oklahoma and ignored her protest that she had observed those in only a small portion of the state. Shannon reassured her, promising that he would keep notes on the birds he encountered on his proposed trip to northwestern Oklahoma and the Panhandle. They eventually compromised, and Margaret agreed to write a preliminary report on the summer birds of the state.[43]

In order to collect all available data, Margaret enlisted the help of the Biological Survey in Washington, DC, for addresses of cooperating ornithologists in Oklahoma, along with copies of nest censuses. With this help, Margaret and Blaine prepared a four-page questionnaire on the status of fifty species and sent it to members of the Oklahoma Academy of Science. The introduction to the questionnaire read:

> The Oklahoma Geological Survey is getting out a preliminary report on the summer birds of the State and would greatly appreciate any information you could give on the subject. Please fill in the following questionnaire. Credit will be given to all collaborators.
>
> Does the following bird breed in your county?
>
> In what other parts of the State do you know of its breeding?
>
> Is it rare, uncommon, fairly common, common or abundant with you?
>
> Kindly give information on any of these birds that you can.

A list of birds followed this introduction.[44]

Although most of the questionnaires resulted in little information, some naturalists provided excellent data. However, Shannon was not one of these. When he returned from northwestern Oklahoma and the Panhandle, his information on the birds was almost useless. Nevertheless, he asked Margaret to prepare a mimeographed list of the summer birds of Oklahoma for distribution at the state fair in Oklahoma City. In response, she prepared an unannotated list of 131 species and subspecies with both scientific and common names. This list was useful because it could be distributed to collaborators for their comments.[45]

Preparing the bulletin absorbed Margaret. She used all available sources, including state lists, her book collection, and government bulletins. Fortunately, she was invited to read a paper at the thirty-eighth meeting of the AOU in Washington, DC. She convinced Shannon to pay for half her trip by persuading him that even though her paper was not about summer birds, conferring with Harry C. Oberholser of the U.S. Biological Survey was essential for this project. This visit had a profound effect on her path to becoming an ornithologist. It was not her talk, "The Nesting of Mourning Doves at Norman, Oklahoma," that was so significant. In fact, she confessed that the talk was less than successful. She later recalled that the colors on her charts did not show up well and that "I was so over-awed that I read rapidly in a faint voice." However, as she had hoped, the meeting afforded her the opportunity to talk to Oberholser. She reported that he "generously spent a whole day helping me with my problems, and this proved the most important part of the trip to me." He showed her the bibliography that the Survey had produced of Oklahoma birds. This "was a revelation to me, particularly in the matter of early explorers." Oberholser provided names of Oklahoma collaborators, books, maps, and portions of his manuscript *The Birds of Texas*. Moreover, this meeting began her amassing of a vast knowledge of the ornithological literature. Nice purchased a complete set of *The Auk* and the *Nuttall Bulletin* for her personal library. She and Oberholser went over her state fair list of "Summer Birds": "What a field day Dr. Oberholser did have in changing scientific names and adding subspecific labels!" He rejected seven birds that she had included, but later all but one were reinstated.[46] One of the mimeographed copies of the list corrected in pencil and ink by both Nice and Oberholser in the fall of 1920 includes the following long paragraph written in ink by Nice:

This is an important document in the history of the Nices and their contributions to Oklahoma ornithology. Mr. C. W. Shannon had financed our 1st camping trip in June & July 1920 to the Wichitas, Arbuckles, & south eastern Okla. And he was determined that we should write a state list covering *all the birds of the whole state* throughout the year. I protested all we could hope to do was to write a popular bulletin on the Summer birds with the object of inspiring people to study the birds of the state.[47]

As Nice worked with Oberholser, she became more clearly aware of her "appalling ignorance" and presumption in attempting to produce such a publication.

"I resolved then and there that no bulletin would be written by us without a great deal more field work. I owe a great debt to Dr. Oberholser for starting me on the straight and narrow path in ornithology and in giving me a different viewpoint from that which I had acquired from from *Bird-Lore.*"[48]

The lessons she learned at this meeting caused Nice to realize that in order to become a professional ornithologist, she must join the appropriate scientific organizations, collect and study the back issues of their journals, and build up her own library. She easily absorbed information about not only birds but also various ornithological techniques and standards.[49]

Nice produced a new Christmas bird census and continued her Mourning Dove project during the spring of 1921. Her correspondence with observers all over the country allowed her to build a network of support that proved more important than her research during this time. Friends who could advise Nice about research and publication outlets and generally help in the advancement of her career were invaluable. Her friend Althea Sherman wrote that she was glad to welcome another woman to their ranks: "Too many women are dabblers."[50]

The more she read in her newly acquired journals, the more Nice craved to publish, but she was still uncertain about the value of her contributions. However, she sent a note to *The Condor* on Mourning Doves (1921) and was encouraged by the response of the editor, Joseph Grinnell. He explained that there was always a place for faithful descriptions of the actions of living birds and noted the scarcity of information on even the most common species.[51] Her confidence was also boosted by the positive reception she and

Blaine received on their joint publication "The Roadside Census" in the *Wilson Bulletin* (1920), and by Sherman's praise of the note in *The Condor*. In this letter, Sherman noted that she was pleased that someone was making use of the motorcar to gather information, explaining that she found cars "an abomination."[52]

The Oklahoma Academy of Science, founded in 1909, was a source of information about birds in Oklahoma as well as a venue for presenting her own research. Margaret and Blaine were elected fellows in 1916, and both were active in the organization. Margaret found the meetings "pleasant and stimulating," and Blaine was elected secretary and "faithfully fulfilled" the office for six years. In a project recording the history of the academy, Blaine collected seven programs (neither Blaine nor Margaret was able to locate the programs for the third and fourth meetings) and thirty-nine papers. In these seven programs, there were fifteen titles on birds. Margaret, always interested in the participation of women, found that not a single woman participated in the first three available programs. The paper Margaret gave in 1916 established a trend, and other women followed her example. Four women participated in 1917, 1918, and 1919; five in 1920; and seven in 1921.[53]

Margaret realized that writing about the summer birds of Oklahoma would be impossible without visiting the northwestern part of the state. Blaine had broken a rib and was unable to go on a proposed camping trip to the area. His absence did not deter Margaret from making the Panhandle trip by train with their oldest daughter, Constance. They started out on May 26, 1922, stopping along the way to observe and to gather information about sources.

This trip was challenging, but so were Margaret's previous camping trips with her brother in Massachusetts and the long hikes she had taken with classmates at Mount Holyoke. Neither Blaine's absence nor the uncertain, fatiguing means of transportation necessary to reach the sparsely populated areas of northwestern Oklahoma daunted her. Twelve-year-old Constance seems to have taken all the difficulties in stride as well.

The pair stopped along the way to get information from knowledgeable sources. They revisited the Northwestern Normal School in Alva, where they met professor of zoology T. C. Carter. He provided Margaret with a copy of his publication "Thesis on Oklahoma Birds" (1908), written with O. J. Trenton, providing her with another source on birds of the area.

Carter and Trenton mentioned 162 species and included brief notes on their occurrence. A visit to the bird collection was only somewhat helpful, because it was inadequately labeled as to dates and localities.[54]

In order to reach their final goal of Kenton, Oklahoma, in the far northwestern corner of the state, Margaret and Constance meandered cross-country. They first traveled by bus and train north from Woodward, Oklahoma, to Liberal, Kansas, and then southwest to Texhoma on the Oklahoma-Texas border. Their transportation included four trains, a bus, and a mail car. The mail carrier took them from Texhoma to Boise City, Oklahoma, and left them forty-two miles from Kenton. They were able to convince another mail carrier to take them from Boise City to Kenton, a small, unincorporated community in Cimarron County, Oklahoma. Located in the extreme northwestern part of the Oklahoma Panhandle, it is approximately three miles east of the New Mexico state line and six miles south of the Colorado state line, on the south side of the river in the Cimarron River valley. The flora and fauna of this part of Oklahoma are unique to the state. The area is dominated by Black Mesa, a landform that extends from Mesa de Maya in Colorado and continues southeasterly twenty-eight miles along the north bank of the Cimarron River; it then crosses the northeastern corner of New Mexico and ends at the confluence of the Cimarron and Carrizo Creek near Kenton. Black Mesa's highest elevation is 5,700 feet in Colorado, and in northwestern Cimarron County, Oklahoma, it reaches 4,973 feet.

As Margaret and Constance rode with the mail carrier from Boise City to Kenton, they passed through country unlike any they had encountered in central Oklahoma. After driving for some time over high prairie dotted with sagebrush and yucca, they suddenly encountered the "breaks," characterized by canyons and sandstone mesas. The flora of the plains consisted mainly of mesquite, yucca, cat's claw, devil's claw, and cholla cactus, while that of the mesas included piñon, juniper, and scrub oak. They stayed with a family, ate at the Kenton Hotel, and made friends with a collector, Mr. Tate, who provided them with valuable information on birds of the area. After observing birds along the Cimarron River, they climbed Black Mesa and found species that were new both for them and for Oklahoma.[55]

Going home was one more adventure. Riding with another mail carrier, they ended up in Clayton, New Mexico, where they took a train to

Oklahoma City and a trolley to Norman. Margaret was ecstatic over the trip and wrote the following:

> I met birds that were entirely new to me; indeed, I had not dreamt that such existed: The absurd little Bush Tit, the sedate Canyon Towhee, the astonishing Lewis' Woodpecker, the Cassin's Sparrow with its exquisite refrain. All these birds were *mine*. For Oklahoma belonged to me in a way it could belong to few others—only those who studied nature in the state. It was mine for I loved it passionately—its pine forests, its flower-studded prairies, its rock-jumbled mountains, its great plains and cedar-topped mesas. I was keenly aware of its soil, and its weather, its contours and rivers, its plants, and most of all, its birds.[56]

Chapter 5

THE BIRDS OF OKLAHOMA

As Nice became more confident in her knowledge of Oklahoma birds, she felt competent enough to modify her narrow project on the summer birds of the state to encompass all its birds, including winter birds and transients. She had developed a network of collaborators, published lists, observed museum specimens, and recorded her own observations from across the state. Her visit to the joint AOU and Wilson Club meeting in Chicago in October 1922 proved valuable on several fronts, but most importantly she had an opportunity to consult with Harry Oberholser again. Her decision to include the birds of the entire state rather than just the summer birds presented problems as to which records were accurate. Because Oberholser was so busy, his answers to questions Nice posed in her letters were not entirely satisfactory. However, as they conferred at this meeting, he was his "kind and omniscient self." Despite all her "labours and studies," he ruled out many species that she had thought safe. She found Oberholser's editing vital "in getting out a trustworthy publication on birds of Oklahoma."[1]

Even though she was prepared intellectually to undertake the task of producing a major work on the birds of Oklahoma, Nice as a married woman with children was denied the luxury of concentrating exclusively on one project. As with many women scientists, her family experience carried over into her professional life, and she found herself involved in many tasks at the same time. Nevertheless, whenever she got the opportunity she continued her travels around the state to gather additional data for her book. Although Blaine coauthored the work, most of the gathering of data as well as the actual writing fell to Margaret. It was not only domestic concerns that slowed Nice's completion of *The Birds of Oklahoma*; other partially completed projects were crying out for closure.

Nesting of Mourning Doves

Although collecting records and recording new observations for *The Birds of Oklahoma* occupied much of her scarce research time, Nice still managed to publish a major study on her old friend the Mourning Dove. Although preservation and conservation concerns first motivated her to begin this project, it soon developed into a much more elaborate study. She described this work as her first major ornithological paper since "The Food of the Bobwhite," published in 1910. Moreover, the two-part paper on Oklahoma's Mourning Doves illustrates the fastidious attention to detail that characterizes all of Nice's works.[2] Since she studied so many birds, nests, and locations, she found it necessary to develop an accurate record-keeping system. This system worked so well for the Mourning Dove project that she later elaborated on it for her Song Sparrow research. Nice's research population of Mourning Doves on the University of Oklahoma campus required a method of keeping track of individual birds and nests. She developed a system using a 10.5" × 11" map of the campus and a large notebook. First, she partitioned the campus into twenty-six areas, each designated by a letter. On the map, she marked the location of each nest with a number and used a new map each month to note changes. Nice then divided the notebook into squares, with columns for the nest number, location, kind of tree, height from the ground, position in a crotch or on a branch, and any peculiarity of the nest or parents. The additional columns were headed by the dates and hours visited. Under each date, she recorded brooding data, the contents of the nest, the size and position of the young, and, if appropriate, the destruction of the nest.

In the first part of the Mourning Dove article, Nice considered information on the nest itself, including its material constitution, the tree chosen, and the height and position of the nest as well as the Mourning Dove's habit of using nests built by other birds. Not only did she provide the data, she also speculated on the cause and significance of the behaviors involved in locating and building a nest.[3] After reporting on variations in the incubation period and in the number of eggs, she included observations on the young birds.[4] Noting that there was usually a size difference in a pair of young squabs, she proposed that this variation could be explained by a one- or two-day difference in hatching time. After charting the weights of the nestlings to note differential growth rates, she found considerable individual variation in the birds, not only in weight gain but also in feather development. She also described feeding behavior, position in the nest, length of brooding time, and the length of time the young remained in the nest.[5]

In the second part of the dove study, a continuation of the first, Nice focused on the behavior of the parents. She described the "broken-wing" ruse exhibited by the doves when frightened. This spectacular behavior involves the bird throwing itself on the ground near an intruder and fluttering around as if it were seriously injured. Nice observed, "The bird flies some distance, perhaps 10 to 30 yards, flutters a little on the ground, stops and waves its wings, then walks along waving its wings, making little flights into the air and then again walking along flapping its wings."

She noted that in some cases, the pretense of injury degenerated into mere form.[6] She explored the reasons some birds exhibited this behavior and others did not. About one-third of the doves observed in Norman from 1919 through 1922 never demonstrated the broken-wing behavior. Approximately one-sixth of the birds showed the behavior throughout the entire nesting cycle, while about one-half showed it with midsized or nearly grown young, indicating a greater concern with the young than with the eggs. She concluded that this behavior typically increased as the nesting cycle advanced, and that if one of a pair showed this instinct, the other usually did.[7]

In considering the breeding season, Nice found that migrant doves usually arrived in Norman in March and left in late September and early October. However, some doves did not migrate and remained all winter. Determining that the nesting season lasted from late March through September and sometimes into October, she concluded that this prolonged season made the Mourning Dove the bird with the longest nesting season in Oklahoma.[8]

From both parts of this paper, it is clear that Nice's research methods were improving. She presented her evidence in the form of tables and even included photographs of the young nestlings. Recognizing that she was working with incomplete data, Nice cited sources from other investigators to support her own tentative conclusions. When this paper was completed in 1923, Nice was able to resume her travels to complete her monograph on the birds of Oklahoma.

In Search of Birds

During May 1923, Nice traveled to northeastern Oklahoma, where she found the birds and plants similar to those of Kentucky and Tennessee.

Among the many birds she observed were migrating Rose-breasted Gros-beaks, a Solitary Vireo (a new state record), and fourteen species of war-blers (several were the first definite records for Oklahoma, and one, the Tennessee Warbler, was the only record). Equally important for her project was a fully labeled collection in the museum of the Northeastern Normal School, consisting of 76 birds collected between 1906 and 1914 by the head of the Biology Department, C. W. Prier.[9]

The fate of the Nices' project on Oklahoma birds was in jeopardy after Charles Shannon, the friend who first suggested the venture and loaned them camping gear from the Oklahoma Geological Survey, was removed from the directorship. Without Shannon's support, the Survey was unlikely to publish the work. The project was saved when the University of Okla-homa agreed to publish it as a "University Study," allowing the Nices to con-tinue their research. They then bought their own camping equipment, and the entire family embarked on an extensive birding trip on June 24, 1923. They revisited the ancient Arbuckle Mountains and then traveled east to McCurtain County in the southeastern corner of the state. After making many fruitful observations in the southeast, they drove to the southwestern corner of the state. At this point they had visited all four corners of Okla-homa and felt more prepared to write about its birds.[10]

Instead of concentrating on her major project, Margaret, as usual, was doing many things at once. Her passion for conservation came to the fore again in 1923, when she was following the fall bird migration and encountered a hunter carrying three Franklin's Gulls. He explained that he thought they were ducks, and that he had to "shoot things" to find out whether or not they were game birds. After reproving this "ignoramus," Margaret wrote a letter to the *Daily Oklahoman*, "What Is a Game Bird?"[11]

Janet: Child Number Five

Margaret was pregnant with their fifth child during the summer's camping trips and the fall migration of 1923. She casually mentioned in her autobi-ography, "Our new baby kindly timed her arrival after the fall migration and before the Christmas census." Baby Janet's arrival did not keep Marga-ret from participating in the Christmas census.

Leaving the baby with her sisters, she and Blaine spent the afternoon of December 23 looking for birds.[12] This story is reminiscent of the expe-rience of another woman scientist, Marie Curie, who was also trying to do

Janet Nice was the youngest daughter, but she too took part in the family's outdoor activities. *Courtesy Michael Thompson Collection.*

Eleanor and Janet Nice, the family's two younger children. Eleanor died of pneumonia at an early age. *Courtesy Michael Thompson Collection.*

Nice children on a family outing. *Courtesy Kenneth Boyer Collection.*

it all. In her case, finding a way to accommodate family and work meant combining pregnancy with a much-needed vacation from research. Marie and her husband, Pierre, relaxed by going on long bicycle vacations. When Marie was eight months pregnant, they left on a long cycling trip. Eventually they were forced to return to Paris, where Marie gave birth to Irène on September 12, 1897.[13]

Although Margaret and Blaine often collaborated on the research on Oklahoma birds, it was Margaret who was the driving force behind the project. The inscription on the James Farley Post Office building in New York City seems especially applicable to Margaret Nice: "Neither snow nor rain nor heat nor gloom of night stays these couriers from the swift completion of their appointed rounds." As we have seen, even pregnancy did not keep her from gathering data. If Blaine was unavailable for an exploratory trip in far-flung parts of the state, she went anyway. It must be noted that when she embarked solo on one of her expeditions, she left the younger children at home with their father. Blaine may have had some babysitting help from students when he was in class, but basically he and the older girls managed to take care of the household when Margaret was gone. He apparently did not resent the situation, although in Barbara's eyes he was overauthoritarian in his parenting style.

Margaret was constantly improving her knowledge of the birds of Oklahoma. Through her many observational trips, her increasing familiarity with the literature, and her attendance at professional meetings where she talked with experts in ornithology, she finally felt competent to write a comprehensive report on the birds of the state.

The Finished Book, The Birds of Oklahoma

On April 24, 1924, *The Birds of Oklahoma,* jointly authored by Margaret Morse Nice and Leonard Blaine Nice, appeared as a 124-page paperbound publication.[14] It began with a physiographic map of the seventy-seven counties of the state, provided by the Oklahoma Geological Survey, and concluded with two plates with two photographs each, taken by the Nices.[15]

Although this work is jointly authored, it bears Margaret's imprint more than Blaine's.[16] A long introduction explains much about her philosophy of natural history, including the interrelationship of living things with their environment and the responsibility of humans as stewards of that environment. Recognizing the importance of understanding the physical and faunal areas of the ecosystem in order to understand bird life, Margaret and Blaine discussed variations in physiography, vegetation, temperature, latitude and longitude, and rainfall. In describing the "Physical Features" of the state, they stressed its diverse character, which included four mountain systems: the Wichitas in the southwest, the Arbuckles in the south-central portion, the Ouachita Mountains in the southeast, and the Ozarks in the northeast. Flat shortgrass prairie characterized the west, and rolling wooded areas made up much of the eastern third of the state. They included other information such as the size (area, 70,057 square miles), the latitude (from 33 degrees 37 minutes to 37 degrees north), and the longitude (94 degrees 29 minutes to 103 degrees west). The elevation ranged from 400 feet in the southeastern corner to 4,500 feet in the northwest. Even though they described the temperature in general as "rather mild," they recognized that it was subject to extremes; the range for the whole state varied from 25°F below zero to 116°F. The rainfall also differed from east to west; the eastern half had an average rainfall of 30 to 45 inches, whereas the Panhandle had an annual rainfall of only 20 to 24 inches.[17] With such variety in the physical environment, the wide diversity in the avifauna became more understandable.

After describing the physical features of the environment, the Nices discussed the birds in different parts of the state. In the wooded eastern part they found an almost exclusively eastern avifauna, whereas some birds, such as the Bobwhite, Western Mourning Dove, Turkey Vulture, Kingfisher, Red-headed Woodpecker, Eastern Kingbird, Blue Jay, Cowbird, Dickcissel, and Bluebird bred over the entire state. Other species, including the Screech Owl, Horned Lark, Lark Sparrow Shrike, and Mockingbird, ranged over the entire state but with different subspecies.[18]

In a historical sketch including quotations from early explorers describing the variety of wildlife they encountered, Margaret and Blaine noted that the earliest mention of Oklahoma birds came from Edwin James's account of Major Long's expedition, which descended the South Canadian River between August 17 and September 13, 1820. He wrote of listening to "the note of a bird, new to some of us, and bearing a singular resemblance to the noise of a child's toy trumpet; this we soon found to be the cry of the great ivory-billed woodpecker (*Picus principalis*)."[19]

Nestled among quotations from other explorers is a particularly descriptive one from Washington Irving in October 1832. He recorded his impressions of Oklahoma birds found near the western border of the state and described the breaking of silence as "the cry of a distant flock of pelicans, stalking like spectres about a shallow pool; sometimes by the sinister croaking of a raven in the air, while occasionally a scoundrel wolf would scour off from before me, and having attained a safe distance, would sit down and howl and whine with tones that gave a dreariness to the surrounding solitude."[20]

The work was more than just a list of Oklahoma birds. It emphasized the loss of bird species since the early observers had recorded their notes. Nice lamented the degradation of the previously rich avifauna: "What about the bird life now? The Passenger Pigeon is entirely extinct, the Paroquet and Ivory-billed Woodpecker have disappeared from the state as well as the Trumpeter Swan, Whooping Crane, Eskimo Curlew, White-tailed Kite, Swallow-tailed Kite and Raven." She blamed humans for the loss: "Such has been the effect of man's occupation—of the tilling of the land, of unwise meddling with nature and most of all, mere wanton destruction." Recognizing that certain birds would never return, she hoped that "from education of the people, from increased respect for law and the development of greater love of nature and of beauty," the situation would improve. Nice reported specific steps that would slow further depredation.[21]

After describing the "Game Laws of Oklahoma" that could protect the birds if they were followed, Nice explained the important state and federal conservation laws and the requirements for hunting licenses.[22] Recognizing that people were more apt to conserve birds if they saw that it was in their financial interest to do so, she stressed the economic value of birds to humans. Although, for her, one of the greatest values was "in the joy they add to life—the pleasure of hearing their songs, of seeing their beauty and of the thrills which come from sight and sound of the wilder, rare ones," she also recognized that she would have a stronger case if she could demonstrate an economic value for birds. Thus, she stressed the importance of birds in the balance of nature because they fed "in large measure upon the enemies of plant life—both insect and mammal." She presented case after case to illustrate the economic importance of birds to humans. One of these examples indicated that the annual savings to farmers in the United States by the consumption of weed seeds by birds had been placed at $89,260,000—and this figure is in 1924 dollars.[23]

Having made the case for the importance of birds, Nice discussed factors necessary for bird life to prosper, such as food, water, nesting sites, protection from enemies, and ways to attract birds and protect them once they arrived. Whenever the opportunity arose to stress the danger that cats presented to birds, Nice did so. In this publication she announced alternatives to having cats as pets: "It's not really necessary to keep cats. A rabbit is a much safer pet for a little child and a dog a much more affectionate and intelligent one for older children and adults."[24]

The main body of the work includes a list of 361 species and subspecies of birds found in Oklahoma. Whenever possible, the Nices described the status, distribution, and records according to counties, including dates and authorities (the source of the record). As for nomenclature, they used the 1910 American Ornithologists' Union Checklist and its supplements, except in a few cases when they chose to accept the classification of Robert Ridgway and Harry Oberholser.[25] The well-documented publication includes a previously unpublished list of observers, and a bibliography of Oklahoma observers.

The university printed 2,500 copies of the publication and distributed them without cost, sending them to the zoology departments of the colleges in the state. It was well received. Emil Kraettli, secretary to the president of the University of Oklahoma, James Shannon Buchanan, reported that there had been a greater demand for this bulletin than for any other published by the university.[26]

Nice had sent a copy of the publication to Alexander Wetmore (1886–1978) on April 18, before it was officially published. Wetmore, who later became secretary of the Smithsonian Institution, studied birds around Minco, Oklahoma, from May 23 to June 2, 1905. The Nices visited Minco, a small town in northern Grady County, in 1923. A handwritten letter from Wetmore to Nice acknowledged his receipt of her book. Wetmore explained that he first became interested in the birds of Oklahoma when he made a "little collection" in Minco in 1905. Consequently, he was "greatly pleased to receive a copy of your Birds of Oklahoma" and wrote, "You have given us an excellent state list, one that comprises knowledge to date on occurrence, and distribution which will be most useful. After reading it I have noted the changes that you indicate in the avifauna of Minco during 20 years as I have often wondered what has taken place there."[27]

Even though Nice had already attained some exposure to the national ornithological community through attending meetings and presenting papers, it was the publication of this work that really first enhanced her reputation. The editor of *The Auk* praised it as an excellent state list, "thoroughly up-to-date" and "carefully compiled."[28] Joseph Grinnell reported in *The Condor* that it "bears the stamp of good workmanship throughout."[29] Many other ornithologists added their praise.

Almost immediately after its publication, Nice began to make new discoveries about shorebirds. An unusual amount of rain had elicited the formation of new ponds, especially one that grew in a low spot half a mile south of Norman. Shorebirds flocked to these new bodies of water, and new records and, in some cases, new species were added to the list. Although the Nices had worked diligently to learn as much as possible about the birds of Oklahoma, the new shorebirds showed them that they had "only made a beginning on this happy, wonderful enterprise."[30] It became obvious to Margaret that a second *Birds of Oklahoma* was needed, although this project was not realized until 1931.

Blaine's Sabbatical Year

Blaine received a sabbatical leave for the academic year of 1924–1925. Since he was to spend this year in Europe, Margaret and the children planned to stay in Amherst near her mother and her sister Sarah. Never considering motels or hotels, the family set out in late June and camped along the way. After establishing the family in a flat near the Morse's house, Blaine left for Europe. During this year, Margaret expanded her knowledge of birds, reconnected with friends from Mount Holyoke and Clark, and attended ornithology meetings. Since the older children were in public school and family members were available to care for the younger ones, Margaret had time to explore the New England countryside. The older girls often accompanied her and on occasion even baby Janet came along. As had become the pattern, the two older daughters continued to do much of the cooking, dish washing, and cleaning.

During the year in Amherst, Margaret made several short trips to visit old friends. She no doubt found it interesting to see how her former classmates had negotiated their lives as educated women in a male world. One of these excursions took her to Boston, where she stayed with her college roommate Lucy Day (Lucy May Day Boring, 1886–1996) and Lucy's husband, Edwin Garrigues Boring (1886–1968). Like Margaret, Lucy had married a professor. However, unlike Margaret, Lucy had earned a PhD degree. Both Lucy and Edwin "Garry" had earned their doctorates from Cornell University, and Edwin Boring had become a distinguished professor at Harvard. Like many women of that time, Lucy never used her degree professionally. Interestingly, as professor of experimental psychology at Harvard, Edwin Boring was notorious for his exclusionary treatment of his female graduate students. His attitude toward women was even more noteworthy since his sister, Alice Middleton Boring, was a respected scientist with a PhD degree.

Nice also traveled to New York City to visit a friend from her Clark University days, Edith Wallace. After graduating from Mount Holyoke, Wallace attended Clark, where she obtained an MA degree in biology. Although she never completed a doctorate, she had a successful career on the fringes of science. Her artistic skill made her a valuable assistant to the well-known geneticist Thomas Hunt Morgan, who was then at Columbia University, and her artistic drawings of *Drosophila* appear in many of his publications. Scientific illustration was an area in which many women interested in science found employment. When she was in New York City, Nice attended the forty-second meeting of the National Association of Audubon Societies (November 9–12, 1925), visited museums, and met with leading ornithologists.[31]

During the winter of 1925, when traipsing around the frigid countryside in New England was less enticing, Nice returned to her research on speech development. In 1923 she had completed a manuscript for a book on the acquisition of language by children. Although this work had been extremely time consuming, she was never able to find a publisher. Her former mentor G. Stanley Hall forwarded the manuscript to many publishers, but it was never accepted. Throughout her life she defended this work, believing "it would have been a useful reference work for college courses" because it contained "much first hand information and a wide survey of the pertinent literature." She complained that "publishers do not necessarily judge a book on its merits," and that her lack of a PhD and "professional status" was more of a disadvantage in psychology than in ornithology.[32] In spite of her lack of success in getting the book published, she continued to publish short papers on the subject, even conferring with Arnold Gesell (1880–1961), the well-known child development psychologist. He inspired her to continue doing this research, and she published sporadically in this field until 1933.

However, Nice realized that she could not easily do "exhaustive work in such different fields"—ornithology and psychology. Still, when she encountered errors in the literature about language development, she felt compelled to correct them, and she continued to keep voluminous notes on Janet's speech development. Nice later recalled that although her studies were mentioned in books on psychology, she often wished she never had been "led astray into this blind alley," perhaps recalling the fate of Althea Sherman. Nevertheless, she was certain that her speech development studies had some value for her ornithological work, providing experience in evaluating the literature in English, German, and French and in recognizing the importance of close observation, "clear thinking, powers of organization, and initiative."[33]

The year without Blaine stimulated Margaret's interest in a variety of fields. Although she explored new areas of study, she never truly moved away from her fascination with birds. Still, after reading some articles in the *Atlantic Monthly* by William Beebe, she resolved to become a more all-around naturalist. She chose ferns as a new pursuit and embarked on a study in which she identified and mounted twenty-one species from the Grey Rocks area. However, she found the birds of Pelham so interesting that she even thought of writing a paper titled "The Summer Birds of Pelham, Massachusetts." She reported her discoveries to the state ornithologist, Edward H. Forbush, who was curious about the presence of Magnolia Warblers at Grey Rocks, because they typically built their nests in spruce. When she discovered a female Magnolia Warbler building a nest in a juniper, she was jubilant and resolved to make her first nest study. "For 26 hours in 17 sessions on 9 days, I watched the little family at distances from five to fifteen feet. Mother fed the three chicks 91 times; Father fed them 118 times and sang 1178 songs."[34]

Return to Oklahoma

In September 1925, Margaret and her family happily returned to their own home in Norman and were able to see "our Oklahoma birds." Clearly, she had identified with this place—it had become home, although she still loved to return to her first home in Massachusetts. To her delight, when they arrived, she found the largest number of occupied Mourning Dove nests in all seven years of fall observations. She spent her research energy on bird studies during the next twenty-one months.[35] During this time she added to her surveys and revisited some of the areas she had been to previously, such as the Arbuckle and Wichita Mountains and the Oklahoma Panhandle.

Meanwhile, *The Birds of Oklahoma* was arousing professional interest, and Margaret's life was proceeding comfortably and was intellectually profitable. In the summers, they visited Grey Rocks and families and then returned to Oklahoma in the fall.

A Move

Returning home in the fall of 1927, a life-changing decision affected both Blaine's and Margaret's careers. Blaine was offered and accepted a professorship in The Ohio State University Medical School in Columbus. Margaret wrote that it was a blow to the whole family to "leave our beloved Oklahoma, our birds and our prairie flowers." But she may have felt it more than the others, except perhaps twelve-year-old Barbara. Margaret wrote, "It seemed as if I were being wrenched up by the roots." Leaving Norman meant forgoing the walks that "had grown to be such a part of me that I did not see how I could be happy or function properly without them, that rather I might become a maimed and stunted creature." She felt "suddenly snatched from my rich field of activities where every walk offered possibilities of discovery, or additions" to her knowledge of Oklahoma birds.[36]

The family's comfortable life was about to undergo an upheaval. It is unclear what part Margaret had in the ultimate decision to move, but she and Blaine managed a united front when explaining the change to the children. Barbara, for one, was not convinced she would ever be happy away from her friends in Norman. She later lamented, "Without warning as far as I was concerned," her parents "made arrangements to move from Norman to Columbus, Ohio, where my father was to be on the faculty at Ohio State." By way of explanation, Barbara understood that the move was necessary because of "something to do with plans to transfer the Physiology Department to Oklahoma City along with the Medical School." She suspected that there were "personalities involved." Although this departmental move to Oklahoma City never came about, "at that time it seemed that it would," and Barbara was devastated by the proposed relocation to Columbus. For shy Barbara, the move meant leaving her close friend Mary behind. It was "a tremendous blow." She added, "I had never dreamed of moving away from Norman, from Mary. She and I had been studying that summer, to skip a grade; we would both go into the eighth grade if plans worked out."[37]

Interpont

The move was less traumatic than Margaret had anticipated because they found a new house that suited her needs perfectly. It was situated on a bluff above the floodplain of the Olentangy River, and the location was ideal for birds. She found the equivalent of her favorite Oklahoma spaces in Columbus, a "wild, neglected piece of flood plain" between the bridge at Dodridge Street and north of the bridge at Lane Avenue. She christened this area "Interpont," between the bridges. Since their house was near that site, Margaret had high hopes that were indeed realized; many of her new neighbors were birds.[38]

An unexpected advantage of Columbus over Oklahoma was its proximity to national ornithological meetings in the East. Nice was better able to attend events such as the 1927 AOU meeting in Washington, where she renewed old friendships and made new ones. Her new friends included the president of the AOU, the well-known ornithologist Alexander Wetmore (1886–1978), and Florence Merriam Bailey (1863–1948), now assistant secretary of the Smithsonian Institution. As a successful woman scientist, Bailey became a model for Nice. Her *Handbook of Birds of the Western United States* had accompanied Margaret on many of her bird-identification trips in Oklahoma. When Margaret was invited to dinner with Florence and her naturalist husband, Vernon Bailey, Florence greeted her as "Mrs. Mourning Dove Nice."[39]

Barbara's Problem with the Move

As perfect as the house and its surroundings appeared to Margaret, at least one of her children, Barbara, found them distasteful. She described the house as "dark" and "frumpy," and on the fringe of town. She did not share her mother's excitement about the proximity of that "excellent" habitat for birds, the new "weed patch." Their street was hardly "more than an alley, disappearing into weeds and a path along a dike leading down to the Scioto River." What for Margaret was ideal was for Barbara unpleasant and even embarrassing. The three houses on their cinder street were "tucked behind other people's backyards." And the two broad fields of weeds between the

Nice house and the "slow and grayish and polluted" Scioto River were not places where Barbara wanted to bring her friends to play.[40]

Barbara's views that her mother put research above family were magnified since she felt that her wishes were not considered in the move. As a child, she did not understand that her mother tried to make the best of a relocation that upset her research. After moving to Columbus, Nice still focused her research interests on Oklahoma birds, but she soon made a new circle of fellow bird-loving friends, a pleasant surprise after the dearth of such in Norman.[41]

Eleanor: A Tragedy

A tragedy struck the Nice family during the winter of 1927. Margaret and Blaine's nine-year-old daughter, Eleanor, died. Although Margaret was outspoken about her feelings when they involved professional problems, her reactions were muted when serious family problems occurred. Few events could be more emotionally wrenching than the death of a child. Yet in letters to colleagues and friends, Margaret informed them of the tragedy but did not dwell on it. It is through Barbara that we know the circumstances surrounding Eleanor's death and the devastating effect it had on the family, and especially on her. She reported that Eleanor had suffered from a persistent cough and cold but seemed to be improving when, after Christmas dinner with visiting Nice relatives, she went ice skating with family members "on a frozen pond in the middle of the weeds below our house." After that experience, she developed pneumonia, and her condition continued to worsen for about a week.[42]

In 1927, families routinely lost children to pneumonia. When a child came down with the disease, it was assumed that palliative care was all that could be done for the patient. William Osler in 1892 considered pneumonia a "self-limited disease," the course of which could not be influenced by any medicine. During the first part of the twentieth century, a new treatment offered a misplaced hope for the pneumonia patient. With the advent of immunology as a science, this new treatment was developed in Germany in 1891 and was known as antipneumococcal serotherapy. The treatment attempted to attack the pneumococcal organism itself by using specific antisera. Because serotherapy represented a "scientific" approach to "curing" the disease, pneumonia was elevated to a public health issue requiring centralized funding, technical assistance, and physician reeducation. The participation of so many different entities, often involving financial profit, caused people to interpret dubious results as success for the treatment. Before the advent of the first of the antibiotic sulfa drugs, Prontosil and sulfanilamide in 1935, when a child developed pneumonia there were only two options: the family could accept Osler's physiological approach or they could actively participate in an uncertain therapy.[43] The mortality statistics for 1927 indicate that pneumonia was a leading cause of death in children; 1,693 children from ages five to nine died of pneumonia that year in the United States.[44]

There is no evidence that Margaret and Blaine tried the new sero-therapy on Eleanor. It is possible that Blaine Nice, as a physiologist, may have been suspicious of the efficacy of this approach and decided to let the disease run its course. There was no mention of a hospital stay for Eleanor.

The stoic front that Margaret and Blaine put forth publicly was merely that—a front. Experiencing her parents' grief while enduring her own was devastating for Barbara. Just before Eleanor died, she found her parents and sisters in the dining room. In his anguish, Blaine cried out, "She's going to die. God I know it." Margaret, whose emotions were usually tightly under control, was in tears. Their parents' distress, so seldom seen, frightened the sisters. At the very end, Blaine called the girls to come to see Eleanor "before she dies." Barbara recalled that Eleanor was lying in the bed in Marjorie's room breathing in heavy gasps. The images of her favorite sister dying and dead especially haunted sensitive Barbara throughout her life. The funeral was held on a bleak, bitter cold day. In the funeral home Barbara put sweet peas around the neck of the fair-haired nine-year-old girl. While to some, viewing the body of a loved one is therapeutic, to Barbara it was a life-changing experience.

Introspective to the extreme, Barbara examined her own thoughts and suspected that if God demanded she give up the thing she loved most, her writing, she might not be able to do so. "My writing? *all* of it? and never be able to write again? words my life. For her? Would God ask that? Could I give it?" These thoughts and her guilt over the fact that she had often quarreled with her younger sister plagued her for many years.[45]

Although Eleanor's death profoundly affected all of the family, the effect on the parents and sisters other than Barbara can only be surmised. Barbara wrote that her parents were "grief-ravaged" but seemed numb and unwilling to talk about their feelings or about Eleanor.[46] Margaret's letters

to friends and colleagues cryptically reported the tragedy, but it is necessary to read between the lines to understand the real impact. Even though
Eleanor's death dealt a wrenching blow, Margaret spent only one short
paragraph in her autobiography on this calamity. Margaret's reticence to
share the details of the tragedy with others means that we do not know
whether she was under the care of a physician. Margaret and Blaine did
what they could to memorialize their daughter. To celebrate her life, they
donated a set of fifty children's books to the State University Hospital in
Columbus (there is no evidence that Eleanor was treated there) and one
hundred children's books to the Norman Public Library.[47]

Chapter 6

A SECOND EDITION OF
THE BIRDS OF OKLAHOMA AND THE
BEGINNING OF A NEW PROJECT

In a new house and with a new and exciting research area in Cleveland, Ohio, Nice banded her first Song Sparrow on March 26, 1928, and christened him "Uno." Little did she realize that she had begun a project that would ultimately ensure her place in the annals of bird behavior. Since Uno's territory was near the house, she could carefully and conveniently observe his behavior. Uno was only one of several Song Sparrows that she

A Song Sparrow; the little bird whose activities made Margaret's reputation as an ornithologist and animal behaviorist. *Courtesy Edward S. Thomas Collection, Ohio History Connection.*

A Song Sparrow nest filled with eggs. *Courtesy Edward S. Thomas Collection, Ohio History Connection.*

banded during 1928, but he was the first. When he returned the following year, she responded with "unbounded delight."[1] At this time she had no idea that much of her lasting fame would derive from the behavior of these small birds.

In 1928, however, Nice was still tied to Oklahoma and its birds. Her most immediate project was completing the revision of *The Birds of Oklahoma*. Assuming that distance from the source would impede her progress, she was pleasantly surprised to find that remoteness had some advantages. Although she missed having people with whom to consult and occasionally felt quite alone as she worked on the project, Nice sometimes considered herself liberated because "there is no one to direct, criticize, nor even make suggestions." This freedom made it possible for her to produce a publication that she hoped would have "the most originality" and "the least copying from other works" and would be filled with original observations.[2]

In May 1929 Nice went by train to visit Oklahoma briefly. She visited old friends, both humans and birds. She wrote to Constance, then a junior at Oberlin College:

It is a great joy to be back in this beautiful country once more and see my beloved flowers and birds. It is really a revelation to me to find how delighted people are to see me. Friends add a great wealth of happiness to life. The memorial for Eleanor of the children's books had made a link that has touched people's hearts.[3]

After this interlude, she returned to Columbus and continued working on her two major tasks.

Nice found that working on the two projects, Song Sparrows and *The Birds of Oklahoma*, simultaneously was a "good combination." Even though there would have been more time to work on Song Sparrows if she had not been involved with the latter project, she found she could do both by "cutting out everything else." After observing Song Sparrows in the morning, she could spend the rest of the day working on Oklahoma's birds.[4]

In spite of being liberated from the ideas of others, Margaret began to have qualms about her ability to attempt such a mammoth task as a second edition of *The Birds of Oklahoma* single-handedly. Although Blaine coauthored the first edition, he had little to do with the production of the second. The undertaking became especially daunting when she learned that the Oklahoma Biological Survey planned to publish this work early in 1931, much sooner than she had expected. Assuming that she had until the end of January to complete it, during the spring of 1930 she had spent most of her time on Song Sparrows. She returned to the Oklahoma bird project only in late June. The leisurely pace that Margaret had envisioned was interrupted by news from Oklahoma that the entire manuscript was due no later than December 1. In order to meet the new deadline, Nice worked constantly on the manuscript. With Marjorie's help, typing sections of the manuscript as they were completed, she sent it off the day before Thanksgiving. The completed project was nearly twice as long as the first *Birds of Oklahoma*, with a much fuller treatment of migration dates and habits.

Proud of her creation, Margaret wrote, "This volume was a tribute of my love and admiration for Oklahoma—the country, the birds, and many of the people." She was especially pleased that she could give credit to early observers who had previously received little or no recognition. The subsequent fate of the manuscript, however, was a horror story. As time passed and she heard nothing from the publisher in Oklahoma, she understandably became anxious. Her first notice of the destiny of the work arrived while she and Blaine were attending a joint meeting of the Wilson Club and the American Association for the Advancement of Science in Cleveland. There she met the professor who was superintending the publication of the book. He admitted that although he had received the manuscript, he had not begun work on it. He promised to have several batches of proofs, including page proofs, sent to her.[5]

Not until February 19, 1931, did she finally received the first batch of proofs. The last batch arrived in March but did not include the bibliography, and she never did receive the page proofs for it. In spite of this omission, the finished publication arrived in her mailbox in the middle of April. Greeted with a full page of errata related mostly to the bibliography, she was horrified. The bibliography was completely mixed up and works were credited to wrong authors. For example, she despaired, "27 of my own 50 references were attributed to Dr. Gould." Even more disturbing, many of the copies had been distributed without the errata page. Gratified that the reviewers "considerately made no mention of the inexcusable negligence that marred the bulletin," she reported that they "emphasized the good features."[6]

While Nice was trying desperately to complete *The Birds of Oklahoma*, she was unable to spend much time on Song Sparrows. Nevertheless, she managed to work on them whenever she had the opportunity. In order to identify the same birds in subsequent years, she trapped and banded them in the winter and early spring.

Nice expanded her study during the season of 1930 to include over thirty acres of the Interpont. She banded 47 breeding adults, discovered 61 of their nests, and banded 102 nestlings that had fledged safely. Her careful observations negated certain theories, both of others and her own, about the behavior of the species. Nice recognized two different populations of Song Sparrows, resident and migratory. She and others had postulated that the resident birds were the offspring of resident parents, and that the migrant birds came from migrant parents. However, after she banded seven young male birds at the Interpont during the winter, she realized that this theory did not hold up. By checking banding data she determined that although one resident son had a resident father, four resident sons had three migratory fathers. She also determined later that residency was not constant, because seven of her banded birds changed their status.

One male migrated for two winters and remained in Ohio for the third. A female was a resident for one winter, migrated the next, and returned the following spring. Two other males remained for two winters but migrated for the third and returned in the spring. She concluded that one factor influencing migration was the weather in October. Mild temperatures appeared to tempt the birds to remain, whereas bleak, cold days influenced them to migrate.[7]

A second question Nice explored in 1930 was the origin of the songs of seven young male birds. In 1924 Aretas Andrews Saunders (1884–1970) had published a paper in *The Auk* positing that the possession of similar songs by birds might indicate relationships. Nice sought to learn whether song patterns were innate or whether they were learned during the first four weeks of life while birds were still being cared for by their parents. Her conclusions were negative on both counts. She discovered that "no son had any song of his father," that two brothers had no song in common, and that bird 58M "possessed a wild and lovely strain unlike any other Song Sparrow" she had ever heard.[8] She determined that the birds began to sing a wide variety of phrases in late winter and developed their individual repertoires by early spring.

Nice became very attached to her subjects and mourned when several of her favorites failed to return. Barbara McClintock also recognized the importance of attachment to her subject. Working with corn, she received the Nobel Prize for her discovery that genetic elements could move from one chromosome site to another. Her discovery of genetic transposition involved hearing "what the material has to say to you," as quoted by Evelyn Fox Keller in her 1983 biography. Most importantly, McClintock also wrote, "one must have 'a feeling for the organism.'" She added, "No two plants are exactly alike. They're all different, and as a consequence, you have to know that difference." Explaining her procedure, McClintock wrote, "I start with the seedling, and I don't want to leave it. I don't feel I really know the story if I don't watch the plant all the way along. So I know every plant in the field. I know them intimately, and I find it a great pleasure to know them."[9]

This type of attachment to the subject might lend credence to the idea of a feminist science, for in fact it may be more common in female scientists than in male, as Keller suggests. However, McClintock would disclaim any classification of her research as different because she was female. She would insist that science is not a matter of gender, either male or female. Keller partially agreed, noting that "the scientific tradition is far more pluralistic than any particular description of it suggests, and certainly more pluralistic than its dominant ideology." Nevertheless, she recognized that since McClintock was a woman, gender must be considered when evaluating her research:

> Because she is not a man, in a world of men, her commitment to a gender-free science has been binding; because concepts of gender have so deeply influenced the basic categories of science, that commitment has been transformative. In short, the relevance of McClintock's gender in this story is to be found not in its role in her personal socialization but precisely in the role of gender in the construction of science.[10]

The same conclusion Keller noted for McClintock can be applied to Nice in her attachment to her subjects and, indeed, to her approach to science.

During the summer of 1931, after banding numerous birds, the family left the Interpont so that Margaret could attend her twenty-fifth reunion at Mount Holyoke College. As usual, they visited Grey Rocks, and she found the time to observe the nests, songs, and fledglings of Black-throated Green Warblers.[11] Upon returning home, she wrote a long, detailed paper on the history of the two nests she had observed that summer, comparing her results with those of others. This study, her last one on Grey Rocks warblers, was the basis for a paper she gave in the fall of 1931 at the American Ornithologists' Union (AOU) meeting.[12]

AOU Meeting, 1931

The venerable American Ornithologists' Union was established on September 26, 1883, with no women among its founders. Other scientific societies had similar beginnings, but during the 1920s, many of the major professional societies began to admit women. On the surface, this move seemed to be a positive step for the recognition of women scientists. However, the societies soon created membership categories, and few women could meet the criteria established for the higher categories of membership.

The AOU represented an excellent example of stratification, with women clustered in the lower ranks. Ornithologist Florence Merriam (later Bailey), the sister and later wife of prominent naturalists, was elected to be the society's first "lady associate" in 1885. For her numerous writings in the 1890s, she was promoted to "member" and in 1912 was unsuccessfully nominated for "fellow." Not until 1929 did she finally achieve this goal.[13] That same year, conflict arose between women ornithologists in the lower ranks and the higher-ranked males. The female members were indignant that no woman had been elected fellow, while the organization simultaneously insisted that there was no discrimination. Nice's associate and friend Althea Sherman wrote to Margaret in 1924, "I have said and believe it, that no woman will ever be made a fellow of AOU." She complained that the men had the ability to pack the meetings and vote for their friends.[14]

Two years after Bailey had been elected fellow there were still only four female members: Mable Osgood Wright, Althea H. Sherman, Elsie M. Naumberger, and May T. Cook. Nice was elected member at this meeting, bringing the number of women members to five. There were many women associates, the lowest category. After years of protests, in 1955 the associate designation was changed to member, while the former members became "elective members." Nice finally became a fellow in 1937.[15]

The 1931 meeting was important to Nice not because she read her paper on warblers, but because she met Ernst Mayr, who was to start working at the American Museum of Natural History in New York City, and the two began an important friendship. A recent immigrant from Germany, Mayr was critical of the quality of most of the papers presented at the AOU meeting. He considered Nice's paper to be in a different category—it not only described ornithological explorations, distribution, and migration but also encompassed the conservation of endangered species. He became a mentor, introduced her to the German periodical *Journal für Ornithologie*, and supplied her with the names and addresses of important European ornithologists interested in life-history work. As soon as possible she sent off letters to these scientists and received friendly replies, many of which included reprints. One of these reprints was especially important for her future work: a classic paper by Oskar Heinroth (1871–1945) on the relationships between bird weight, egg weight, set weight, and length of incubation (1922).[16]

A Friendship Develops: Nice and Mayr

After returning to Columbus, Nice began an extensive correspondence with Mayr. Interested in birds from his childhood, Mayr had become a competent observer by the time he entered the University of Greifswald

in 1923 to study medicine. He claimed that he chose Greifswald because
it was situated in an ornithologically interesting area. Mayr had previously
made a positive impression on ornithologist Erwin Stresemann of Berlin
when he was able to identify a rare species of bird. In 1925, at Professor
Stresemann's suggestion, he gave up medical school and completed his
doctorate in ornithology at the University of Berlin. A year later, at the
age of twenty-one, he accepted a position at the Berlin Museum. Stresemann, who had become Mayr's mentor, introduced him to the banker and
naturalist Walter Rothschild (1868–1937). Rothschild asked Mayr to lead
what became an extraordinarily successful expedition to New Guinea on
his behalf and that of the American Museum of Natural History. Mayr
returned to Germany in 1930, and when Nice met him at the AOU meeting
in 1931 he had accepted a position as curator at the American Museum of
Natural History in New York City.[17]

At Nice's request, Mayr supplied her with an application form for membership in the Deutsche Ornithologen-Gesellschaft. She was delighted that
her application was accepted, especially because of her admiration for the
German ornithologists. Unhappy with the state of American ornithological studies, she exalted the European investigators: "I am much impressed
with how the Germans know all that we are doing . . . while we know almost
nothing of what they are doing."[18]

Nice always answered her correspondents immediately. If they were
dilatory about replying she did not hesitate to send a follow-up letter, as she
did once to Mayr. "I wonder whether my letter and reprints reached you?"[19]
Mayr apparently felt appropriately chastised for his delay in replying and
wrote apologetically, "I feel terribly guilty for not having answered your
kind letter of last November, and for not having thanked you for the package of reprints." Mayr also favored international cooperation but realized
that "as long as people who study birds do not learn foreign languages
they cannot expect to understand the scientific work of other countries."[20]
Nice's education in languages prepared her to read and translate German
and French works, an advantage she had over many of her colleagues in
the United States.

Europe, 1932

Nice soon had an opportunity to meet many of her correspondents in person. Her husband's International Physiological Congress met in Rome in

late August, making it financially possible for him to bring Margaret and their three older daughters with him. While Margaret familiarized herself with European birds and talked to ornithologists, the girls acquired a general educational experience. Margaret sought advice from Mayr about their planned itinerary, writing, "It will be a great help to us in our plans if you can answer promptly as you did last time."[21] The family, minus eight-year-old Janet, who stayed with Margaret's mother and sister Katharine, sailed for Europe on June 26, 1932.

With Mayr's help, they finalized their itinerary. Their first stop was France. Although Margaret spoke French, she found her printed bird guide woefully inadequate for bird identification. Upon reaching Paris, she wrote to M. Jacques Berlioz (1891–1975), assistant director of the laboratory of ornithology of the Museum of Natural History (Muséum National d'Histoire Naturelle), and included a letter of introduction written by Mayr. Unfortunately, the introduction was not helpful, for Berlioz replied that he was about to depart for Canada and could not show her around personally.

Left to her own devices, Nice, armed with Berlioz's reply, went by herself to the venerable museum, which was originally founded in 1626 as a royal garden of medicinal plants (Jardin du Roi) and later expanded to incorporate a museum to house the king's natural history collections. Georges-Louis Leclerc, Comte de Buffon (1707–1788) became *intendant* (director) in 1739 and was instrumental in converting the Jardin du Roi into a major research center and museum. He enlarged the original area by arranging for the purchase of adjoining parcels of land and acquired botanical and zoological specimens from all over the world. After the French Revolution, the tradition of the Jardin du Roi continued, but in 1793 its name was changed to the postrevolutionary Muséum National d'Histoire Naturelle.

When Nice visited the museum, she found that the birds were not arranged by taxonomic or habitat groups but were organized in rows, much as they would have been in Buffon's time. The guards were not helpful; one was asleep and the other three were busily conversing with each other. After inducing one guard to show her *les oiseaux de la France* (the birds of France), she was taken to a small room that contained large birds on shelves near the floor, but the smaller birds were arranged close to the ceiling. The only access to them was through a gallery, and she could see no stairway. Since her purpose in going to the museum was to see small passerines, she was frustrated. To make matters worse, the guards informed her that access was only for the professors. After showing the guard the letter in English from Berlioz, he pretended to understand it and agreed to take her to the "sacred gallery," as Nice described it. Although he informed her that she could visit for only ten minutes, she talked him into fifteen. From her exalted position above the main gallery, she could hear arguments and recriminations against "her" guard for letting her into a forbidden area. In spite of all the problems, she discovered the French names of many birds as well as the identity of several birds she had observed outside.[22] Trying to identify unfamiliar French birds in the field was difficult, but Dr. Hans Scharnke, a student of Professor Erwin Stresemann, led her on a bird-watching trip to Saint-Germain-en-Laye.

While the family enjoyed a journey on the Rhine, Margaret took a train to Berlin, where she found disturbing political posters everywhere. She reported that the Communists and National Socialists were vying for power, calling each other "liars, murderers and so on, while another party attacked them both."[23] Although troubled by these developments, she temporarily put politics on the back burner and tried to ignore the ominous political overtones. At the time of her visit, although Adolph Hitler had already replaced his Austrian citizenship with German, the seeds of his vicious ascent to power were not immediately apparent to visitors. Like many other visitors from the United States, Nice was impressed by the friendliness of the German people, the fragrance and beauty of the flowers and trees, and the sophistication of the scientific institutions. She found Germany a superb place to learn about birds and their behavior. The ornithologist Erwin Stresemann welcomed her warmly, as did Ernst Mayr, who was visiting his former teacher. Stresemann invited Nice to use his extensive library, where she worked for ten days.

George Steinbacher and Werner Rüppell, students of Stresemann, took Nice on two birding expeditions. Although these trips were interesting, as was her tour through Oskar Heinroth's institute and the zoo, guided by Heinroth himself, who was director of the Berlin Aquarium, she claimed that the most important benefits of her visit were her conversations with Stresemann.

These conversations were especially useful to Nice, for in Norman and even in Columbus she had little interaction with other ornithologists. The only organization in Columbus that could have provided her with feedback was the Wheaton Club, but it was open only to men. She had little opportunity to try out her ideas on colleagues. Although it would have been more satisfactory to share ideas in person, she had previously had to rely on correspondence; especially helpful was her correspondence with Mayr. For example, she wrote Mayr, "My Song Sparrows are proving more and more interesting. I am getting many returns now, especially of my nesting males banded one and two years ago."[24] Coming across the German term *Strichvogel*, Nice asked Mayr about its meaning.[25] She was interested in finding out whether the term might apply to her Song Sparrows. Mayr replied:

> We call Strichvogel in Germany those birds which leave their breeding grounds during the winter but do not migrate to any fixed winter quarters. . . . As a matter of fact, there is no definite line between the residents and Strichvogel and Strichvogel and migrants. In certain species of birds, as, for example, in our European blackbird, the more northern populations are regular Migrants. The southern-most populations are strict residents, while birds in intermediate localities are Strichvogel. . . . You will see that many of your American birds can also be called Strichvogel.[26]

The term proved applicable to Nice's work on Song Sparrows, as she attempted to understand why some birds remained resident and others were migratory. If Nice had had knowledgeable colleagues at home with whom to discuss the situation, it would have been most helpful. In April, shortly before her European trip, she reported that she had banded over seventy adult nesting males and over sixty females. "I have 60% return—or survival—of the adult males, 50 per cent of the females and 13 per cent of the nestlings this year—11 per cent last year."[27] Although correspondence of this sort was immensely useful to Nice, the person-to-person contact on this 1931 trip to Europe provided an entirely new dimension to her research.

Stresemann listened carefully to her descriptions of the Song Sparrow study and made valuable suggestions. Nice complained that it was difficult to publish long papers in the United States because, regardless of merit, the editor of *The Auk* published most of the short papers and rejected the longer ones. Stresemann replied that although he rejected over two-thirds of the papers submitted to him as editor of the *Journal für Ornithologie*, the oldest continually published ornithology journal in the world, length was not a criterion for acceptance or rejection. He invited Nice to send him her paper on the Song Sparrow and promised to have it translated into German. Stresemann's statement that it could be one hundred pages long if she wished delighted her. He agreed that since *The Auk* published nothing longer than twenty pages, a paper so short could not adequately present her material.[28] Stresemann's enthusiasm provided Nice with the push she needed to prepare the paper when she returned home.

The Girls Tour Europe

After Margaret's visit to Berlin, the family met in Munich but then separated again, with the girls traveling to Venice and Blaine and Margaret to Switzerland; here the Nice parents went birding with ornithologist Josef Bussman and his wife. The three Nice girls who went on the trip, Constance, Marjorie, and Barbara, were twenty-two, twenty, and seventeen years old, respectively, and apparently Margaret and Blaine thought they were old enough to travel around Europe on their own. All the family members spoke some French, but Constance and Marjorie became the trip historians. However, it was Barbara who gave an account of the trip in her autobiography. She noted that she and her sisters were "receptive to some extent to the impact of an old culture, and all the material evidences of earlier ages." She recalled exploring the Norman coast, "the dankness in the dungeons of Mt. St. Michel, and the light melodic voices of French girls walking along the wall." She also remembered their pension in Paris, and meeting her French correspondent Paul. Apparently, Paul had been designated to help Barbara (and perhaps the older girls) navigate France. Barbara was afraid to meet him and felt "horrifying [sic] inept and stiff and frightened." Although "he talked good English," she declined "a real opportunity" to visit his home. Barbara described her adventures "bumping along third class on a German train," and over the steep Austrian hillside. In Rome, she lay on the benches in the Sistine Chapel "to make out the paintings on the ceiling." Although the three girls traveled together, they also separated according to their different interests. Barbara was alone at least some of the time, for she mentioned striking up a conversation with a solitary visitor at the Forum, "alone like me, and I believe a German." In Venice, Barbara recalled Marjorie arguing about the fare with a gondolier in Venice.

In Naples, Barbara had a romantic adventure. She met "a lean dark slight English boy" only a year older than herself and accompanied him to Capri. They spent "an utterly heavenly day upon the ferry, climbing over the hump, swimming (and burning) in rented bathing suits." She arrived back at the pension, where she worried because her sisters had not returned from their excursion. Although she met the boy, Douglas, in London again, she recognized that their romance was doomed. "There was an air of foreordained tragedy about this tenuous drawing together." Douglas's "dark coloring" was inherited from his Indian father. Because he was half Indian, she noted that societal constraints dictated that she would never be able to marry him:

> My parents, "They," public opinion, and the climate in which I had lived, my own lack of courage and knowledge of the world; I should never be able to be with him. It was unadulterated tragedy; I wept in my room downstairs; my father sent for me to come to their rooms upstairs.

Barbara found it "impossible" to disregard Blaine's summons. From this incident a glimpse of family dynamics emerged. Barbara fully expected an insensitive response from her father and a supportive one from her mother. She was surprised when she had his sympathetic understanding. As she expected, Margaret was compassionate. However, even with the support of her family, the prejudices of the prevailing culture ensured that Barbara's assessment was correct. Nevertheless, she was gratified to find that "feelings for once . . . were respected."[29] Douglas and Barbara wrote to each other for about a year after she returned to the United States.

When Margaret and Blaine arrived at the Physiological Congress in Rome, Blaine gave his talk on changes in the specific gravity and chemical elements in the blood after emotional excitement. Meanwhile, before returning to London, Margaret practiced her Italian with her fellow bird banders. The family came together in England. After visiting London, they returned to the United States and landed in New York, where they were reunited with Janet, and returned to Interpont on September 27, 1932.[30]

Strategies for Intercontinental Cooperation

Back in Columbus, Nice was still starry eyed from her European experience. She thanked Mayr for starting her "on the road to acquaintance with European bird literature and ornithologists." She waxed ecstatic over Berlin: "Never before (nor since) have I found people so uniformly courteous and friendly." Nice contrasted the help she received on her problems in

Germany with what she had experienced in the United States.[31] The trip to Europe was vitally important for two major aspects of Nice's future career: intercontinental collaboration and inspiration to continue her Song Sparrow research. After making friends with European investigators, she became passionate about increasing the cooperation between the Europeans and Americans. Her attempts at establishing this association helped guarantee her place in the history of science. The effect of this cross-fertilization also had a direct influence on Nice's own research on the Song Sparrow. Through meeting European ornithologists and behaviorists, she was inspired to continue her research with renewed vigor.

After an unsuccessful attempt to convince the president of the Wilson Club, Jesse M. Shaver, to join the Deutsche Ornithologen-Gesellschaft, Nice decided to embark on some missionary work during the club's meeting to try to change minds.[32] She recognized the need to bridge the gap between European and American ornithology by developing effective strategies. She stated to Mayr that although the first step should be the interchange of information, to ensure that this exchange would occur she must first educate her recalcitrant American colleagues. Thus, she gave a talk to the Wilson Club describing her European experiences and followed it up with an article for the April issue of *Bird-Banding*, "telling something of the birds, the people, the institutions, the fine work that is being done, etc. and urg[ing] people to keep in touch with what is being done across the ocean."[33] The Wilson Club attendees evidently responded positively, for they suggested that she write an article for the *Wilson Bulletin* indicating the most important periodicals and books that American ornithologists should know about.[34]

The language problem explained much of the lack of cross-Atlantic scientific exchange. Understandably, the German journals presented a problem to most Americans, but it did not explain why *British Birds* did not have a wider circulation in the United States. Nice did not attempt to explain the problems with British periodicals, but she tried to convince Americans that "scientific German isn't so very hard," even while adding the caveat that American ornithologists would have to be "willing to work" at it. Determined to improve international communication, she asked Charles L. Whittle, the editor of *Bird-Banding*, to invite European ornithologists to contribute to the journal. This idea set Nice along the path she would follow throughout her life, that of reviewing foreign articles for various American publications. Although her early attempts to convince Americans of the importance of cooperation across the Atlantic met with resistance, she was eventually successful in convincing others that research in foreign countries was applicable to American ornithology.[35]

Initially Nice faced formidable opposition from the American journals, which were set in their ways and not interested in change. As she had complained to Stresemann, *The Auk* made it difficult to publish good papers and did not really critique those papers that it did publish. She faulted the editor for being too kindly and "too courteous to criticize adequately contributions sent him or to judge the many publications he mentioned in his journal." On the other hand, the editor of *Bird-Banding* was eager to include any article that might improve ornithology. This journal became a venue for Nice's determination to present foreign ideas and publications to the American ornithological community. With the blessings of editor Whittle, she produced a review section for the journal that included foreign publications.[36] Her new method of presenting the reviews by subject rather than alphabetically by author annoyed those who found all change disagreeable, but many readers approved of the idea. Still, her mainstream parochial colleagues failed to see the need for American ornithologists and behaviorists to understand the European literature. She approached the resisters by persuading influential American scientists of the importance of more exchange and encouraging them to lobby for the cause.

One man whom Nice considered vital as an advocate for her cause was the highly respected Joseph Grinnell (1877–1939). Grinnell served as the director of the Museum of Vertebrate Zoology at the University of California, Berkeley; he also edited one of the publications of the Cooper Ornithological Club, *The Condor*, for forty-three years. Using herself as an example, Nice explained in a letter to Grinnell that she realized the importance of an international exchange of scientific papers only after it became apparent that although she was very familiar with the American literature on life-history studies, she knew "practically nothing of foreign work." She proceeded to make her case: "Too many American ornithologists have despised the study of the living bird; the magazine and the books that deal with the subject abound in careless statements, anthropomorphic interpretations, repletion of ancient errors and sweeping conclusions from a pitiful array of facts."[37]

Nice continued by reporting that she had begun the project by ensuring that *Bird-Banding* would publish a series of articles from foreign bird banders. Since *Bird-Banding* did not have the same prestige as *The Condor*, she drew on Mayr's name to convince Grinnell to publish foreign articles in that journal. She wrote that "Dr. Mayr and I" realized that a journal that published papers of a "non-banding" character would be most important. After making as strong a case as possible, Nice asked the influential Grinnell if he would be willing to publish European papers in *The Condor*.[38]

Although Grinnell had not answered Nice's letter by early January 1933, he did respond to Mayr. Nice was not offended that Grinnell had responded to him rather than to her, but rather was delighted that he appeared interested. In a letter to Mayr she asked: "Aren't we having fine success with our plans?"[39] Gender as well as Mayr's reputation probably entered into Grinnell's decision to reply to him rather than to Nice, even though she had initiated the correspondence. Grinnell's positive reply to Mayr included a series of queries.

Since Nice had put off writing the article for the *Wilson Bulletin* because she was working on her Song Sparrow paper, she was inspired by Grinnell's response and resolved to finish the article as soon as possible.[40] Mayr wrote, "The whole matter looks very promising now, and I agree with you that we should attack the matter at once." He also agreed to translate the papers "if such papers are not too long and not too numerous."[41]

Deepening Friendships

The friendship between Nice and Mayr deepened and expanded to include their families. Since Marjorie Nice attended Columbia University in New York and Mayr was at the American Museum, he asked for her address, and they developed a friendly relationship.[42] It was through Marjorie that Margaret learned of Mayr's engagement. She offered her congratulations and added, "I am anxious to know more of your fiancée. Is she a naturalist?" The congratulatory statement was hidden in a letter filled with information about publications and birds. She obviously felt guilty about how she viewed the relative importance of the engagement news and research news. "I did not mean to tuck in the comment on the great news of your engagement in the middle of this letter; I meant to have it the climax! But afterwards, I thought of several other things."[43]

The professional relationship between Nice and Mayr gradually became more of one between equals. Although she always considered him her mentor (a position he was happy to accept), he began to ask her to critique some of his material. In a letter to Nice, Mayr included a manuscript of his paper "Bernard Altum and the Territory Theory," later published in the *Proceedings of the Linnaean Society of New York*, and requested her comments and advice. This paper initiated Mayr's historical writings. Nice praised it as a fine piece of work and "inserted suggestions here and there as to the English—a few commas, etc. which seemed needed." She also enclosed a general critique of the work. That he asked for her assessment of this work illustrates his increasing respect for her opinions. However, in spite of the exchange of papers and ideas between the two, there remained an unequal quality in their relationship. Throughout their lives they both considered Mayr to be the mentor and Nice the learner.[44]

Chapter 7

PUBLISHING THE
SONG SPARROW RESEARCH

The 1932 meeting with European ornithologists and behaviorists in France and Germany inspired Nice to continue her research on the Song Sparrow with renewed vigor and determination. Although she was determined to present Stresemann with a completed manuscript as soon as possible, her progress was impeded by too many activities: convincing U.S. journal editors of the importance of international cooperation, carrying on an extensive correspondence, and writing reviews. To make matters worse, the city of Columbus, mired in economic woes spawned by the Great Depression, sought ways to mitigate the hunger of many of its citizens by planting gardens in unpopulated areas. One such area was the Interpont.

The good intentions of the city of Columbus resulted in unintended consequences, for the Interpont to which Nice returned in 1932 was not the same place she had left the previous year. The city had cleared the area along the riverbank of trees and underbrush. In her journal she lamented, "The most beautiful spot on all Interpont has been demolished. 'Janet's Mountain' leveled. The weeds cut down; a desert made. I'm thankful I was 4,000 miles away this summer." Although she was able to convince the authorities to retain some of the most important habitat, many of the Song Sparrows had been driven away and others were forced to shift their territories to areas that had not been denuded. Nice had hoped that the authorities would forget their garden-cultivating plan, but such was not the case. Just as she was beginning to relax, men arrived with plows attached to tractors. On June 6, most of the Song Sparrow nests held two- to three-month-old nestlings. One brood of four was almost ready to fledge, and in hopes of protecting the young Nice slipped them into a stocking and released them into a nearby grove of cottonwood trees. Two of the rescued birds survived. She relocated many young birds, hoping that at least some would live. The entire season of 1933 seemed to be plagued by one calamity after another. A late spring followed by two floods also destroyed many of the nests. The rebuilt nests were then ruined when tractors plowed the Interpont.[1]

Zur Naturgeschichte des Singammers

In spite of the problems, Nice spent whatever free time she could find working on her Song Sparrow paper. By organizing her activities well, she was able to spend an hour outside observing and the rest of the day writing. Aside from the necessary activities of eating, sleeping, preparing breakfast and lunch, and a modicum of housework, she worked full time on the manuscript. Rather than hindering her progress, her daughters helped by preparing dinner and washing the dishes. As she worked, she sometimes felt elated but at other times was discouraged and convinced the work would never be finished.

In November Nice wrote Mayr that although she had a good start on the paper, an immense amount of work remained. As she organized and summarized her earlier research, she realized how much more reading she needed to do. "I fear I may not be able to finish the article next month as I had hoped to do."[2]

Nice began typing the manuscript on February 26, 1933, and mailed the completed product to Stresemann on March 18. Triumphantly, she informed Mayr, "The *Melospiza-Forschungen* started for Germany last week; it has been a mighty task, but it has been a most valuable experience for me, for I can go on with my problems now much more intelligently than before."[3] Stresemann, pleased with her "magnum opus," offered his "heartiest congratulations" and gave the manuscript to Dr. Hermann Desselberger to translate into German.[4] However, getting the manuscript to Stresemann was just a first step in the long process toward publication.

Editing, translating, adding new data, and providing up-to-date maps delayed the actual appearance of the paper in the *Journal für Ornithologie*. In a letter, Nice credited Mayr with an important role in its final production; he had provided suggestions for improving a revised version with its new data.[5] After he received this amended copy, he sent his comments to Nice. In response, she wrote him that she felt cheered because he had extravagantly reported that the manuscript left him "speechless."[6] The translating proved to be a major task, and Desselberger planned to send his entire translation to Mayr for advice on some "Americanisms." Stresemann had previously told Nice that the first part of the paper would not appear before the *"Oktoberheft."*[7] Even this prediction was overoptimistic because it was November when it finally appeared.

Nice's major treatise in German appeared in the *Journal für Ornithologie* under the title *Zur Naturgeschichte des Singammers.* Because of its length, the treatise was published in two separate issues of the journal and occupied the entire issues. The first part appeared in November 1933 and the second in January 1934.[8]

In the introduction Nice credited Stresemann, Mayr, and Desselberger for making publication possible. She also familiarized the reader with the Song Sparrow and explained her choice of the bird as a research subject. Although the entire species had a wide geographic range, Nice studied only one race or subspecies, the Mississippi Song Sparrow, *Melospiza melodia beata* Bangs. After briefly recounting its appearance and habits, including food preferences, she noted that in spite of the bird being relatively common, attractive, and friendly, little research had been done on Song Sparrow biology. Her goal was to rectify this gap. Choosing the Song Sparrow as the object of her research was especially convenient, because Nice had only to walk out her door to encounter her subjects. Contextualizing the study for her European readers, she described her research area and included a map of the region she studied and a photograph of a Song Sparrow.

Research Methodology

Nice explained her thorough research approach, including the capturing, banding, and releasing of birds and the recording of data. From her earlier work on the Mourning Dove, she was well aware of the importance of a consistent, convenient, and clear method of research. She elaborated on and modified her previous scheme as she discussed capture and banding. Her later English-language version of the Song Sparrow study included the same methodological material as the German.

Experimenting with different types of traps, Nice found that a funnel trap that allowed the bird to enter in order to get the bait and subsequently become trapped inside worked best. Sometimes, however, the bait (a mixture of seeds, baby chick feed, hemp, millet, bread crumbs, crackers, and rolled oats) was an insufficient incentive to attract them. In these cases, Nice used other birds as decoys to lure the subject Song Sparrow into the trap. She used different iterations of this ploy, but one involved using the young as bait, either by putting a large trap over a nest when the offspring were about six days old or placing the young that were ready to leave the nest in a small cage inside the trap. As the parents checked on the young they found themselves trapped.

Occasionally Nice took advantage of the cowbird's habit of laying its eggs in the nests of other birds by placing a seven- to ten-day-old Brown-headed Cowbird (*Molothrus ater ater*) into a Song Sparrow nest for a short time. She then put the baby parasite in a trap beside the nest and trapped the adoptive parents when they came to tend to their charge. By using these and other methods, Nice was usually able to catch the birds, although she reported that a few stubborn ones refused to enter the traps. After catching a bird, she brought it into the house in a small cage with a black cloth wrapped around it. She then banded and weighed it, measured its wing and tail, and released it from a window.[9]

The second part of Nice's research involved banding the birds, or as the Europeans called it, "ringing." She used numbered aluminum bands supplied by the U.S. Biological Survey. For nestlings, the bands were placed on the right leg, and on the left for adults. In addition, Nice positioned colored celluloid bands on the trapped birds but not on the nestlings. She made her own celluloid bands or used poultry bands produced for baby chicks. Nice recommended vivid colors (red, blue, green, black, and yellow), with the admonishment that they must not fade. Two celluloid bands on each bird worked best, so that if one band was lost the bird could still be identified. A great number of combinations were possible, depending on the position of the celluloid band above or below the aluminum band and whether or not it was on the right or left leg. She used these colored bands in addition to the numbered aluminum ones because the latter were difficult to read in the field.[10]

Although bird bands were not Nice's innovation, the use of colored bands may have been. Certainly, the way she modified colored bands to suit her own needs was unique. The banding of birds in order to understand their movements is credited to a Danish schoolteacher, Hans Christian Mortensen. In 1899, he was the first to band birds in a systematic attempt to study migration. He marked a great range of species, and by the time of his death in 1920 he had banded 5,000 individuals of thirty-three species. His innovation quickly spread throughout Europe.[11]

Recognizing the importance of identifying individual birds, Nice devised an impressive system of record keeping that was much more elaborate than the one she had used previously for Mourning Doves. To the casual reader this system seems unnecessarily complex and has considerable overlap. However, she considered redundancy good insurance against error. Her records included a Banding Record, Card Catalog, Key Tables, Daily Record, Field Notebook, Maps, Nest Records, and Plan of Work. To help the reader understand the system, she painstakingly noted in the article what each category included and how and why she used it.[12]

Plan of Work

When Nice explained her Plan of Work in the published paper, there is no doubt that those who praised her work on the Song Sparrow were correct. Her thorough research on all aspects of these birds' lives inspired trust in her observations. The amount of time she spent in the field was impressive. She did not have a break in the winter; Song Sparrow observation was year round since not all Song Sparrows migrated. In late fall and winter Nice observed them every day for one to two hours. She recorded the birds she saw and set traps for new birds. Every morning from February on, she visited all of Upper Interpont to look for new arrivals. In the spring and summer Nice spent the entire morning and often part of the afternoon and evening observing the birds. She also took a census at various times of the year. Her census methods involved identifying each bird by its field number and recording its location on the map. She explained that there were optimum times to conduct the census for various categories of birds such as resident males, summer resident males, or females (before incubation and when the leaves were not yet out). This time-consuming work would have been almost impossible for a person with a full-time position and perhaps incited some envy among those ornithologists who were unable to devote so much time to their research. However, when one takes into account Nice's domestic responsibilities and additional professional tasks, her freedom to work as required was remarkable.

With such a meticulously organized methodology, it is obvious why this publication was so widely praised, especially in Europe. Although Stresemann recognized that part 1 of the publication was very important, he was even more effusive in his praise for part 2, claiming that he did not know a similarly oriented study as full of substance or one that would so greatly advance science.

It was not Nice's complex research method, but her vision of the importance of following the same birds over a period of years and studying every aspect of their behavior that made her work so valuable. As historians know, it is dangerous to credit someone as being the "first" to do something. It is also unfortunate to designate a study as the most important in its area of research. Since natural history is a venerable field, people have studied the behavior of birds for many centuries, beginning at least during the time of Aristotle (384–322 B.C.E.). In the nineteenth century, British amateur ornithologists observed birds in the field and attempted to interpret their behavior. For example, naturalist Edmund Selous (1857–1934) believed in the value of patiently watching the behavior of a single bird species; one of his favorite subjects was the Nightjar (*Caprimulgus europaeus*). Selous's approach to bird study was neither as methodical nor as long term as Nice's. As much as possible, he took notes in the field and elaborated on them later under more comfortable circumstances.[13] Another British amateur, Henry Eliot Howard (1873–1940), helped demonstrate the scientific importance of fieldwork. Howard's two-volume work on British warblers (1907–1914) made use of his extensive observations of these birds to refute Darwin's views of sexual selection. The book includes full-page plates, with some of the rarest warblers depicted in color.[14] There were also numerous field studies by Americans that concentrated on close observation, such as Arthur Allen's work on the Red-winged Blackbird (1914).[15] Even with the publication of earlier and concurrent ornithological studies, Nice's work received a great deal of credence when it was praised by acknowledged experts like Stresemann and Mayr.

Competing Activities

After mailing both parts of the manuscript to Stresemann, Nice spent more time on other activities. As if writing papers, giving talks, caring for her family, and keeping up a voluminous correspondence were not enough, she began a new project of "broadcasting." In the spring of 1933 she produced a twenty-minute weekly program over The Ohio State University's station WOSU, which she characterized as "missionary work." She hoped to popularize ideas about bird protection and proposed a series of nature talks by naturalists. Nice organized the project, arranged for speakers, and prepared the announcements. Although she wrote that the talks on a wide variety of subjects were excellent, she regretted that the response was not great. Nice had hoped for a greater reaction from the public and evidence that people had actually listened to the programs.[16]

The summer of 1933 was infinitely more satisfying than the spring. Finally, the two parts of the paper for Stresemann were published, and the Nice family embarked on a five-week trip to Oklahoma, New Mexico, and Arizona. While they were in Norman, Nice received a book by the Dutch ornithologist H. N. Kluijver on the biology and ecology of the European Starling. Since the volume was in Dutch, Nice used the University of Oklahoma's library resources to puzzle out the essence of the book. After this experience, she felt competent to read and review factual studies on birds in Dutch, but not theoretical discussions. She reviewed Kluijver's book in *Bird-Banding* (1933).[17]

In early November, Margaret traveled to New York City both to visit her daughter Marjorie, who held a graduate resident fellowship in history at Columbia University, and to attend the fifty-first meeting of the AOU at the American Museum of Natural History. On this trip she met five young ornithologists who were later to become important colleagues: Joe Hickey, William Vogt, Roger Tory Peterson, Bob Allen, and Warren Eaton. She also presented a paper, "Problems in the Study of Song Sparrow Eggs."[18]

AOU Memorial Volume

At this same meeting, the AOU presented a memorial volume, Fifty Years' Progress of American Ornithology: 1883–1933, to which Nice had contributed an invited paper, "The Theory of Territorialism and its Development," a topic that was of great interest in the 1930s. In this paper, Nice summarized the ideas of previous ornithologists who had contributed to various theories of territoriality. After British ornithologist H. Eliot Howard's Territory in Bird Life was published in 1920, American ornithologists had become preoccupied with the idea of territoriality. Nice complained that ornithologists since then had been in danger of going "territory-mad." Although Howard had "captured the imagination of the bird students of the world" and Nice recognized the importance and influence of his work, she was upset that students used the term "territory" too broadly and loosely. She stressed, as had Howard, that if a bird's range was not defended, it was not a territory.[19]

Nice concluded that no one theory could explain territoriality in all birds and that overgeneralization could lead to error. She provided a historical context and discussed different ways that territoriality had previously been explained, including the view accepted by many ornithologists of that time that the purpose of territoriality was to ensure that the young would have an adequate supply of food through spacing of the nests. If this was the case, she asked, why did the male drive out rivals of only his own species and tolerate those of different species whose young would be fed the same sort of insects as his own? She also noted that if the overall explanation for territoriality was only a question of food, only those birds that collected prey close to the nest would have any need for territories. Nice found some value in the often-derided idea that territories were established because of males fighting over females; this notion suggested that the food aspect may have been overstated, and that attaining a mate was "of more importance" than was realized. Not wanting to be misunderstood, Nice wrote, "The males do *not* fight over the females; they fight for territory." However, she also insisted that for some birds, establishment of territory was as essential for ensuring that the orderly sequence of the nesting cycle would proceed without interference as it was for safeguarding the food supply.[20]

Nice insisted that the only way to really understand the role played by territoriality in the lives of birds was to engage in detailed field studies of many different species. Since different birds establish their territories in different ways, she realized that generalization was impossible. Nice's Song Sparrow work had revealed that these birds had a definite procedure for establishing territory, whereas other studies showed that different birds established territories in different ways with different purposes. She could not arrive at one theory of territory that applied to all species and did not believe that anyone else could either.

Nice's most productive research period began when she returned to Columbus after her European trip in 1932. The encouragement she had received from European colleagues, especially from Stresemann, inspired her to produce her first major Song Sparrow work, which was published in 1933 and 1934. The chapter on territoriality included in the AOU anniversary publication not only discussed earlier theories on the subject but expressed some of her own ideas. Nice's reviewing experience was helpful in her evaluation of the theories of others for this retrospective publication; she had grown accustomed to evaluating the ideas of others, while also including new findings from her own research.

Chapter 8

A POPULATION STUDY
OF THE SONG SPARROW

Pleased with the European reception of her two-part German-language monograph on the Song Sparrow, Nice returned to additional research on the subject for the Linnaean Society of New York's *Transactions*. The success of her German publication also encouraged others to invite her to present papers on the Song Sparrow at meetings.

Oxford Conference, 1934

As president of the Eighth International Ornithological Congress, Erwin Stresemann invited Nice to give such a paper in Oxford, England, in July 1934, for she was now acknowledged as *the* expert on the Song Sparrow. Although flattered to be invited, she was apprehensive and reached out to Mayr for support and help. "What kind of paper is it best to give? My paper at the last AOU had far too much in it, was too concentrated for people to grasp when they heard it read. I believe it's better to give just a few points and elaborate them."[1] But she was still uncertain as to whether this approach was the proper one. Perhaps, she anguished, it might be better to give a general paper on the Song Sparrow. Since Mayr's answer to Nice's request is unavailable, it is unknown which of these alternatives, if either, he favored.

Margaret and her sister Katharine left for Germany, Scandinavia, and England on May 26. Although her ultimate destination was the Oxford Congress, her first stop was in Germany, where she was saddened by the change in the country since her first visit. She later wrote, "*Heil Hitler* has taken the place of *Guten Tag* and *Aufwiedersehen*."[2] In spite of the gathering storm, Nice was able to hike in an area near Berlin with the ornithologist Gottfried Schiermann, who had conducted a bird census of the area. She also finally had the opportunity to meet Hermann Desselberger, the translator of her Song Sparrow manuscript for the *Journal für Ornithologie*. After her stay in Germany and before traveling to England, she spent two and a half weeks in southern Sweden and Norway, visiting museums and enjoying the spring flora and fauna.[3]

Meeting Konrad Lorenz

Fortunately, when they reached Oxford on July 1, Margaret and her sister were assigned to the same boardinghouse as Konrad and Margarethe Lorenz. Although they had never met in person, Margaret had read Lorenz's paper on the ethology of social corvids in the *Journal für Ornithologie*, and he had read her Song Sparrow paper in the same journal. Their familiarity with each other's work made it easy for them to develop a comfortable friendship.[4] Nice later opined that Lorenz was the most important new friend she had made at the meeting, and his theory that "a display releases or inhibits action in another animal of the same species" was a fundamental tenet of animal behavior.[5]

Ethology, the New Field of Animal Behavior

The term "ethology," from the Greek *ethos* (character) and *logia* (the study of), was first used in modern times by John Stuart Mill (1806–1873) in his *System of Logic* (1843) to portray a category of ethics, the study of character formation. It evolved to mean the biological study of animal behavior and officially took its place as a new component of the biological sciences in 1973 when Lorenz, Niko Tinbergen, and Karl von Frisch were awarded the Nobel Prize in Physiology or Medicine. Although Lorenz and Tinbergen usually receive the credit for establishing ethology as a discipline, they were not the first to study behavior from a biological, rather than a psychological, perspective. However, Lorenz is credited with laying the conceptual foundation for ethology during the 1930s.

THE ORIGINS OF ANIMAL PSYCHOLOGY

The forerunners of Lorenz's ideas came from different disciplines, including that of the nineteenth-century empiricist philosophers who posited that the mind was originally a blank slate (tabula rasa) and developed (i.e., became filled) only through associations among sensory perceptions. John Stuart Mill added to the empiricists' assumptions by suggesting that compound ideas were formed through the association of two simple ideas, and that the result varied from its two constituents in the same way that water differed from its two components, hydrogen and oxygen. Mill's notion allowed philosophers to retain their belief in the fundamental role of the associative process (the process that leads to the connection between events, thoughts, behavior, etc.) as well as explaining why human and animal minds had different degrees of complexity.[6]

The real support for studying the comparative abilities of different animals, including humans, came from the evolutionary perspective that was "in the air" during the nineteenth century. Although Jean-Baptiste Lamarck (1744–1829) and Robert Chambers (1802–1871), among others, had postulated a progression of life forms, they were unable to arrive at a believable mechanism to explain the changes. Alfred Russel Wallace (1823–1913) and Charles Robert Darwin independently arrived at natural selection as the explanatory mechanism for evolution. It was Darwin rather than Wallace whose work became more often associated with natural selection. His ideas gave a boost to animal psychology after the publication of *On the Origin of Species by Means of Natural Selection* (1859) and became even more relevant after *The Descent of Man, and Selection in Relation to Sex* (1871) was published.[7] Historian of animal psychology Robert Boakes wrote that unlike Wallace, Darwin considered "the difference in mind between man and the higher animals great as it is, . . . is one of degree and not of kind."[8]

By the end of the nineteenth century, the efficacy of natural selection was reevaluated. Newly acquired evidence seemed to make it impossible for natural selection to be the only way in which evolution could occur. One problem was that an enormous amount of time was required for evolutionary changes to take place. Although the hypothesis of a very old earth that would allow the needed time for profound change seemed possible to some in 1859, by the 1870s physicists had revised estimates of the earth's age, based on newly accepted principles of thermodynamics. Even Darwin recognized that a younger earth would not provide sufficient time for natural selection to be the sole mechanism causing evolutionary change, although he was not completely convinced by the physicists' evidence. In addition, if the contemporary (late-nineteenth-century) view of genetics based on the idea of blending inheritance was accepted, new species could not arise by the continuous selection of small variations. Before Mendelian genetics was rediscovered in 1900, this model prevailed. The following example describes the ultimate reason that blending inheritance could not work. If a tall parent and a short parent were to produce a child, its height would be intermediate between the heights of its parents. In the next generation this child's height would represent one of the limiting boundaries for the following generation. This process would continue down the generational line, until eventually in every family the potential for variation would be less for each subsequent generation and would eventually disappear. In this case, the final result would be a single height for all members of our hypothetical family. In addition, blending inheritance failed to explain recessive characteristics—why certain traits disappear from a family's lineage for several generations and then reappear later.

Along with the issues of time and heredity, the possible atheistic implications of this chance-driven theory had always added to the difficulties of its acceptance. Thus additional credence was given to Lamarckian ideas of the inheritance of acquired characteristics. Darwin himself even placed some emphasis on this type of inheritance as an agent for change, along with natural selection. Wallace, however, continued to believe that natural selection was the sole mechanism for evolution in nonhuman animals, but he believed that the human brain was an exception that could be explained only by the intervention of a higher intelligence.[9] To many who followed Darwin, an evolutionary perspective was just as valid for mental as for physical changes. For example, the Scottish philosopher and psychologist Alexander Bain (1818–1903), an associate of John Mill, accepted this view.

According to Boakes, Bain was the first person to devote most of his life to the study of the mind. In his books *The Senses and the Intellect* (1855) and *The Emotions and the Will* (1859), Bain attempted to establish psychology as a natural science rather than as a division of philosophy. Profiting from new ideas on the physiology of the nervous system, he sought to discover the relationship between psychological phenomena and the mechanisms of the brain through studying subjective experience.[10] By proposing that all knowledge and mental processes were based on both spontaneous thoughts and actual physical sensations, Bain suggested that he could explain subjective behavior by separating the feelings of movement from actual movement. Although he advocated the use of experiments to study psychological phenomena, he did not run experiments himself.

Herbert Spencer (1820–1903), often linked with social Darwinism, became associated with Bain, although he differed in his emphasis. He found his own answers in a steady, progressive evolution from the simple, undifferentiated beginnings of the nervous system to the complexity of the human brain. Spencer did not accept subjective experience as a useful tool in explaining behavior. In the first edition of his *Principles of Psychology* (1855), he was concerned with mental evolution and proposed that a study of animal behavior was important in understanding this phenomenon. Although Spencer and Bain both tried to understand how mental processes worked, they differed in their theoretical perspective. Nevertheless, Bain and Spencer were similar enough that some of their ideas were grouped together as the Spencer-Bain principle of learning. This principle postulated that the frequency or probability of a behavior increased if it was followed by a pleasurable event and decreased if it was followed by a painful one.[11]

Spencer's evolutionary ideas emphasized instinct and put him at odds with the majority of the philosophers of the mid-nineteenth century, Mill and Bain among them, who had a definite bias favoring the influence of environment on behavior. Bain theorized that seemingly instinctive responses were actually not innate but had been acquired rapidly at an early age. However, there was no experimental evidence to support this idea. Douglas Spalding (1840–1877), who attended some of Bain's lectures, devised a series of experiments to test these ideas. He hooded newly hatched chicks to deprive them of visual and auditory stimuli and found them just as capable of pecking accurately and moving toward insect food as chicks that had previously experienced these sensations. His results convinced him that these activities were entirely instinctive. Spalding also found that when chicks and ducklings had their hoods removed shortly after hatching, they would follow him around throughout their lives, but if he waited three or four days to remove the hoods, they feared him. Many years later, this phenomenon, which Spalding called "imperfect instinct," was rediscovered by Jakob von Uexküll and Lorenz and called "imprinting." Spalding discovered other innate behaviors that were modified by early experience (imperfect instincts), such as a chick initially pecking at its own excrement and later stopping, but both he and Spencer concluded that instinct was inherited.[12]

Thomas Henry Huxley (1825–1895) supported Spalding's findings. Both men agreed that psychology should not be based on subjective experience and could advance only if it was restricted to the study of behavior. In spite of the objections that treating animals, including humans, as objects determined by both present and past events eliminated free will, the views of Huxley and Spalding survived and developed into the behaviorist movement some fifty years later, in the early twentieth century.[13]

During the 1880s, the disciplinary home for the study of animal behavior was debated. Should it be considered a division of natural history or of psychology? Two important investigators arrived at different conclusions. Although George Romanes (1848–1894) considered it a part of natural history, Conwy Lloyd Morgan (1852–1936) was convinced it should be a category of psychology. This question was not successfully resolved and persisted well into the mid-twentieth century.

A second problem, the attempt to define both instinct and intelligence and determine the types of studies that would distinguish the two, also concerned nineteenth-century investigators. In retrospect, solutions to these problems were also difficult because so little was then known about genetics. Originally both Morgan and Romanes were concerned with the same question of whether behavioral characteristics as well as physical ones could be transmitted to offspring. However, the younger man, Morgan, disagreed with Romanes's use of anecdotal evidence to determine whether a behavior was instinctive or learned. One of the most important disagreements between the two was Morgan's endorsement of the Lamarckian view of the inheritance of acquired traits, while Romanes continued to accept the basic principles of Darwinian natural selection.[14]

Boakes carefully documented the many other contributors who became a part of the developing field of animal behavior. Even though early English investigators stressed the importance of experimentation in the study of behavior, few devised the appropriate tests. In Germany, however, after an early-nineteenth-century conflict between those promoting idealist philosophy and others practicing laboratory science, the latter was more fully endorsed, and experimental psychology became a successful academic pursuit in universities. However, with the exception of Ernst Haeckel (1834–1919), German experimentalists seemed to be little influenced by evolutionary ideas. They tended to be interested in well-controlled experiments in physiology without any evolutionary considerations.[15]

Konrad Lorenz and the General Intellectual Climate

While Konrad Lorenz was exposed to German debates about animal behavior, he developed his own research agenda with little awareness of the general intellectual climate at the time. As a boy, he had always appreciated the outdoors, loved animals, and enjoyed raising them. His appreciation of nature, however, did not lead him to want to be a field biologist, for he much preferred to simulate natural conditions in a controlled situation.

At his father's insistence, Lorenz obtained a medical degree, but he had no intention of becoming a doctor. During his studies of comparative anatomy, he had instead become interested in the possibility of constructing phylogenies on the basis of homologous organs. He thought he had an original idea when he extrapolated from anatomy to behavior and concluded that behavior patterns could be used to determine evolutionary relationships, just as homologous organs were. He later realized that Charles Otis Whitman (1842–1910) in the United States and Oskar Heinroth in Germany had previously reached similar conclusions.[16]

Lorenz's early research on the Jackdaw (*Corvus monedula*) brought him to the attention of Heinroth, who later became his mentor, and Erwin Stresemann, one of the most important figures in European ornithology. Determined to make a career of studying animal behavior, Lorenz prepared himself by enrolling as a doctoral candidate in the University of Vienna's zoology department, where he then worked in the anatomical institute; he also took courses in psychology from Karl Bühler (1879–1963). Lorenz's research on the behavior of the Jackdaw corroborated Heinroth's ideas that behavioral patterns were innate, not learned, and could be used to reconstruct phylogenies.

As Lorenz's reputation grew, he sought companions who he felt shared his knowledge of animals. There were few people whose ideas he respected, but he found that the radical Estonian biologist Baron Jakob von Uexküll (1864–1944) supported many of his ideas and stimulated him with new ones.[17] Uexküll's experiments on the feeding behavior of the tick especially reinforced Lorenz's own thinking.[18] Terms that were later adopted as an important part of Lorenz's framework were derived from Uexküll, such as "releasers" and "companions."[19]

Although Lorenz was becoming well known in Europe when he met Nice at the Oxford meeting, he was not as recognized in the United States. Nice and Julian Huxley (1887–1975), whom Lorenz also met at the meeting, introduced him to English-language research he had previously been unfamiliar with; his English-speaking colleagues then informed others about his research. Huxley provided Lorenz with English-language research papers and Nice introduced his ideas to researchers in the United States. These contacts allowed him to become familiar with previously unknown ideas from other countries. By incorporating new concepts, Lorenz became better prepared to write his *Kumpan* monograph and also grew assured that Americans would be more open to accepting his conclusions.

In this monograph, Lorenz organized his many detailed observations into 202 pages that appeared in two successive installments in the *Journal für Ornithologie* in 1935. Dedicated to Uexküll, this publication described many of the concepts that became so important to the future of ethology and provided the conceptual basis for Nice's 1943 Song Sparrow work. Nonhuman animals, according to Lorenz, most often did not act from insight but instead through instinctive responses. Central to these responses was the concept of the "releaser" (*Auslöser*), the element in the environment that served as a stimulus and elicited an instinctively determined response. This response had been evolutionarily selected for its survival value. Lorenz used the term "releaser" to mean all the characters that activated the innate schemata (or patterns of response) in the subject. These releasers could be morphological structures or behavior patterns or some combination of each. Lorenz posited that although releasers resulted in instinctive (i.e., innate) behavior, learning could influence the intensity by which an instinctive behavior could be released. However, the form of the instinctive action never changed.[20]

Kumpan, or "companion," was another of Uexküll's terms that became an important part of Lorenz's theoretical framework. Lorenz observed that every Jackdaw had a number of social drives in which other Jackdaws played the part of "companion," and these differed according to what part of the life history was involved. No general Kumpan existed. A Kumpan linked one Jackdaw to another in only one kind of behavior; for example, there could be a sex Kumpan, a parent Kumpan, or a social Kumpan, and they could be represented by different birds for one Jackdaw. Although a Jackdaw could provide the stimulus that released the appropriate instinctive behavior patterns in another, the Kumpan did not have to be another Jackdaw; Lorenz noted a case in which the parent Kumpan and sex Kumpan referred not to another Jackdaw but to a human. The Kumpan concept could be even more complex. For example, in some birds the parent Kumpan was further divided. To a young bird, the parent was sometimes a different Kumpan at different times, such as a feeding Kumpan, a warmth Kumpan, or a leader

Kumpan, depending on factors in the environment. Lorenz noted that the external situation (environment) had to be considered separately for each individual response.[21]

Lorenz stressed that ethology was a biological science. He insisted that it was important to focus first on instinctive behavior before proceeding to learned behavior. In his *Kumpan* paper, he described one phenomenon that could be classified as neither instinctive nor learned; he called this imprinting. Lorenz observed that newly hatched Greylag goslings did not instinctively recognize adult Greylags as members of their own species. If the goslings at an early age were exposed first to a person rather than to an adult goose, they accepted the human as their "parent." The young goose would then respond to its human "parent" in the same way it would react to a goose. However, if it imprinted on a fellow goose, the process would provide a suitable releasing mechanism and cause certain irreversible, instinctive behavior patterns in the gosling. Since a young bird is usually exposed first to members of its own species, imprinting ensures that it will acquire needed information.

Lorenz's theories of releasers and innate releasing mechanisms represent a hypothetical innate system in which an animal responds to a stimulus in the environment that produces a preprogrammed, stereotyped behavior pattern; these mechanisms embody the core of his view of ethology.[22] Although Lorenz recognized that it was dangerous to generalize from one group of animals to another—for instance from birds to lizards—he still intuited that his theory was more universal.[23]

Although Lorenz did not meet Niko Tinbergen until 1936 during the Leiden Instinct Symposium, they had corresponded the previous year. Their approach to behavior differed, but they also had many ideas in common. Unlike Lorenz, who preferred to study captive animals, Tinbergen favored field studies. To Tinbergen, studying animals in captivity was rather boring. He became more sympathetic toward those studying captive animals after reading papers by A. F. J. Portielje, the director of the Amsterdam Zoo, in the Dutch ornithological journal *Ardea*. He grew impressed with Portielje's ability to handle animals and probably accepted the author's views that a good zoological garden had more to offer to the study of behavioral phenomena than most zoologists admitted.[24]

It was not from Lorenz that Tinbergen learned of the ideas of Oskar Heinroth and Jakob von Uexküll, but through the publications of his fellow countrymen Jan Verwey and Portielje. Consequently, when he met Lorenz they had a common intellectual background.

Even though Tinbergen was first interested in birds and continued this early pursuit by studying Snow Buntings and Herring Gulls, he broadened his behavioral research to include a variety of animals, including the digger wasp *Philanthus triangulum*. Tinbergen studied its homing behavior for his PhD thesis. One of his best-known research projects was on the behavior of the common freshwater fish known as the stickleback.

The three-spined stickleback (*Gasterosteus aculeatus*) proved to be an important animal in Tinbergen's research, for it possessed distinctive innate behavior patterns. He and his students concluded that much of the Stickleback's behavior consisted of these patterns being released by a limited number of special sign stimuli. Courtship involved a "reaction chain" in which the male and female received stimuli from each other in a characteristic sequence at the appropriate time. When a female appeared in a male's territory, it elicited the "zigzag dance" of the male. This dance then caused courtship behavior on the part of the female, which resulted in the male leading her to the nest; that in turn elicited the female following.[25]

As an assistant in the Department of Zoology at Leiden, Tinbergen always had both graduate and undergraduate students available to help with research. In the spring and summer, when his research subjects were active, he and his students conducted research. During the fall and winter, he taught and wrote up the results of the previous spring and summer's research. It would have been easy for Tinbergen to settle into this pleasant and productive routine, but he wanted to expand his research experiences. He was able to spend three months working with Lorenz at Altenberg in 1937 and in 1938 managed a trip to the United States, where he learned more about American studies of behavior.[26]

Tinbergen clearly had an active research program before he met Lorenz, and he was already familiar with the research of Lorenz's predecessors. Nevertheless, Lorenz's theoretical framework had a very important influence on Tinbergen. At the 1936 Leiden meeting when they finally met, each realized that their talents were complementary.[27]

Nice did not meet Tinbergen until long after the Oxford conference in 1934, but Lorenz's friendship was especially helpful to her during that meeting, allowing her to navigate the overwhelming maze of papers, receptions, dinners, and excursions. When Nice, Julian Huxley, and Lorenz shared an enjoyable lunch at the Oxford conference, she probably did not realize just how important Lorenz would become in providing a new foundation for understanding bird behavior. However, she was the first American to recognize the overall significance of his work, and she made it her business to introduce his ideas to English-language readers. She first did this by introducing Lorenz to the American animal psychologist Wallace Craig. Craig then introduced Lorenz to the work of his American colleague Charles Otis Whitman, a zoologist and behaviorist. This chain of events was especially important to the Americans, because although the new discipline of ethology was vibrant in Europe, it was then relatively unknown in the United States.[28]

Because of her friendships with her European associates, Nice had a positive experience at this conference. However, she observed that those Americans attending who were not well known in Europe probably felt lonely because "no one at the Congress wore his name [tag] and there was little interest in introducing people." Nice credited Ernst Mayr, Erwin Stresemann, and the Song Sparrows for ensuring that her experience was memorable. In spite of early trepidation, she reported that her paper "Territory and Mating in the Song Sparrow" was well accepted.[29]

After the conference, Nice spent additional time in London, working in the Natural History Museum, reading and copying notes in its library, and visiting Lord Rothschild's museum in Tring with its collection of bird skins. She and Katharine left for the United States on July 28 on the SS *Bremen*, reached New York five days later, and visited family in Pelham, Massachusetts, before returning to Columbus on September 20, 1934.[30]

A Population Study of the Song Sparrow:
To My Friend Ernst Mayr

Nice had concentrated on the life history of the Song Sparrow for many years before her two-part German publication *Zur Naturgeschichte des Singammers* appeared. This publication had inspired such effusive praise from both Stresemann and Mayr that it led Mayr to promise that an updated version of this "finest piece of life-history work, ever done" would be published in the *Transactions of the Linnaean Society of New York*, "even if it runs to three volumes."[31] Mayr was true to his word about facilitating the publication, which eventually appeared in 1937. Eight years elapsed between March 1928, when Nice banded her first Song Sparrow, and 1937, when the first of two volumes of *Studies in the Life History of the Song Sparrow* was published. During the intervening years she collected a large amount of data, gave talks, published a major monograph in German (*Zur Naturgeschichte des Singammers*), and wrote many short papers.

After working so hard on the German-language Song Sparrow paper, Nice had fallen behind in her other commitments. She was equivocal about when she might be able to finish the Song Sparrow manuscript for the Linnaean Society of New York, but Mayr accepted her vague schedule for its completion: "I have to have only a very approximate idea in order to plan the printing schedule of the Linnaean Society." Nice was concerned about committing to an absolute time schedule, because this publication was to be more than a simple rehashing of the German work. She wrote Mayr in 1934 that she had an immense amount of new data to go through, warning that "it's going to take a long time." The proposed first part of *Studies in the Life History of the Song Sparrow* would include new data, which had to be collected in the spring and early summer (1935).[32]

DRAFTS

In spite of many glitches, Nice finally completed a draft of the Song Sparrow manuscript, minus the charts and maps. She sent it to Mayr in January 1936. Dissatisfied with the introduction and conclusion, she asked him to tell her "frankly" what he thought of it. Although she never stated it openly, Nice often sought validation from Mayr. She never forgot that she lacked a PhD degree, and this preyed upon her self-confidence. She also had to have been aware that it was unusual for a woman scientist to publish a major piece in such a respected journal. She wrote apologetically, "I hope you weren't too discouraged at the dreadful length of the mass [*sic*]," and "do you like the title?"[33] Mayr's first response must have been reassuring. He declared that although he had not had time to read it carefully, what he had seen so far "pleased" him "tremendously." He promised to read it closely and provide suggestions. Answering her specific concerns, he thought that the title was "fine" and that the manuscript was not too long. Still, she agonized over the printing details.[34]

After Mayr had time to read the manuscript thoroughly, he was even more enthusiastic, pronouncing it a "wonderful piece of work." He added, "There is little that I can say in criticism of it." Mayr asked for a description of the subjects she planned to treat in the second part in order to ascertain that the first volume would not overlap the "life history studies intended for the second volume." While suggesting some revisions in her chapter structure, he assured her that they were not necessarily an improvement on her arrangement, "but it is always good to have other peoples [sic] opinion in regard to one's work." As editor, he discussed additional housekeeping chores that had to be decided, such as the size of the edition, noting that the "normal edition" for the *Transactions* was five hundred pages. The format and style also had to be determined before he could present the manuscript to the council of the Linnaean Society of New York for printing approval. Believing that there would be a large demand, he suggested that they "print a larger edition," or more than five hundred. He proposed a price of two dollars for the volume and recommended that they use the aesthetically pleasing format of the *Proceedings of the Linnaean Society of New York* rather than the "cumbersome and unattractive" format of the *Transactions*.[35]

In answering Mayr's letter that included his advice, Nice expressed her satisfaction with his comments on the manuscript. She accepted his suggestions gratefully, noting in particular that his thoughts on rearrangement of the chapters were not only interesting but reflected her "problems clearly." As far as the number of copies to print, "Dr. Nice [Blaine] and I thought 1000 might be the proper number." Reflecting the culture of the time, Margaret included Blaine in the publication decisions and referred to him by his title, "Dr. Nice." They both agreed with Mayr that a price of two dollars was acceptable, and they concurred with his opinion that it was a good idea to use the format of the *Proceedings* rather than that of the *Transactions*. As Mayr had requested, she included an outline of the topics to be included in the second volume.[36]

Nice sent out drafts to many colleagues, and most of them proposed minor changes in the manuscript. She never seemed to resent their suggestions and dutifully made the changes when she agreed with them and explained herself to her critics when she did not.

As the last-minute arrangements were being made for publication, Mayr and the ornithologist and ecologist William Vogt (1902–1968) agreed that the charts should be prepared in Columbus under Nice's supervision. A careful reading of the manuscript led Mayr to query some twenty points that he had not mentioned previously. Because the next meeting of the council of the Linnaean Society of New York was not until March, he informed Nice that she did not need to hurry her reply to the various proposals.[37]

THE "POPULATION STUDY" IS FINISHED!

As is always the case with a publication, just when it seems that it is complete, new issues invariably arise. With Nice's work, getting the charts and maps completely correct, constructing the indices, and adding new material all caused delays. Nevertheless, she sent the manuscript to Mayr on June 25, 1936, and jubilantly proclaimed: "Behold the mss at length and at last. It is all here, I believe but the two indices, which are not yet ready, although planned out." Even then there was still much work to be done. It was essentially finished, but Nice continued to add new material and requested Mayr's suggestions on the charts.[38] Almost a year later, on April 15, 1937, in the midst of family activities, including Barbara's wedding, Margaret finished checking the page proofs of the "Population Study." Still there were more decisions to be made, including the color of the binding and the price. When Mayr suggested a bright blue cover, Nice agreed that his choice was clearly the most beautiful but not the most practical, since "we live in a sooty climate, not a clean place like New York." Instead, she suggested dark gray as more serviceable. She was pleased when Mayr reported that the price of the volume would be $1.50.[39]

Even then there were further holdups. Mayr wrote on April 26, "The publishing of your paper has, unfortunately, been somewhat delayed due to a mistake at the printing of one of the plates."[40]

The work was finally published in the spring of 1937 as *Studies in the Life History of the Song Sparrow, Volume I: A Population Study of the Song Sparrow and Other Passerines*. The dedication read, "To my friend Ernst Mayr." Mayr responded, "To have this paper dedicated to me makes me more proud than any honorary fellowship could do."[41]

Although Nice hoped that her study would have a wide appeal, an October letter to Mayr reveals that this was not the case, at least at first. She expressed disappointment that the "Population Study" had not sold better, blaming the lackluster sales on what she considered the small number of "real ornithologists" in the United States.[42] Since at this time the ornithological community was still made up of a wide group of people with different types of interests in birds, ranging from hobbyists to those who sought to support the AOU's struggle to forge a professional discipline, it is not clear exactly what Nice meant by "real" ornithologists. She would not necessarily have excluded herself from their ranks because she did not have a paid professional position or a PhD degree. It is apparent, however, that Nice derided American ornithologists who did not wish to become informed about European studies. It seems probable that Nice was referring to what she considered Americans' general ignorance of European theoretical advances in bird behavior.

The Work Itself

In the introduction to the first volume, Nice explained (as she had in the German work) that her observations were based on recognizing individuals in the field by using colored bands, repeatedly checking the status of the community, and examining birds that she captured. Her goal was to study what actually happened to birds in the wild without collecting them and with minimal experimentation. As she had done in the previous German publication, she explained how by trapping and banding the birds she could follow individuals throughout their lives, thus establishing family histories.

In investigating population issues, Nice included the following topics: the relationship of the Song Sparrow to its environment (comprising climate, habitat, and other animal species), weights and measurements, the migratory status of the Song Sparrow on the Interpont, spring and fall migration, territories throughout the year, and territories from year to year. She also covered relations between the sexes, nests, the start of laying, eggs, incubation, care of the young, nesting success and failure, the relationship to the Brown-headed Cowbird, survival of the adults, survival of the young, age attained, and population problems.

While recognizing the value of spending an extended period concentrating on a single species, Nice also understood the deficiencies of such an approach. The subject was difficult and complex and was made even more so by "the fact that it was undertaken by one person alone." She regretted "the meagerness of data on various points, the failure to find certain important nests, the uncertainty as to the exact course of events with particular pairs, and many other unfortunate gaps."[43] Even allowing for these problems, Nice hoped to provide a model for others studying the living bird of any species. The scope and depth of her study provided a remarkable prototype, as suggested by the number of birds she banded in the breeding season of 1932. In that year her attempt to band every adult Song Sparrow on the Upper Interpont nearly succeeded, for she banded all sixty-nine males and most of the females.[44]

Factors That Influenced Song Sparrow Populations

After setting the stage by presenting the reasons she had chosen Song Sparrows for her study, Nice explained how various fundamental environmental factors, such as temperature, precipitation, and sunlight as well as flora and fauna important in the life of the Song Sparrow, all affected the birds' activities and their timing. Nice concluded that the most important factors in regulating the Song Sparrow's "calendar" were changing day lengths and changing temperatures. Low temperatures stimulated migration in the fall and flocking in the winter. They inhibited song in the spring and fall, slowed migration and territorial activities in the spring, and delayed nesting. The inverse proved true of high temperatures. Although the birds bred, nested, and brooded at approximately the same time each year under normal temperatures, these activities occurred later when temperatures were lower than usual and earlier when they were higher than normal. Although day length was important in regulating the birds' activities, she did not find the percentage of sunshine during a particular season significant. The amount of precipitation, however, had an effect on the activities of the birds. The drought in June and July 1930 caused premature molting, and a drought in May and June 1932 resulted in the young starving in the nest. On the other hand, the flood in mid-May 1933 destroyed numerous ground nests.[45]

The habitat of Nice's study area at first satisfied the basic needs of the birds; food, shelter, singing posts, and nesting sites were all abundant. During much of the period covered by the study, the area was "largely waste land supporting a rank growth of weeds, many shrubs and some trees."[46] These circumstances were favorable for the Song Sparrow, but as the land was cleared for growing food, conditions grew progressively worse. The population changed from a "well situated, thriving population with . . . excellent survival" to an "exposed population, subjected to many perils and unable to reproduce itself."[47]

PREDATION

Even when Song Sparrows had plenty of food, predation was a constant peril to their survival. "Both a predator and victim," the Song Sparrow ate a "great variety of invertebrate forms," Nice wrote, but was parasitized or eaten by others. Although it dominated small birds, other creatures preyed on its eggs and young.[48]

Nice concluded that three introduced predators—Norway rats, feral dogs, and "most destructive of all, cats"—were responsible for most of the

Song Sparrow losses. She found that House Sparrows also had an unfortunate effect; they competed with native birds for food, and people often confused the introduced brownish House Sparrows with the native brownish Song Sparrows and did not hesitate to shoot either.[49] Other impacts on the birds occurred when people altered the habitat, when boys shot the sparrows, and even when Nice herself conducted her investigation.[50]

TERRITORIALITY

Nice's observations established that territoriality was innate and essential to the life and reproduction of the Song Sparrow. Through song, display, and fighting, territories were recognized, and they allowed the reproductive cycle to carry on without interruption. The birds were highly territorial during the six months that encompassed reproductive activities. However, those birds that did not migrate tended to remain near their territory permanently and in the fall and winter were more social. Nice observed that Song Sparrow pairs seemed to remain together during one season, but it was unusual for a bird to choose the same mate in a subsequent season. Since Song Sparrows cannot recognize the sex of members of their species by appearance, they rely on behavior.[51] The male's activities include defending the territory, finding his mate, bringing nesting materials to the female, and participating in feeding the young. The female's major activities are building the nest, incubating the eggs, and brooding and feeding the young.[52]

Before and long after publication of the population study, Nice continued her research on territoriality in birds; this interest was one she shared with many bird behaviorists. In her 1933 contributed paper to the AOU's *Fifty Years' Progress of American Ornithology (1883–1933)*, she complained that since British ornithologist H. Eliot Howard had published his *Territory in Bird Life* in 1920, bird students had been in danger of misusing the term.[53]

As Nice described various theories of territoriality, she concluded that it was impossible to arrive at a single theory that applied to all species. It was obvious to her that since birds establish their territories in different ways, the only reasonable way to proceed was not to generalize, but to conduct careful studies on many different species of birds, as she had done for the Song Sparrow.

Later, ecologist G. Evelyn Hutchinson (1903–1991), in *An Introduction to Population Ecology*, explained the importance of her historical information on territory. He interpreted Nice's ideas as follows:

The theory of territory in bird life is briefly this: that pairs are spaced through the pugnacity of males towards others of their own species and sex; that song and display of plumage and other signals are a warning to other males and an invitation to a female; that males fight primarily for territory and not over mates; that the owner of a territory is nearly invincible in his territory; and finally that birds which fail to obtain territory form a reserve supply from which replacements come in case of death of owners of territories.[54]

Both Nice and Hutchinson agreed that males do, in part, fight over mates, although the acquisition of territory is the most important result of competition.

Unique Aspects of Nice's Research

Most ornithologists who collected data on birds during the early twentieth century worked with museum specimens and therefore tended to tabulate wing measurements rather than overall specimen weight. It was much more common for ornithologists to describe characteristics generally than to collect precise data on the living bird. Nice's careful observations of both the physical and the behavioral characteristics of the Song Sparrow set a high standard for ornithologists. From her data she noted which characteristics provided the most information about this species. Although she measured the birds' wings (there was a significant difference in the length of the wing in males and females), she found that weight changes provided more useful information. She weighed a total of 746 adult Song Sparrows, noting seasonal variations. During the fall, Nice established a "standard weight" for each bird. She found that weights began to increase in December and reached their maximum in January. Then they decreased to another standard weight in April. In general, female weight increased just before and during egg laying and remained slightly above the standard during incubation. The weight of both males and females decreased while they were feeding the young.[55]

Reception

Like most authors, Nice was never sure how her work would be received until the reviews appeared. She regretted not having asked ornithologist Robert A. McCabe (1914–1995) to review the work after he wrote, "It is of course the most important in the behavior field since Howard's Territory [H. E.

Howard's classic book on territoriality]." Nice asked Mayr, "Why didn't we think of him as a reviewer?" A review by Jean Delacour in *L'Oiseau* praised the work as "a model of clarity; in its substance it is perhaps the most important contribution yet published to our knowledge of the life of a species."[56]

Aldo Leopold (1887–1948) wrote a review in the *Canadian Field-Naturalist*, surprising Nice, who had expected to see it in *Science*. His review was important because of his reputation as a writer, environmentalist, and ecologist (his best-known book is *A Sand County Almanac*, 1949). In his review Leopold regretted the lack of prestige attached to natural history and stated that it would be necessary to read hundreds of publications in order to determine the origin of this unfounded prejudice against this subject. He credited Nice for potentially eliminating the stigma that tainted natural history with her *Studies in the Life History of the Song Sparrow*. He praised it as "a complete and convincing integration of . . . field observation, controlled experimentation, and scientific deduction," accompanied by conclusions that challenged those of other investigators. Leopold found the work especially significant for the following reason: "Mrs. Nice is an amateur. No one paid her to blaze a new by-path for ornithological science, or to search the libraries of the world for its direction and route."[57]

Historians of science usually agree on the dangers of using the terms "amateur" and "professional" indiscriminately, and a large amount of literature discusses the subject. However, in describing Nice as an amateur, Leopold equated the terms "amateur" and "layman," meaning that she was not being paid for her research, nor did she have all the formal training usually associated with being a professional. By the time Nice was studying and writing, it was possible, but hardly likely, that a woman could have the qualifications often associated with professionalism. As noted, she lacked both a PhD and a paid position, but she worked in the observational sciences, where amateurs were more able to thrive. However, Nice's work went far beyond mere observation. Leopold's comments no doubt referred to the quality of the work—her research utilized all the tools of a "professional" ornithologist.[58]

Other reviews by leading behaviorists and ornithologists especially pleased Nice. She fretted, however, because "some of the reviews seem to be very slow in coming out."[59] Nevertheless, when they did appear, they were almost uniformly favorable. Paul Errington reviewed the volume for the *Wilson Bulletin*; "G. M. A." for *The Auk*; and Lawrence E. Hicks for *Bird-Banding*.[60]

Since Mayr had been instrumental in ensuring the publication of the Song Sparrow volumes by the Linnaean Society of New York, he worked very hard to see that the publication succeeded. He wanted to widen its distribution to include Europe, so he was pleased to report that noted British ornithologist Henry Forbes Witherby (1873–1943) had written him that the "Population Study" would be reviewed by another British ornithologist, Edward Max Nicholson (1904–2003), and published in the December (1937) issue of *British Birds*, the journal that Witherby published and edited. Mayr sent ten copies to Witherby "to be on hand" if he received any orders. He wrote Nice that he was "preparing a circular to be sent to universities, libraries and ornithologists, containing an appraisal" of the work and selected items from the most notable reviews.[61]

Competition for Time: Family Events and Professional Obligations

With all the obstacles Nice faced, her successful completion of the first part of the Song Sparrow monograph for the Linnaean Society of New York was remarkable. In addition to her usual professional responsibilities, she encountered some personal time-consuming roadblocks, including a family wedding. On June 29, 1935, Marjorie married Carl Boyer (1906–1976) at the same place Margaret and Blaine had married twenty-six years previously—Margaret's parents' home in Pelham, Massachusetts. Marjorie's three sisters were bridesmaids. At the time of their marriage, Carl was an instructor in mathematics at Brooklyn College (he was a full professor of mathematics from 1953 until his death in 1976), and the two had met in a seminar course in the history of science at Columbia. Boyer was to become a respected historian of mathematics and would write a number of books on the subject. Both Marjorie and Carl were working for their doctorates when they married, and they planned to live in New York City when they returned from their honeymoon in Canada. Marjorie was the first daughter to be married, followed by Barbara and Janet. Constance never married.

Margaret's family obligations began to wind down by 1935 when only one daughter, Janet, was still living at home. Constance was attending a teachers' college in Iowa, and Barbara was a junior at Massachusetts State College in Amherst. In 1936 Barbara announced her engagement to Stanley Thompson, a senior at Amherst College.[62]

Chapter 9

THE WINDY CITY
Move to Chicago

The first volume of Nice's monograph on the Song Sparrow had just been submitted when the family left Columbus for Blaine's new job in Chicago as head of the physiological and pharmaceutical departments of the Chicago Medical School. The reasons for leaving Columbus are unclear. Although Margaret did not explain why they left, she observed that Blaine loved teaching and as long as he had contact with students, he would be happy. "As in his other teaching positions he was loved by his students because of his warm sympathy for them."[1]

In their last year in Columbus (1936), Margaret continued to work on the second part of her Song Sparrow project, but when it came time to move she had to forgo making additional observations. Although primary among her many regrets about leaving Columbus was the loss of her convenient and much-loved Interpont research area, she also missed the "friendly naturalists," many of whom were members of the local Audubon Society. She was not, however, sorry to leave the all-male Wheaton Club. Even though she benefited from the expertise of club members by attending lectures, she resented the lack of opportunity to discuss her research there with colleagues. Shortly before they left the city the situation began to improve; Blaine was elected Wheaton Club president, and Margaret received the designation of "unofficial honorary member."

Even though Nice had published many important works and was known and respected by many of the world's top ornithologists and animal behaviorists, her gender had hindered her opportunities to communicate effectively with local elite experts. Denied the benefits of networking where she lived, she shared the problems of many women scientists around the globe. Because of her extensive correspondence with European and American ornithologists and behaviorists, she was able to mitigate some of the difficulties. Nice received several national and international honors in 1936 reflecting the respect her work elicited. She became an associate editor of *Bird-Banding*, was elected a corresponding member of the Royal Hungarian Institute of Ornithology, and was promoted from corresponding to honorary membership (*Ehrenmitglied*) in the Deutsche Ornithologen-Gesellschaft. Although Ernst Mayr had recommended her for the editorship of *Bird-Banding*, she declined because of responsibilities relating to the move.[2] One way Nice compensated for her lack of contact with local professionals was by becoming active in the local Audubon Society, and she was slated to become the Columbus group's next president.[3]

Getting Settled

Although the move to Chicago severely curtailed Nice's ability to do observational field research, there were definite advantages to the move. The family purchased a "fine house" at 5708 Kenwood, with a study that Margaret could use in both summer and winter. For once she had enough room to establish an elaborate scheme for cataloging reprints, references, and her innumerable cards for the reviews. In a letter to Mayr, Margaret bragged about her "gorgeous study," where she finally had room for all her books and journals: "I'll be able to arrange my possessions so as to work efficiently." She rationalized leaving Interpont, explaining, "We had no control over most of it, for our land comprised only about one of its sixty acres."[4]

According to Margaret, the rest of the family also seemed pleased with the new arrangement. Janet liked her school because it was close to home, and Constance enjoyed attending the Gregg Secretarial School. Blaine appreciated his new position and was happy teaching. Margaret's reputation followed her to Chicago, and the natural history community embraced her immediately. She attended the Zoo Club at the University of Chicago, the weekly Ecological Seminar, the Chicago Ornithological Society, and the Illinois Audubon Society; she soon found herself a director in the latter.[5]

From Nice's autobiography it would seem that life was going smoothly and that family members were adjusting appropriately to their new lives. Nice's daughter Barbara, however, had a different take on the situation. In the introduction to her own autobiography, she presented a less idyllic view of her family. Margaret's cryptic description of Constance's attendance at secretarial school did not explain her lack of success in other areas. Barbara was convinced that Constance would never become an "able, aware, productive woman."[6] Although Margaret seemed to have tapped her oldest daughter to follow in her footsteps (Constance had always been her mother's helper in working with birds), somehow as an adult, even though she attended several colleges, Constance, according to Barbara, never seemed to succeed.[7] Although Janet may have enjoyed her new school, Barbara, without explicit examples, suggested that she did not live a "normal, productive life."[8] Blaine may have been happy in his teaching, but as Barbara noted, the position was at a small, unrecognized medical school.[9] Although Margaret may have presented too rosy a picture, she surely must have been relieved that the new situation was at least workable. Nevertheless, she confessed to Mayr the reasons she declined to accept the editorship of *Bird-Banding*. She acknowledged that she was somewhat overwhelmed and did not have time to commit to "working over other peoples' studies." The time that she had apart from family responsibilities ("you know I have to look after my family and Janet is finding she needs lots of help from me now that she is in public school") could best be spent on her own research.[10]

Although Nice missed studying native birds near home (there was no wild area close by), she still could observe birds at Jackson Park or in one of the forest preserves such as the Orland Wildlife Refuge or Long John Slough. These preserves surrounded Chicago on three sides and were established from 1904 to 1915 by the Cook County Forest Preserve District, following the plans of the landscape architect Jens Jensen (1860–1951). When Jensen drew up his plans he could not have predicted that the city would expand as it did.

Nice also found that the Morton Arboretum and the Indiana Dunes were good locations for bird-watching.[11] Nevertheless, it was difficult for her to carry on a long-range project such as the Song Sparrow work. Instead, she concentrated on the ornithological literature and speculated about the meaning of the behaviors she had observed in the Interpont. She continued to publish small papers and expanded her reviews.

In late October 1936, Margaret returned to Columbus to visit Barbara, who was then a senior at The Ohio State University. Perhaps she was trying to establish a better relationship with her perpetually depressed and introspective daughter. According to Barbara, her early college years were typical, although she fretted over her perceived inadequacies. For her junior year, Barbara convinced her family that she should attend Massachusetts State University, where her future husband, Stanley Thompson, was a student. However, after the family moved to Chicago she returned to Ohio State to finish her senior year.[12]

After visiting Barbara, Margaret drove with a colleague to the fifty-fourth meeting of the AOU in Pittsburgh, where she presented a paper titled "Do Young Birds Return to the Place of Their Birth?" This question was of particular interest to Nice because the American and European birders disagreed on the answer. She claimed that the Song Sparrow was usually faithful to its birthplace and especially to its specific nesting place.[13]

Early Professional Activities in Chicago

True to form, Nice remained active in ornithological organizations and was elected first vice president of the venerable Wilson Ornithological Club when it met in Chicago from November 27 to 29, 1936. This club originated in 1886 when a group of bird enthusiasts formed the Young Ornithologists' Association. In 1888, they formally affiliated with Harlan H. Ballard's national network of natural history societies and changed the name to the Wilson Ornithological Chapter of the Agassiz Association. Their main interest was the study of the living bird, and in 1902 they withdrew from the Agassiz Association and became the Wilson Ornithological Club.[14] After Nice's Population Study of the Song Sparrow was published in 1937, she was elected the club's first woman president.[15]

Much of Nice's time was spent preparing reviews for *Bird-Banding*. This task was exceptionally time consuming but followed her early commitment, linking the European and American ornithological communities through the literature. By reviewing European articles, she kept American ornithologists abreast of European developments. When Nice was unable to find anyone else to write the reviews in a way that pleased her, she wrote them herself. Thanks to her successful efforts to convince *Bird-Banding*'s editor of their importance, the journal became the most popular (and sometimes the only) venue for European reviews. Although editor Charles L. Whittle always appreciated her efforts, the numbers began to overwhelm her. She got some help with the large volume of work from Thomas T. McCabe, a research associate in botany at the University of California, but Nice complained that his reviews, while entertaining, often failed to provide the gist of the author's contribution. McCabe eventually tired of constantly writing reviews, and his last contributions appeared in April 1940. Nice wrote that although he had often been a trial to her, "he had also been a help" in her "heavy, self-imposed task." In fifteen issues of *Bird-Banding*, from April 1936 through April 1940, the journal published 111 of McCabe's reviews and 719 of Nice's.[16]

When assessing a great quantity of material, a reviewer is likely to offend some of the authors. Nice realized that some of her reviews "were not welcomed by the authors criticized." The Norwegian Thorleif Schjelderup-Ebbe, the pioneer in the study of pecking order in barnyard fowl, was especially indignant. His description of pecking order was similar to the phenomenon that Nice had observed in her chickens as a young girl. Her harsh review was not about his original work on pecking order, but rather on *Social Behaviour of Birds*, which she reviewed in April 1936. After recognizing Schjelderup-Ebbe's pioneering work, she wrote that "he makes the mistake . . . of applying his findings too widely, as [W. Clyde] Allee has shown, and as, indeed will be evident to any careful student of the behaviour of wild birds." She referred to his view that pecking order was a universal phenomenon in nature and that every bird in a flock knew its exact place in the hierarchy. Schjelderup-Ebbe demanded that Nice correct what she had written and asked her to please send the corrections to him. He signed this letter "with a big red seal beside his name."[17] Allee joined the fray and sent Schjelderup-Ebbe reprints of his own article. These reprints illustrated that his own research results and those of his students differed from Schjelderup-Ebbe's. In defending her review, Nice replied, "The role of a critic is not merely to give praise, but to point out errors and weaknesses. In this way scientists can help each other in their common search for truth." Although Schjelderup-Ebbe did not answer Nice, he wrote to Allee complaining that the observations made by him (Allee) and his students must have been incorrect because they differed from his own. A description of this controversy was recounted by Nice.[18]

Barbara Marries

During a trip to New York in March 1936, Nice participated in Barbara and Stanley Thompson's wedding, visited with family and friends, saw plays, and visited the Metropolitan Museum of Art. The simple wedding occurred in sister Marjorie's apartment and was also attended by Margaret, Barbara's maternal grandmother, Margaret's sister Katharine, Barbara's friend Edith, and the sister of brother-in-law Carl. Barbara was conflicted about both the size of the wedding and her own motives for marrying. The chip on her shoulder was heavy as she wrote, "I should have liked the stability of a real home and community, real friends to have as bridesmaids." In her own mind she lacked these things, so she was glad that the wedding was small. Although she felt that marrying Stan was the right thing to do, she also harbored the fear that marriage was an escape from "a world basically and perplexingly hostile."[19]

Nice the Popular Writer: The Watcher at the Nest

Nice had always been interested in the popularization of ornithology. She was convinced that if people only "knew" birds, they would appreciate the importance of caring for both them and their environment. During her first year in Chicago, she began work on a popular book, later titled The Watcher at the Nest. One of the reasons she undertook this project was financial. She hoped that a popular account appealing to the wider public would provide a small profit. Since she had never had a paying job and her labors on birds "during the last 18 years or so had meant considerable outgo of money but very little income," she hoped to change the situation. Encouraged by the editor of Bird-Lore, William Vogt, she published three articles in that journal in 1936: "The Way of a Song Sparrow," "The Nest in the Rose Hedge," and "Uno and Una Return." The naturalist and illustrator Roger Tory Peterson (1908–1996), originator of the Peterson field guide series, supplied the illustrations, and the conservationist and writer Aldo Leopold praised it: "It is not often that one who has done anything scientific succeeds in giving it literary expression." Pleased with the reception of the articles, she undertook to expand them into a book.[20]

When Margaret popularized her fieldwork she often used anthropomorphic terms to describe the birds. In order to distinguish one bird from another she gave them names and equated their individual characteristics with those usually associated with humans. Her fieldwork in 1935 centered on a bird she had identified as Song Sparrow 4M. She had carefully recorded information about his songs and when they occurred. When a mate arrived, 4M always stopped singing. In The Watcher at the Nest Nice described this mate as a "cold, old-maidish creature, tyrannizing over her fine husband like a veritable Xantippe [the shrewish wife of Socrates]." After Nice tried unsuccessfully to trap Xantippe in order to replace her with a more tractable individual, 4M's mate surprised Nice by finally beginning to nest in the neighbor's raspberry patch. Although Xantippe laid eggs, they were punctured by House Wrens, and "4M's poor excuse for a wife disappeared never to be seen again." After her disappearance, 4M again began to sing "gloriously every day." Once he found another mate, the singing stopped again. Sparrow 4M's new "wife," Dandelion, produced eggs, but the pair was not successful in rearing young.[21]

Although Nice described the activities of the birds in anthropomorphic terms in her popular works—naming each bird and writing about marriages, thievery, and other traits shared with humans—in her formal papers she kept fastidious records of the behavior of these birds and generally refrained from using such descriptions. In *The Watcher at the Nest*, Nice designated the behavior of the heroes of her story, Uno and 4M, in terms of "their conflicts with each other and their other neighbors, their luck with their wives and devotion to their babies, the exuberance of their glorious singing—not to mention the fortunes of their sons and daughters, grandchildren and great-grandchildren."[22] She rightly assumed that by telling her birds' stories using human qualities or activities, she could interest an audience of nonprofessionals.

Writing a popular book was more difficult than Nice had ever imagined. Because she had so much information, at first she tried to include it all. Her sister Katharine convinced her that readers would be confused and suggested that she limit her narrative to Uno, 4M, their mates, and descendants. In an early draft, she concluded the book with a "burning plea for conservation." However, her daughter Constance convinced her that this chapter would antagonize readers. Her suggestion, to which Margaret acquiesced, was that an "enthusiastic account of our recent trip to Oklahoma incidentally including propaganda for saving choice samples of prairies and swamps" would accomplish the same goal without provoking readers. Afterward, Margaret, who would not have minded irritating readers for a cause she believed in, said strongly in response to Constance's arguments: "You write it." By working together, mother and daughter "made a satisfactory final chapter." The book, illustrated by Roger Tory Peterson, was published in 1939. Although Nice found writing this kind of popular account interesting at times, she also found it frustrating, so much so that she vowed never to attempt another book of that kind.[23]

However, in this popular book, Nice highlighted certain activities and traits she had developed or would still develop in her scientific writings. The interaction between two male birds, 4M and Uno, afforded Nice the opportunity to reprise her conclusions on territoriality. Although Uno was the first Song Sparrow she had banded, he was soon joined by others. The second year, Uno's territory had been usurped by 4M. The bird called 4M had claimed two territories and seemed "to take special delight in singing" right next to the Nice house. Nice lamented that "poor Uno" was a mild-mannered Song Sparrow, and she did not know how he would defend his territory against the aggressive interloper.[24]

The idea of changing dominance (one bird showing dominance by originally claiming territory, but later losing his claim to another bird) had fascinated Nice since her childhood, when she had first observed pecking order in her hens. She observed a similar pattern in the Song Sparrow. At first the two birds were in the southeastern corner of Uno's territory, "down on the ground and in the weeds" and puffed out. Uno was singing rapidly, steadily, and not loudly. The bird 4M was quiet but attacked Uno about every minute, though "not fiercely." Uno responded by flying a few feet away. They kept up this behavior for approximately ten minutes. Then 4M became more aggressive and they came to blows, each "falling to the ground and fighting furiously." Neither bird seemed to have the advantage, and the dispute was decided when each bird returned to his original tree and apparently agreed to accept the other bird's claim to his original territory. "Each sings and sings and sings." Nice was also interested in how the birds would recognize a possible mate, "since both sexes are dressed alike." She wrote that she "looked forward eagerly to learning what form of courtship display and special song he would use to win the lady."[25]

Nice's anthropomorphic treatment of her Song Sparrows in her popular writing did not mask her original, meticulous, and consistent observations of the lives of these birds. In fact, the chapter titles in *The Watcher at the Nest* inspired budding ornithologists to become aware of the importance of conservation and realize that they too could contribute to knowledge of the life histories of birds. While she was in Europe in 1938, Nice received the news from Bill Vogt, the editor of *Bird-Lore*, that *The Watcher at the Nest*, a title suggested by her sister Katharine, had been accepted by Macmillan for publication. This popular book that had presented Nice with so many problems in the writing finally appeared in the spring of 1939. The reviews were positive, as the following letter to Nice from the nature writer Donald

Peattie (1898–1964) exemplified: "*The Watcher at the Nest* is a joy and a delight. I have read it all and am reading it again. Your art of telling it is so good that it conceals how good the science is. My warmest congratulations."[26]

As gratifying as the reviews were, *The Watcher at the Nest* did not prove to be the financial success that Nice had envisioned. After receiving a pre-publication payment of $80 from the publishers in July, instead of receiving another check, she was told that she had been overpaid $41.60. *Bird-Lore* editor Vogt, who was originally involved in finding a publisher, had left the country early in 1939 to study Peruvian guano birds and was therefore unable to help with the publicity. Her second check, for $79.24, was sent in January 1940.

Babies: Happiness and Heartbreak

Two babies important to Margaret were born in 1937 and 1938, a girl to the Mayrs and a boy to Barbara and Stan. The fates of the two children were quite different. Mayr's second little girl was born in 1937. He reported to Nice "the good news of an addition to the Mayr family, a strong little girl of 7 pounds 8 ounces." He commented that his first child, Christel, "will be delighted to have a little playmate." Nice congratulated him on the new baby and agreed that the two would be "fine playmates."[27] Margaret and Blaine's new grandson was born on January 18, 1938, and was christened Malcolm. Barbara was euphoric after the birth of the baby. She and Stan had produced the family's first boy; she may have felt that surely her life finally had meaning. Barbara received much-desired attention from Margaret: "Mother wrote me numerous letters, as well as a telegram the first day, and a check." She basked in being the center of attention. However, Barbara also felt that her good fortune was undeserved and too good to be true. Unfortunately, things began to go awry as soon as they left the hospital to take the new baby home. Stan had neglected to check the gas gauge and they ran out of gas; she felt "miserable, rejected, and thoroughly inadequate to the care of this new life, now sleeping in the car with me."[28] Both Barbara and Stan doted on baby Malcolm, but he developed a dangerous form of asthma. After an especially severe attack, the baby, just over a year old, died. His death had a profound effect on the family, which was partially mitigated by the later birth of three healthy sons to Barbara and Stan.[29] Barbara later wrote a poem to these sons in November 1977 as she was dying of cancer, finally at peace with herself.

> I see the things I might have done
> And didn't.
> Once I would have said
> I couldn't
> Today I know that where I was
> Was where I was.
> I look at them,
> No longer needing me.
> Their lives, their hope, their aims
> Aside from me.
> I am not needed now.
> Yet I am glad
> That I may know them now,
> As men[30]

Margaret coped with Malcolm's death in much the same way that she had previously dealt with her daughter Eleanor's death—but in this case, she did not discuss it in her printed works and perhaps not even in her surviving correspondence. She did not mention the death of this grandson in her autobiography, nor was he included in the family tree at the end of *Research Is a Passion with Me.*

Writing a popular book, corresponding with colleagues, composing reviews, and dealing with concerns about family and friends occupied much of Nice's time during her first years in Chicago. Still, she always realized that her other major project, the second volume on the Song Sparrow, was barely progressing.

Chapter 10

PREPARING FOR SONG SPARROW, VOLUME TWO

Thoughts about how to proceed with the second volume of the Song Sparrow monograph, which would be on the behavior of the Song Sparrow, lurked in the back of Nice's mind as she carried on her many other activities. She needed additional types of difficult-to-acquire data that required a controlled environment. Because it was impossible to control the variables in the field and also because she no longer had access to her Interpont research area, Nice wanted to learn techniques of studying captive birds. For this information she turned to Konrad Lorenz, who was well known for his success in raising birds. Ernst Mayr had written her that Dutch animal behaviorist Nikolaas Tinbergen had spent several months in Altenberg, Austria, working with Lorenz. This letter from Mayr planted the idea in Nice's mind that she too might spend time with the Lorenzes in Altenberg.[1]

A Visit to Konrad Lorenz's Home

Since the Ninth International Ornithological Congress was meeting in Rouen, France, from May 9 to 13, 1938, Nice hoped to combine the conference with a visit to Lorenz at his home in Altenberg.[2] She proposed the idea to Lorenz, who quickly agreed: "We should be very happy indeed, if you would come to Altenberg for a few months as Tinbergen did." However, he warned her that she should not expect "too much in the way of a large bird collection because financial necessity has caused us to reduce our live birds to such species as are strictly necessary for my present work."[3]

At this time, the situation for scholars in Austria was uncertain, to say the least. On March 13, 1937, Hitler had arrived in Vienna and had taken formal possession of the country. Lorenz was without a position, although he was hoping that the Kaiser Wilhelm Institute would finance and develop a station similar to the one he had created at Altenberg. Konrad, his wife, Margarethe, and their two children—Thomas, nine; and Agnes, seven—lived with Konrad's professor father, Adolf, and his mother in a large house in Altenberg overlooking the Danube River. Margarethe was a physician and worked in a Vienna hospital.[4]

Lorenz apologized to Nice for asking her to pay for "the cost of the food and the washing and heating of your room," but he claimed it was necessary since he and his family were "living as permanent guests in the house of my father, so that we cannot simply invite you to be our guest for the time of your stay." He lamented, "It is a sad thing that our finances are as low as that."[5]

Money was a problem for Nice as well. She fretted that steamship rates were very expensive—$200 round trip on the *Europa* and "no nice excursion rates as there were four years ago" when she had last been in Europe.[6] Nice arranged to finance part of the trip herself by putting together a group of eleven ornithologists to travel to the ornithological congress in Rouen. Because she arranged for the others to travel, she got her passage free. On May 8 they landed at Le Havre and barely made it to the opening of the congress. It is not surprising that Margaret enjoyed the international conferences, for in addition to hearing and giving papers, she was able to not only see the sights of the city where the conference was held, but also observe birds, both in museums and in the field.[7]

The major purpose of this trip was, of course, to spend time with Lorenz. Nice was so enthralled with the opportunity to visit him and his family that she was either ignorant of, or chose to ignore, his political views. In 1938, National Socialism was a very powerful force. She also seemed unaware of the extent of his ideas about eugenics. Traveling on the train to Vienna, she was met by Lorenz, who drove her to his orthopedic surgeon father's house, which seemed "a cross between a castle and a palace." Not only did this estate provide shelter for two families, it also housed numerous birds. Lorenz's colony of Jackdaws lived on the roof of Lorenz Hall, and the guest room (and sometimes the kitchen) was home to young birds. The porch served as a brooder for young birds of all kinds, and since the food was mixed in this area it also attracted great quantities of House Sparrows. When Nice asked Lorenz whether he ever did anything to cut down on their numbers, he replied that he never killed birds and was a friend of successful species, even weeds.[8] This exchange, with its emphasis on "successful," is interesting from the point of view of National Socialism. Nice often explored the bird-filled area around the house with Lorenz.

It was important for Nice to observe the development of healthy young birds in order to distinguish between innate and learned behavior. To carry out this project she had to procure a nest with young birds, learn to keep them alive and healthy, and observe their behavioral development. Although birds were anything but scarce on the Lorenz estate, it was still difficult to find nests with young the right age for her study. After many failures, she finally obtained a nest of European Redstarts with "six babies just the right age!" Lorenz retrieved three of the young from the nest in a crevice near the top of a chimney and carried them to the ground nestled in a handkerchief. He contrived a nest, and Margaret spent much of her time feeding and observing the babies.[9] She named them *Gelb* (Yellow), *Rot* (Red), and *Blau* (Blue) according to the color of their bands. When they were fourteen days old they climbed out of their makeshift nest, and Margaret installed them in a large cage. A fourth Redstart several days younger than the original three joined the group after Lorenz found him abandoned in the grass. Nice kept a detailed record of the accomplishments of the Redstarts, including the age when they learned to sing. She also worked with another group of young birds; these were Serins, which were difficult to raise by hand. Nice wrote that she had learned what she had hoped to and was "ready to raise and study baby Song Sparrows."[10]

Return to the United States

Before returning to Chicago, Nice was reunited with her family at Grey Rocks, Massachusetts. Although birds of many different kinds were abundant there, Margaret was searching for a Song Sparrow nest with eggs in order to try out her new baby bird–raising skills. Just as in Austria, it was difficult to find a nest with eggs that would hatch at the right time. She finally located a nest with three eggs, which was two and a half feet from the ground in a small hemlock. She visited it daily, and on July 24 two tiny babies appeared, and a third hatched the next day. On July 30, she transferred them to a basket and carried them home to a nest she had prepared that was similar to the one Lorenz had created for the Redstarts. As was her custom, she named the babies according to the color of their bands: the seven-day-old babies were called Redbud and Blueboy, and the six-day-old baby, Yellow Puccoon. She and Janet gathered fresh insects for the babies and "we developed great respect for the young birds."[11] A letter from Lorenz confirmed the status of the birds she had worked with during her visit, and she was pleased to find out they were healthy and well.[12]

As she had for the Redstarts, Nice kept accurate records of the behavior of her young birds. She was especially impressed by the early age at which the Song Sparrows began to sing. Redbud sang at thirteen days—"the youngest definite age of starting to sing that I have been able to find for a bird of any species." Blueboy followed his sibling by warbling for four minutes at a stretch the next day. Since male song sparrows were known for their singing, clearly Redbud and Blueboy were both males. Margaret's hopes that Yellow Puccoon was a female were dashed when he too began to sing.[13]

On August 8, the Nices packed the three brothers in a bamboo cage and began the long drive back to Chicago. They caught grasshoppers at each relative's house where they stopped along the way. Because of the August heat, they carried the young birds inside every time they stopped to eat. Nice paid their young nephews and nieces in southern Ohio a penny for every ten insects they caught. For the first time since babyhood, the young Song Sparrows heard singing from adults of their species. A near tragedy occurred when Puccoon almost got lost at the house of another relative. Nice was attempting to put a bathing dish into his cage as it stood on the lawn, and he escaped and landed on a bush. To her great relief she was able to pick him up. The little birds seemed very happy when they arrived in Chicago after their long journey, for they could leave their cage and stretch their wings again.[14]

The three brothers were entertaining subjects, and Nice carefully monitored and recorded all their activities. In a letter to Lorenz, she wrote that her three male Song Sparrows gave her great pleasure and had the freedom of the study, but she regretted she still did not have a female. Nice had asked a friend to trap some birds, but "so far he has not brought me any."[15] After the birds gained their adult plumage, they began to quarrel more frequently and established a straight-line hierarchy with Blueboy at the top, Redbud in the middle, and "Pucky" at the bottom. Their quarrels resulted in an unhappy ending on October 14, when the family found Redbud dead. Margaret assumed that in a wild chase he had banged himself against the window. She left the two remaining birds in Janet's care while she and Constance attended the AOU meeting from October 17 to 22,

1938, in Washington, DC. Meanwhile, dominance shifted back and forth between Blueboy and Pucky.[16]

Soon after Margaret returned from the AOU meeting, she, Blaine, Janet, and a bird-watching friend drove to the twenty-fourth meeting of the Wilson Ornithological Club in Ann Arbor, Michigan. When they returned to Chicago they found the house frigid; the furnace boy had neglected his job, and they almost lost the Song Sparrows. Blueboy and Pucky stopped singing—a bad sign—but they recovered after the furnace warmed the house.[17]

On the morning of February 1, 1939, they found Blueboy dead on the floor—probably another victim of the window—leaving Pucky as the lone survivor of the trio. Nice noted that although he sang constantly and his six songs were typical of wild sparrows in their form, length, and timing, the quality was "inferior." She speculated that this could have been because he had not heard an adult Song Sparrow song in the fall.[18]

Only on occasion did Nice keep her wild birds caged. She had allowed them free access to the house during her student days at Clark, when her first Bobwhite, Loti, was granted this freedom. Her visit with Lorenz corroborated her idea that to confine a bird was to inhibit its natural behavior. Nowhere in her accounts does she mention the obvious problems that such freedom presented to the human occupants of the house.

The Hunt for a Female Song Sparrow

Since the three captive Song Sparrow brothers had taught Nice so much about their behavior, she was determined to raise a female sparrow during the summer of 1939. To search for a female, she spent June with her friends and colleagues Miles and Lucy Pirnie at the W. K. Kellogg Bird Sanctuary on Wintergreen Lake near Augusta, Michigan. In a letter to Mayr, she wrote that unfortunately she had struck an "inbetween [sic] time when everybody has young out of the nest or eggs, so I have not accomplished much."[19] Because Song Sparrow nests were exceedingly difficult to locate, Margaret vowed next time to study a bird with nests that were easy to find. The Chipping Sparrow, she jested, would have been a much easier subject because it built its nests in more accessible places than the Song Sparrow.

Brown-headed Cowbirds used both Song Sparrows and Chipping Sparrows as foster parents for their own young. Nice found a nest with one very large baby Cowbird cohabiting with several small Chipping Sparrows.

In order to give the small chippies a chance, she adopted the baby Cowbird and applied the techniques of bird rearing she had learned from Lorenz to "Chippychild," as she named it.[20] In spite of the lack of new Song Sparrow babies to rear, Nice wrote to Mayr, "it is proving a delightful vacation with the kind Pirnies and doing my health a world of good."[21]

On June 10 Nice's luck began to change; she found several Song Sparrow nests and monitored them continually. Experimenting with the new film technology of motion pictures, she shot film of the nests with a movie camera, showing the parents feeding the young and later leaving the nest. Although most of the nests were victims of one disaster or another, she managed to band three chicks with red, blue, and yellow bands (Scarlet, Flax, and Goldilocks). Since Goldilocks did not thrive in captivity, Nice placed her in another nest, where the parents cared for her as their own. Dewberry came from another nest and joined Flax and Scarlet as research subjects.

Nice took the new birds back to Chicago by car, where they met Pucky, who had been alone since February. Pucky approached the newcomers with his tail spread, perching on one cage and then another. He was hostile toward the babies and pulled out their feathers when he had the opportunity. Eventually Flax had only a few tail feathers left and Scarlet had none at all. Dewberry ended up with two remaining tail feathers. Poor Chippychild had died after Janet overfed her. Margaret blamed herself for not warning her "against over-feeding the enthusiastic beggar."[22]

Finally, a Female!

After a quick trip to Grey Rocks to visit Marjorie's new baby, Hugh, and another trip to New York to visit herpetologist and behaviorist G. K. Noble and evolutionary biologist David Lack, who was visiting from England, Nice returned to Chicago to find molting, somewhat subdued Song Sparrows. On September 19, 1939, she found Scarlet dead, and Flax followed two days later. She did not speculate on the cause of death of either bird. Since there was not a female in the group, Nice was still on the lookout for one to rear.

The problem was solved when a bird-banding friend in Columbus offered to give her a young female Song Sparrow named Jewel that he had nurtured from the age of eight days. He also supplied her with two hand-raised Goldfinches. Nice took possession of them in Louisville, Kentucky, where the Wilson Ornithological Club met from November 24 to 26, 1939.

At this meeting, she illustrated her paper "The Development of Song Sparrows and a Cowbird" with her experimental motion pictures.[23]

The use of motion pictures as a tool for understanding animal behavior had a history dating from the late nineteenth century. Early cinematic technology may have begun with the chrono-photographic gun, invented in 1882 by the French physiologist Étienne-Jules Marey (1830–1904). This device could record the motion of birds in flight on a single plate. By taking twelve photographs in one second, Marey was able to document movements that were not visible to the human eye.[24]

Earlier, American (born English) photographer Eadweard Muybridge (1830–1904) had responded to a bet that Leland Stanford, then California governor, had made with a friend, arguing that all four feet of a galloping horse left the ground at the same time. Muybridge devised a way to solve the problem by establishing an array of twelve cameras that photographed a galloping horse in a series of shots. He thereby determined that all four feet did indeed leave the ground at the same time, no doubt pleasing Leland Stanford. Muybridge contributed to a technology that had both educational and scientific possibilities. However, by the early 1900s inventors and promoters had made cinema a venue for entertainment as well as for education.[25] Movies soon obtained a reputation for causing moral turpitude and societal decadence, raising the ire of families and clergy. According to historian Gregg Mitman, natural history movies of animal life served to counter the new "morally and socially corrupting" influence of the entertainment movie enterprise, for they were both educational and entertaining.[26] The wider application of cinematic technology to the study of animal behavior in addition to entertaining animal movies was realized somewhat later.

The use of motion pictures to record bird behavior began in the spring of 1929 when Peter Paul Kellogg (1899–1975), a graduate student of Arthur Allen, the founder of the Laboratory of Ornithology at Cornell University and an instructor at that institution, became intrigued by electrical sound equipment. In May 1929, Kellogg was approached by the Fox-Case Movietone Corporation for his assistance in recording the song of wild birds to demonstrate the new technology. Allen agreed to help, and he, Kellogg, and the Movietone crew recorded the songs of a Song Sparrow, a House Wren, and a Rose-breasted Grosbeak. Although the results were disappointing and the equipment heavy and expensive, Kellogg and Allen found the possibilities fascinating. This experiment initiated the use of audio technology to enhance the study of bird behavior.[27]

These opportunities expanded when a broker on the New York Stock Exchange, Albert R. Brand (1888–1940), quit his job in 1928 and came to Cornell to study ornithology under Allen. Interested in sound recording and with the financial means to support that interest, he began buying, testing, and modifying recording equipment with the help of an undergraduate, M. Peter Keane (1910–2014). Brand and Keane recognized that motion-picture film with sound presented the best medium for recording sounds, so they concentrated on sound cinematography. Two years after they began their investigations, they had recorded over forty species of birds, and at the 1931 annual meeting of the AOU, Brand presented his *Preliminary Report of a New Method for Recording Bird Songs.* As exciting as the possibilities for this new technology were, because of the limitations of the equipment, the sound quality remained poor.

During the next winter, the ornithologists at Cornell collaborated with three local electrical engineers and redesigned and rebuilt the equipment. An idea of Peter Keane's, along with the assistance of the Cornell Physics Department, proved helpful. Inspired by a visit to the Radio City Music Hall, where parabolic reflectors were used to record voices of individual singers, Keane suggested that the signal picked up by a microphone could be intensified by a parabolic reflector. The Cornell Physics Department supplied some parabola molds, originally made for the detection of approaching enemy planes during World War I, and a reflector for bird song was soon built. In 1932 Allen and Kellogg used the new tool for a behavioral study of the Ruffed Grouse. They combined both sound and pictures and made a film that was presented alongside a paper at the 1932 AOU meeting.[28]

Nice was not the only one to take advantage of this new technology— seven of the thirty-seven papers presented at the 1939 Wilson Club meeting also included motion pictures. In Nice's presentation, her motion-picture experiment did not go smoothly. She lamented, "When the projector was turned on, the film proved to be in backwards!" Nonplussed about the mishap, she "kept talking about Chippychild" during the rewinding.[29]

Nice found herself very busy as president of the Wilson Club at these meetings, and not just because she presented interesting papers. The presidency required that she spend much time on administrative details.

She was proud of her many accomplishments as president but declined to continue for another term. In a letter to her mother, she wrote:

> Many people were shocked and grieved that I was not to continue as President. It has been an honor and an opportunity, and with the help of excellent fellow-officers we have been able to achieve a number of important things. Of one new feature I am especially proud—the establishment of the Wildlife Conservation Committee.[30]

The committee that Nice referred to proposed to print regularly in a section of the *Wilson Bulletin* a summary of the information gathered on the preservation of wildlife "in its totality." It solicited opinions and factual contributions of the society's members.[31]

Jewel and the Boys

When Nice arrived home from the Wilson Club meeting, she found that the recently acquired Jewel had upset the established dominance relationships. Although at first Pucky had ignored Jewel and Dewberry had shown only moderate interest in her, this situation soon changed. Pucky found his previous dominance over Dewberry challenged after Nice shut him into a large cage to medicate him. Dewberry immediately began to warble loudly by Jewel's cage, waving his wings. In response to his attention, she moved to the back of her cage. Dewberry then flew to Pucky's cage and warbled even more loudly and waved his wings. Pucky then formed a ball with both wings up and sang softly. Dewberry raised his crest and Pucky rushed at him and drove him away.

The competition for dominance continued for two days, during which Dewberry sang short songs to intimidate Pucky, who flew back and forth in his cage with a raised crest. Dewberry then puffed up and sang very loudly while vibrating his wings. Ten minutes later he started to make a "tchunk" sound, a "sure sign of dominance." However, Dewberry's dominance did not last, for Pucky eventually regained his position. Nice postulated that Pucky originally lost out to Dewberry only because he was not feeling well.[32]

Nice conducted numerous experiments on the Song Sparrows' acquisition of song. Since Pucky's and Dewberry's songs were so similar, she postulated that Dewberry had imprinted (see chapter 13 for discussion of imprinting) on Pucky. Other experiments included the responses of hand-raised birds to predators such as owls. Nice put a stuffed and mounted Barred Owl on the piano, and the birds were clearly alarmed. Even after the owl was removed from the piano, the little birds regarded the instrument with mistrust.

The female Song Sparrow, Jewel, had a "personality" different from that of the males. Although she was basically a quiet animal, occasionally she would threaten one male or the other. Nice also noticed that in late February and early March she became restless. She posited that Jewel's behavior might have been migration restlessness since she had hatched in central Ohio, where most of the female Song Sparrows were migratory.[33]

After an extensive trip during the spring of 1940, Margaret and Blaine returned home and found that both Jewel and Dewberry had died by "accident" three days before. A postmortem dissection by Nice on the pair indicated that although their diets had been similar, Jewel was much heavier, lending credence to the idea that she had been preparing for migration. If she had lived, she might later have shown "some specifically female behavior."[34] The last key member of the hand-raised Song Sparrow group, Pucky, died in the late summer of 1942 after a veterinary surgeon accidentally caused his death while attempting to remove a lump under his bill.[35]

Nice Meets Tinbergen

Although Nice and Tinbergen, the cofounder of ethology with Konrad Lorenz, had corresponded, they had never met in person. Tinbergen regretted that he had not able to see her "up till now [1938]," because she was one of the people he "was most anxious to meet." Appreciative of Nice's reviews in Bird-Banding, he explained that the only reason he subscribed to the journal was because of her reviews. Under a separate cover, he sent her a copy of Ardea (the official journal of the Netherlands Ornithologists' Union) that contained a paper on old Dutch methods of capturing migrating birds that would be new for American bird trappers. He volunteered to translate it and said that "one of the interested Americans could do the final revision."[36]

Tinbergen and Nice finally met at the fifty-sixth meeting of the AOU in Washington, DC, October 17–22, 1938. This meeting with Tinbergen was the most productive part of the conference for Nice. She raved about the paper he presented on the sociology of the Herring Gull, calling it the most outstanding presentation of the meeting.[37] Although Nice had planned to read a joint paper with Lorenz at the meeting, he had failed to submit his section to her, and without the "theoretical portion of our joint paper," she was unable to present it.[38] Too late for the meeting, Lorenz finally provided the theoretical basis she needed. However, the paper was never published because of Lorenz's delay.[39] In place of the planned joint paper, she read another one, "The Social *Kumpan* and the Song Sparrow."

After the meeting she wrote, "Dr. Tinbergen is a delightful man, so unassuming, yet so brilliant. I wished I could have had much more time to consult with him; a week would have been none too long."[40] The compliments were mutual, for Tinbergen praised Nice's paper. In a letter to Lorenz he reported that her paper was "absolutely excellent." Lorenz relayed Tinbergen's praise to Nice, reporting, "He is a very hard critic, so you may really feel rightly flattered by this! I am very glad you like Tinbergen, he is really one of THE BEST in every respect scientifically and personally."[41]

Chapter 11

"DEAR EDITOR"

During the time Nice was preparing the second volume of her Song Sparrow monograph, World War II was wreaking havoc on the European scientific community. At the same time, Nice was experiencing health difficulties. She was overworked, concerned about her European friends, and generally exhausted by life. With all the demands on her time, Nice was often frustrated as she tried to complete the second volume of her Song Sparrow monograph, *The Behavior of the Song Sparrow*, for the Linnaean Society of New York. She recorded her moods in her "Plans Book," a combination journal and diary that she excerpted in her autobiography. On July 17, 1941, she wrote, "SS II is a nightmare. It is the last—I hope—big task—rather—enormous task. I've achieved hard things before. I cannot fail now." Her mood seesawed from depression to eagerness. On January 10, 1942, she recorded, "The best week I've ever had." But on January 12 she wrote, "Tired this morning; have worked at too terrific a pace." By January 21 things were "going splendidly—way ahead of schedule." But on February 20, when she finally began to accomplish what she had set out to do, she was interrupted by having to take "four days off for Reviews."[1]

Illness

Nice always had an excess of energy, working incessantly on her research, publishing her results, writing endless reviews, corresponding with colleagues all over the world, and dabbling in conservation politics. However, the fast pace finally caught up with her; after she spent three months in the hospital in 1942 with a diagnosis of coronary thrombosis, her physicians told her to curtail many of her activities. Field research became out of the question, and she was required to do most of her work at home during the next five years. As it turned out, these precautions were unnecessary.

In 1947 her heart specialist reexamined the electrocardiograms taken in 1942 and concluded that she had not actually had a "real attack of coronary thrombosis," and that her problems were the result of a "labile [unstable with episodes of hypertension] sympathetic system and too many drugs." His advice was to "take up your bed and walk."[2]

Nice spent the years of uncertain health finishing some articles on her observations at Interpont and her experiences in Europe for the *Chicago Naturalist* (1940, 1944–1946) and the *Bulletin of the Illinois Audubon Society* (1940–1944).[3] During this period, the Nices also downsized their living space by moving three blocks east of their old house to a smaller dwelling on Harper Street. Margaret was positive about the move. Even though the new house was small, it was "more modern." It forced her to downsize her possessions, a process she claimed was constructive. She gave away about two-fifths of her ornithological library to the Wilson Club library and to her friends. Her new house's proximity to Jackson Park made it possible for her to carry on small projects with birds while convalescing.

Letters

Nice had always been interested in the politics of science, and during her convalescence spent time railing against what she considered to be the idiocy of the uninformed. Previously, her frenetic pace had not allowed her to express her opinions freely in the popular press or to complain of injustices to politicians. Freed from some of her other responsibilities, she was now liberated to pursue other passions, and she engaged in an orgy of letter writing. For example, she disagreed with the stance of the humane societies that attempted to prevent medical schools from "utilizing stray dogs in their goal of prevention of death and cure of disease." In a letter to the editor of the Chicago Sun, she claimed that this attempted prevention was reminiscent of the "persecutions of the Dark Ages." Experimentation on animals, she wrote, was the basis for "the conquest of diphtheria, typhoid, small-pox, cholera, rabies, plague, tetanus." Other miracles of modern medicine, such as the use of insulin, sulfa drugs, penicillin, and blood transfusions, were possible only because of research on animals. "Instead of hampering these men and women who are devoting themselves to the welfare of mankind, the grateful public should do everything possible to help them." She closed the letter with a comparison of the so-called "humane" individuals in the United States to those in Europe. "When I was in Austria in 1938, I was told sarcastically by physicians and medical students: 'Medical Schools in Germany can no longer use dogs for experiments or demonstration. Hitler has forbidden it.' He had just too tender a heart."[4]

Her lack of sympathy for domestic animals did not carry over to wild-life, whose conservation and preservation she deemed essential. She railed against those who proposed "ridiculous" ideas that would harm wildlife and the natural environment. In a letter to Harold Ickes, secretary of the interior, she maintained that it was important not to relax safeguards on waterfowl: "It is essential that we give the birds further protection. The season should be shortened and the entire country once again made into a winter sanctuary for all waterfowl." She insisted that Wood Ducks be given complete protection, because "their numbers have been markedly depleted by the inexcusable opening of the season on this most beautiful of all our ducks." She asked Ickes to state publicly that baiting and live decoys would never be allowed. She also proposed that hunters be forbidden to use lead shot. Recognizing that farmers had a legitimate complaint that migrating ducks destroyed their crops, she suggested that "oscillating beams of light be used" to protect the farmland.[5] She sent a similar letter to Dr. Ira N. Gabrielson, director of the U.S. Fish and Wildlife Service, in Washington, DC.

In another instance, Nice wrote to the editor of the popular magazine *Coronet*, praising the color photographs of birds in the May edition. She then launched into a tirade about the accompanying story by Leonard Dubkin as "an insult to intelligence." Poor Mr. Dubkin had complained about people supplying colored ribbons for nesting material. This practice, he wrote, made a robin's nest "a glaring landmark to all the cats in the neighborhood." Nice wrote, "Mr. Dubkin does not seem to know that cats are color-blind." Dubkin also worried that crows would pull the nest to pieces in order to get the ribbons. "What, pray," wrote Nice, "would crows want of ribbons?" She proclaimed that he would do well to become acquainted with his neighborhood birds: "Perhaps then he would not class cardinals and tufted tits as migratory." Nice took issue with his supposition that bird lovers and legislators did more harm than good for the birds they professed to love.[6]

From the time Nice had been a young girl, she had realized that cats killed her beloved birds. As an adult, she continued a diatribe against cats and their owners who allowed them to run free. This time she wrote a letter to the editor of the *Chicago Sun* about the problem with cats and birds. Nice claimed that it made no sense to make people pay fines for destroying birds or nests while the law allowed them "to keep with impunity carnivorous animals [cats] that slaughter many birds a year." She found it unfair that the owners were held responsible for the bad behavior of most domestic animals on other people's or public property, yet "the most dangerous creature of all [the cat]" was exempt. She proposed that the owners be fined from $25 to $300 for each bird killed by each of their cats. That action, she asserted, would surely solve the problem.[7] Much later she wrote a congratulatory letter to Illinois governor Adlai Stevenson for the "cat bill" passed by the legislature, which made "the trespassing of cats illegal."[8]

Nice wrote a letter to the *Reader's Digest* lambasting the magazine for an article titled "Quacker Comeback." The article posited that there was no reason to limit the season on the "pitifully few" ducks at Poland Park [in Chicago], because the numbers were actually increasing. Not so, cried the incensed Nice. "I am very much concerned over the situation." She agreed with the experts who believed that only a completely closed season would save the ducks. The *Reader's Digest* gave "entirely the wrong impression." She complained to Mayr, "If only they'd publish a statement of the real facts it would do much good."[9] She claimed that because of the magazine's enormous circulation, the article had done incalculable harm to the preservation of these ducks. The *Digest*, she claimed, was a bad influence in the world because it habitually published "false articles and never retreats." The article did not refer to a specific population like the one in Poland Park, but it considered the accomplishments of a group of sportsmen who established an organization that since 1938 had "boosted the continent's duck population by 500 percent."[10]

Nice did not confine her opinions to natural history. Invariably outspoken and confident in her ideas, she chastised those she thought were being unfair. In the immediate pre-McCarthy era, she outraged conservative politicians with her views. With a letter to *Life* magazine on April 1, 1947, she admonished the magazine for its treatment of the Soviet Union by "rendering signal disservice to humanity by consistently fomenting hatred of Russia." She targeted a book by former radical and later right-wing political philosopher James Burnham (1905–1987), called *Struggle for the World* (1947), as a "shockingly misleading war-mongering" example. Burnham had called the Soviets' victory over the Japanese "cheap," thus infuriating

Nice. She called it "an ignoble deed to be fostering suspicion and enmity against our ally, a country that is doing its best to give the common man and woman a chance with no distinction as to race." Nice wrote that naturally, "capitalists are terrified of Communism—we conveniently forget that it was practiced by the Early Christians—for it means sharing their money bags." She concluded her letter by asking whether capitalists would "really be better off in the long run when they have succeeded in wrecking the world?" Instead of war and hatred, "the only hope for mankind lies in cooperation and friendship between nations."[11]

Nice addressed another letter to author and professor of philosophy Barrows Dunham (1905–1995), in which she praised him for his book *Man against Myth* (1947) "as a liberal and well-wisher for humanity." Dunham's political philosophy was similar to Nice's, and later, on February 27, 1953, when he was called before the House Un-American Activities Committee for his views, he refused to answer any questions, invoking his Fifth Amendment privilege against self-incrimination. Temple University, where he was a professor, fired him for refusing to cooperate with the committee. Although he was eventually acquitted, Temple did not reinstate him and he was blacklisted from academic employment for fourteen years. However, Nice's letter was written before the indictment. After praising him, she felt obliged to point out what she considered two serious flaws in his book. First, she felt that he gave a false impression of the General Semantics movement, which was "earnestly laboring to dispel 'myths.'"[12] As a scientist, she was disturbed that he ignored "*the* basic problem of the world—over-population and the concomitant decrease of arable land." She proposed the following: "Until we balance the ledger by birth control and soil and wildlife conservation, all efforts to improve living conditions and social relationships are mere palliatives." In order to steer him in the right direction, she recommended William Vogt's report titled *The Population of Venezuela and Its Natural Resources*. Vogt was the editor of *Bird-Banding* and later (1948) published a well-respected book on population control, *Road to Survival*. Nice included a copy of the review of Dunham's book that she had prepared for *Bird-Banding*.[13]

Nice was not shy in expressing her views to those in the highest political positions in the country. She wrote to President Harry S. Truman on July 28, 1948, protesting the treatment of the board members of the Joint Anti-Fascist Refugee Committee, demanding that they "not be sent to jail for upholding the tradition [upon] which our country was founded." She found it "bitterly ironical" that the United States was now persecuting those of its citizens who "are working against this evil." By this time McCarthyism was gaining traction, and Nice proclaimed, "We will have lost the war in the most tragic sense if we in America, the bulwark of democracy, adopt fascism ourselves."[14]

Life magazine reappeared on Nice's radar screen in October 1948, when she excoriated its editors for their views on two extraordinary books on conservation, William Vogt's *Road to Survival* and Fairfield Osborn's *Our Plundered Planet.* "It is just such blindness to basic realities as shown in your editorial that is bringing the world inevitably to disaster, unless we change our ways, promptly and radically."[15] She turned her attention to *Time* magazine the next month, claiming that Henry Luce, the editor, had "maliciously misrepresented the exceedingly important book of William Vogt's, the *Road to Survival.*" She accused Luce of a "vicious and slanderous attack [that] is evidently motivated by religious prejudice and sympathy with Big Business which wishes to continue to exploit the natural resources of the world without the slightest concern for the good of the people of this and all future generations."[16]

Others of Nice's many letters were more local in scope. She wrote to the editors of the *Chicago Sun-Times,* deploring the "indifference to civic pride" as evidenced by a "half dozen Pennsylvania Railroad engines at the round houses . . . belching forth black smoke." She also complained about the "continuous heaps of tin cans" that disfigured the Southwest Highway between Western and Kedzie Avenues.[17] The mayor of Chicago was the recipient of one of her letters, which criticized the city for destroying "the splendid hedge that protected" the circular garden in Jackson Park next to Stony Island from "the noise and dirt of the streets."[18]

In addition to writing letters to editors, reviewing papers, and catching up on writing papers for publication, Nice engaged in another important activity during her convalescence. During the war years and immediately after, she spent much of her time organizing American ornithologists and behaviorists to send aid to their European colleagues.

Chapter 12

EUROPEAN ETHOLOGISTS, ORNITHOLOGISTS, AND WORLD WAR II

World War II complicated friendships for European scientists. Accustomed to sharing ideas across national boundaries during the prewar years, many friends and colleagues took sides in the conflict. The situation was reminiscent of the Civil War in the United States, when family members were often on opposite sides of the struggle; in many ways Austrian Konrad Lorenz and Dutchman Niko Tinbergen were like brothers before the war, but the conflict essentially destroyed their friendship.

Lorenz and Tinbergen

Lorenz's position on National Socialism during the war years is problematic. We know that he applied for membership in the Nazi party on June 28, 1938, claiming to be a "German thinker and scientist [and] always National Socialist."[1] But what did party membership at the time actually mean for Lorenz? Scholars vary in their treatment of his career during this time. Some totally ignore his wartime conduct, others consider him a politically active biologist who endorsed Nazi thinking, while still others presume that he cautiously tried to slip anti-Nazi ideas into his writings.[2] British historian of science Jonathan Harwood asserts the inadequacy of attempting to categorize individuals as either "Nazis" or "anti-Nazis." He suggests that the majority of academics did not fall into either camp, but into a middle ground between the two extremes. After 1933, only a handful of German academics opposed Nazi policies publicly. Over half the staff at most universities was composed of party members—most had joined in order to further their careers. Harwood concludes that the majority of scientists were neither "ideologically committed Nazis nor political opponents, but rather politically indifferent individuals whose primary concern was the well-being of their discipline." He believes they were willing to compromise to varying degrees in order to secure resources or protect themselves.[3] So the question becomes, was Lorenz just a pragmatist doing what many German scientists were doing to be able to continue their work, or was there a darker side to his thinking?

Lorenz's activities during the war still polarize historians. For example, British historian of science Michael Ruse offended Austrians in a blog written after he left Vienna precipitously in 2010 before giving an invited talk, claiming that his visit left him "feeling a bit grubby."[4] Ruse's insulted hosts immediately responded. Gerd Müller, chair of the Konrad Lorenz Institute for Evolution and Cognition Research, chastised Ruse for departing without notice before his lecture at the institute in Altenberg, and to make matters worse, Ruse had the temerity to write "a moral piece on Austria." In this blog, Ruse claimed that Lorenz might have worked as a physician in one of the death camps, a possibility that Müller denied, and one that is open to interpretation. Ruse lamented that in today's Austria, "it is possible to name a scientific institution after a war criminal." Müller considered this criticism totally unfair and one sided, because Ruse chose not to mention that ever since the founding of the institute in 1990 it had supported historical inquiries into Lorenz's behavior during the war. He challenged Ruse to present factual data indicating that Lorenz was active in the death camps. American historian of science Mitchell G. Ash at the University of Vienna also disagreed with Ruse and concluded his own article with the following charged statement: "Given his [Ruse's] demonstrated ignorance of and apparent disdain for what is actually happening in his own field, I find his text intellectually lazy, and his decision to publish it morally and politically irresponsible." In this highly emotional exchange, both Ruse and his detractors praised Richard Burkhardt's book as presenting a measured and fair interpretation.[5]

The evolving situation in Germany eventually had an effect on Nice's research and on that of many of her European colleagues. Adolf Hitler had gained power after two failed parliamentary elections when Germany's president, Paul von Hindenburg, had reluctantly agreed to appoint him chancellor in 1932. During 1933, Hitler's Nationalsozialistische Deutsche Arbeiterpartei (NSDAP, abbreviated NAZI in English) continued to consolidate power but could not secure an absolute majority. Hitler had to be content with a coalition government with the Deutschnationale Volkspartei (DNVP, or German National People's Party). After a suspicious fire that destroyed the Reichstag and was blamed on the Communists by the NSDAP, Hitler's party was able to push through the so-called Enabling Act, Ermächtigungsgesetz. The passage of this act allowed Hitler's cabinet to gain full emergency legislative powers for four years; the act also included significant deviations from the constitution. In order to ensure the two-thirds majority necessary to pass the Enabling Act, not only Communist delegates but also Social Democratic delegates were kept from participating in the proceedings. Much of the opposition was thus purged, including Ernst Rhöm, head of the Sturmabteilung (SA), during the so-called Night of the Long Knives. With the opposition eviscerated, the NSDAP was declared the only legal political party in Germany on July 14, 1934. The last legal obstacle for Hitler was overcome when the second president of the Weimar Republic, Paul von Hindenburg, died on August 2, 1934. On that day, Hitler became Führer and Reichskanzler. The office of president was abolished and its powers merged with those of the chancellor, essentially giving Hitler absolute power.

Since Lorenz was so important to Nice, we will explore some of his more questionable ideas relating to Germany's political situation and speculate on the effect they may have had on both her work and their friendship. Perhaps, as Harwood argued, pragmatism was the great motivator in Lorenz's politics. Even while Lorenz was gaining fame among biologists and animal psychologists, he was still unable to obtain a paid academic position and remained an unpaid lecturer in Karl Bühler's institute of psychology at the University of Vienna. Lorenz blamed his lack of success in obtaining the positions he wanted partially on the Austrian regime of Chancellor Kurt von Schuschnigg (1897–1977). According to Lorenz, Schuschnigg's attempt to keep Austria independent from Germany was misguided, to say the least. Lorenz had long wanted to find a position in Germany to avoid the "damned Jesuit rabble" in Austria who were in political control.[6]

As far back as 1937, Lorenz was angling to get the Kaiser Wilhelm Institute in Berlin to finance and develop a biological station similar to the one he had created at Altenberg. He wrote Nice that if "they should succeed, I should be the happiest man on earth."[7] When this plan did not materialize, he continued to look for other ways to encourage the government to sponsor his projects. After the *Anschluss* (forced union of Austria and Germany) of March 1938, Lorenz was delighted. He saw the possibility that his dream of an institute sponsored by the Kaiser Wilhelm Institute might indeed become a reality. In a letter to Stresemann, Lorenz emoted: "I believe we Austrians are the sincere and most convinced National Socialists after all!"[8] This statement is quite damning, even if he was thinking mostly about his own institute.

Although many of Lorenz's hopes did not materialize, his behavior indicated that either he believed sincerely some of the statements in his papers or he was willing to prostitute himself in order to attain what he considered to be a higher goal. When his former mentor Karl Bühler lost his position because he had lied about his wife's Jewish ancestry, Lorenz was not only unsympathetic but schemed to be appointed to Bühler's chair of psychology and the directorship of his institute of psychology at the University of Vienna. When this did not happen, he sought other avenues, including joining the Nazi party.

Some of Lorenz's lectures and papers written during this time emphasize his attempt to show others that his research supported the Third Reich's ideas regarding race hygiene. In a lecture at the 1938 joint meeting of the Society for Animal Psychology and the German Society for Psychology in Bayreuth, Lorenz posited that the degeneration of instinctive behavior patterns that he observed in domesticated ducks and geese corresponded to the genetic and cultural degeneration of civilized humans. This presentation earned him the friendship and support of Erich Jaensch, professor of psychology and director of the Institute for Psychological Anthropology at Marburg. Jaensch interpreted Lorenz's conclusions as supporting his ideas that so-called invirent, or weak, types in a society could threaten its health much as cancerous cells could destroy a human body, and he was convinced that Lorenz's ideas upheld the postulate that the Nordic movement was "a countermovement against domestication damages in civilized man."[9]

After Lorenz's 1938 Bayreuth talk postulating that degeneration of instinctive behavior patterns caused domestic animals to be inferior to their wild counterparts, Lorenz published a series of papers applying this idea to conditions of civilization, including modern medicine. He argued that so-called advances in medicine allowed inferior people to live and pass on degenerate genes to their progeny. From his experiments on crossing and backcrossing pure-blooded Greylag geese with domestic geese, he found that if a goose possessed only 1/32 of the blood of the domestic goose, the offspring would exhibit "degenerative features of domestication." He used this experiment to warn that it "took only a small amount of tainted blood to have an influence on a pure-blooded race."[10] These ideas and others espoused by Lorenz during the wartime years made it apparent that his conclusions were compatible with the Third Reich's glorification of racial purity. If anyone remained in doubt about his eugenics views, an article he wrote for the journal *Der Biologe*, "Nochmals: Systematik und Entwicklungsgedanke im Unterricht" (1940), would put that notion to rest. Lorenz, however, argued that he was just doing "good" science.[11]

Lorenz, along with many biologists from all over the world, including the United States, accepted many of the tenets of eugenics. The notion that the human species was becoming degenerate because of the addition of undesirable genes for characteristics such as criminality and feeble-mindedness was not limited to Germany. In 1928, the American geneticist E. G. Conklin (1863–1952) anonymously wrote the following in *Harper's Magazine*: "We cannot avoid the conclusion that although our human stock includes some of the most intellectual, moral, and progressive people in the world, it includes also a disproportionately large number of the worst human types." One of the reasons for this decline was the immigration of what he called "undesirable" people into the United States and the uncontrolled breeding of "defectives," such as the "feeble minded," the insane, criminals, and the physically handicapped.

By the 1930s, many American geneticists had modified their views when they became concerned that the American eugenics movement was being co-opted by nonprofessionals. Even Conklin became somewhat apprehensive that racial prejudice and restrictive immigration issues were dominating the eugenics movement. Geneticists Raymond Pearl (1879–1940) and L. C. Dunn (1893–1974) were more skeptical than Conklin about the ability of eugenics to improve the human race. As Hitler's excesses became more and more evident, the reputation of eugenics in the United States grew tarnished. Because Lorenz amalgamated his ideas on genetics with the social doctrines of the Third Reich, his credibility in the rest of the world also became blemished.[12]

However, the question still arises about Lorenz's motivation for his increasingly strident monographs. Was he being totally pragmatic by establishing his ideological purity in order to get support from the regime? In 1937 his application for additional funding from the German Research Organization (Deutsche Forschungsgemeinschaft, or DFG) was denied. Ostensibly he was turned down for financial reasons. But one of his enemies (vertebrate paleontologist Othenio Abel) questioned both his "politics and ancestry" and those of his wife. Perhaps he countered this possible blot on his character by not only presenting a clearly Aryan family tree but also designing his talks and papers to convince those in power that he was one of them, both politically and scientifically.

The animosity between Abel and Lorenz stretched back to the time of Lorenz's doctoral examination. Since Abel was not asked to be a member of Lorenz's examination committee, Lorenz assumed that Abel disliked him because of this omission and carried a grudge that manifested itself later.[13] However, as much as Lorenz wanted Nazi support, his ideas on the mixing of races and domestication preceded his attempts to demonstrate his philosophical agreement with the Nazis. They shared a common ideological background. He was probably correct when he later claimed that he got his ideas not from the Nazis but from his own experience and experiments, but he appeared to be unable to understand the cultural origins of his assumptions and seemed incapable of self-criticism. Finally his ambitions were achieved when he was appointed to a professorship at Königsberg, a position he could not have gotten in Austria either before the *Anschluss* or in later years, even if his "purity" (through his wife's supposed Jewish connection) was unquestionable.

In October 1941 Lorenz was drafted into the German military, first as a motorcycle messenger and, after the "powers" realized that he had been a psychology professor, as a military psychologist administering tests to those who aspired to become officers. This position was discontinued, and in 1942 he was appointed to the Department of Neurology and Psychology at the military reserve hospital in Poznań, Poland, where he worked as a physician and psychiatrist.[14] After the German invasion, much of western Poland was incorporated into the Third Reich. The policy of separating Germans from Poles then created a new apartheid in Poland. Burkhardt describes a test created by the race psychologist Rudolph Hippius designed to sort out the various people the Germans might encounter as they moved eastward into Russia. Although Lorenz was an honorary examining psychologist, the extent of his involvement remains unclear.

During his time in Poznań, Lorenz completed a major manuscript, "The Inborn Forms of Possible Experience"; although it stressed the desirability of racial purity in humans, it included many other subjects. He attempted to synthesize the themes he had written about during the previous eight years. Denying that he was a materialist, he explained his profound appreciation of the creativity of nature and his understanding of the ways in which humans distinguished themselves from the rest of the living world. In spite of this assertion, he assumed that humans experienced the world as a function of their organ systems, which were themselves products of organic evolution. Lorenz posited that the function of releasers and innate releasing mechanisms in the behavior of birds and fish presaged the recognition of the biological source of aesthetic and ethical judgment in humans. The general tone of his paper was different from that of his earlier writings, especially the 1940 paper "Domestication-Caused Disruptions of Species-Specific Behavior." Absent was the praise for the Nordic movement, although some of the same elements did reappear. Those who seek reassurance in denying Lorenz's political identification with the Nazis could use this monograph for support. But those who are critical of his wartime philosophy could also use it for reinforcement for their ideas.[15]

Nice was greatly influenced by the ethological views of both Lorenz and Tinbergen, especially Lorenz, in developing her own theoretical framework. Although the two men's approach to animal behavior was quite similar, Tinbergen's experience during the war years was very different from Lorenz's. In May 1940 Germany invaded his native Holland, and in just five days the Dutch surrendered. In spite of the invasion, Tinbergen took his students into the field during the summers of 1940 and 1941. During the early years of the war, Tinbergen continued to correspond with Lorenz. In March 1942 Tinbergen published a paper in the Dutch journal *Bibliotheca biotheoretica*, in which he stressed that ethology was about studying the causes of behavior. He distinguished his own ideas from those of the American animal behaviorists as well as the European psychologists. According to Tinbergen, the Americans were misguided because they considered only a few animal species and were prone to extrapolate other animal behavior from that of humans. However, the European animal psychologists were also ill advised because they were not interested in the *cause* of behavior. Tinbergen insisted that the proper way to study behavior was to apply physiological methods to determine the causes.[16]

Tinbergen's paper on this subject was his final attempt during the war to explain how ethology differed from other forms of behavioral studies, because German authorities then targeted the faculty at the University of

Leiden and replaced the incumbents with Nazis. Tinbergen, along with 80 percent of the faculty, resigned in protest. He was sent to an internment camp, where he remained a prisoner for two years until the camp was liberated. Although Lorenz considered the possibility of using his personal connections to free him, Tinbergen refused. Tinbergen and his family suffered enormously, as did his friendship with Lorenz.[17]

Nice and the War

Nice's loyalty to both Lorenz and Tinbergen was absolute. In spite of evidence to the contrary, she gave Lorenz the benefit of the doubt. She did what she could to help her friends, both German and non-German, on the other side of the Atlantic. During the actual fighting, information about the status of the European ornithologists and animal behaviorists was scanty. During the war Nice was aware of only some of the many tragedies that befell her European colleagues. One exception was the fate of Dutch naturalist Jan Joost Ter Pelkwyk, who visited the Nices in 1940 on his way to Dutch Guiana, where he planned to study the wildlife and work on his dissertation at the University of Leiden. While Ter Pelkwyk was visiting, Holland was invaded and his plans disrupted. His interim strategy, to study at the University of Chicago under ecologist Clyde Allee (1885–1955), also changed soon. In the fall of 1941 he received an appointment from the Netherlands government in exile, as ichthyologist at the Fishery Research Station in Batavia (today Jakarta, Indonesia). For several years he corresponded with Nice and other colleagues and friends. His last letter was written from Sumatra on January 22, 1942, and his fate was unknown until after the Japanese surrender. One report stated that as he was leaving Batavia for Australia in a small motorboat with a staff of officers, they were ambushed by a group of Japanese boats and Ter Pelkwyk was killed.[18] However, his mother wrote Nice that her son was killed "in a bombardment over Batavia in Mar. 1942."[19]

Immediately after the war the bad news outweighed the good. The lack of accurate information on the fate of the European ornithologists and behaviorists distressed Nice, and she was concerned that the ornithological journals were not doing more to help. It was "a pity," she reported, that little news of foreign colleagues and museums appeared in *The Auk*. None at all was reported in the *Wilson Bulletin*. She also blamed the journals for "the way that obituaries were recorded for deceased AOU Fellows and Members."

Even if an obituary was recorded (many were missed), the information was often inaccurate.[20] Mayr agreed and replied:

> It had been considered the duty of the [AOU] secretary to handle the matter. The current secretary, of course, is incompetent to handle such an assignment. Actually such matters have been handled rather informally in the A.O.U. and anybody who feels like writing an obituary can do so and send it to the editor of the *Auk*. He, no doubt, will be glad to publish it. Chapin, for example, is thinking of writing one of old Professor Neumann. Incidentally we never found out when he died and how long he was gravely ill before his death.[21]

Since mail connections between Europe and the United States were not restored immediately, many of the reports about German science and scientists were only partially substantiated, and others reflected mainly gossip. Nice belatedly learned that Oskar Heinroth had died on May 31, 1945, from pneumonia. He had been a mentor of Lorenz and, as Nice put it, was "a great pioneer—a wonderful student of animal behavior." She had profited from "good visits with him in 1932." Nice was unable to get a clear report on the fate of museums in Germany for many months. She "heard that the Zoologisches Museum in Berlin was 'virtually undamaged'" but sought information about the Museum für Naturkunde; it had been mentioned in the The Auk that it was destroyed.[22] The Auk's information about this museum proved to be only partially correct. Although the collections were damaged severely by the Allied bombing, with the east wing suffering the most destruction, the museum as a whole was not destroyed.

A letter from Nice to Mayr illustrates how difficult it was to get accurate information, especially from a defeated Germany. She referred Mayr to an article in *Nature* in which Huxley had quoted Stresemann's report that Lorenz had "gone missing" in Vitelsk [*sic*] "in the summer of '44, and is presumed dead." She grieved because both Stresemann and Lorenz were brilliant students of animal behavior and "both dear friends of mine."[23] Fortunately, Stresemann had survived relatively unscathed, and in spite of air raids his own house was almost untouched. He spent the immediate postwar years in the Soviet Zone.

The fate of Lorenz was not established with certainty until several years after the end of the war. After months of thinking him dead, Mayr informed Nice that he had good news from ornithologist Jean Delacour (1890–1985), who reported that he had received a letter from an English friend in Vienna indicating that Lorenz was alive and living in that city.[24] However, Tinbergen still thought Lorenz was dead in 1946. In a letter to Nice, Tinbergen noted that he and Lorenz had been very good friends, and he worried about the fate of his family. However, as he learned more about Lorenz's activities during the war, he became less tolerant of him and his behavior. As for the other German ornithologists, Tinbergen vowed that his

> connections with German ornithology will not be taken up again so long as Nazis like SS-man Niethamer and Ministerialdirigent Ludwig Schuster play a part in it. Beware of the spirit of Prussian militarism and of the nazi-Geist. One of the surprising and discouraging lessons taught us by this war is the knowledge that a man may be a most degenerate criminal while in ordinary circumstances making the impression of a reliable, friendly, honest man. A very discouraging experience but it is *true*! It is a pity that we have lost our naivete in this respect but it has brought us at least better insight in human nature.[25]

Nice received a letter from Tinbergen that described his imprisonment with twenty other Leiden professors for two years. During those years he occupied himself by writing "a little book on animal sociology" as well as several illustrated books for children from four to ten years old. He had originally intended to give them to his own children "as a letter from me during my captivity, one page each week, but forming coherent stories." The other ornithologists who were imprisoned with Tinbergen all survived the war, although two of them almost starved to death. Tinbergen was eager to restart international cooperation and hoped to arrange for a small conference with interested researchers.

Beginning in 1945, the Nice family began sending food and clothing to their Dutch friends, but Margaret credits Joseph Hickey with trying to persuade the AOU and the Wilson and Cooper Clubs to appoint committees for European relief. In spite of the difficulty of navigating the mail system, some packages made it to the countries formerly occupied by Germany early in 1946. Letters began to reach Nice thanking her for her long-distance help. Many boxes found in the Nice collection at Cornell and in the Mayr correspondence at Harvard are filled with letters attesting to the gratitude that the ornithologists and their families felt for her contributions. The letters were handwritten; in an attempt to save paper every margin was often filled with writing. Stresemann called her "the mother of international ornithology." He also wrote, "Your correspondence must have reached a tremendous voluminousness!"[26]

Nice received material help in sending packages to the families from naturalist Frances Hamerstrom (1908–1998), who had responded to a request from Joe Hickey and Nice.[27] She and her husband, Frederick, were invaluable to the effort, but as Fran Hamerstrom wrote, "There are several who hold misconceptions: i.e., that we started the Action. We didn't, it was M. M. Nice and J. J. Hickey."[28] Nice especially appreciated her participation because with Hamerstrom's superior knowledge of the German language she could write directly to Europe for names of needy families, determine the ages and sexes of their children, and relay the information to those in the United States who wanted to help. Nice wrote in retrospect, "It is almost incredible what she accomplished."[29]

In 1947, Nice and the others were still trying to find a way to match donors with those who needed help, and to avoid thievery. In a letter that Frederick Hamerstrom (Hammy) wrote to the many involved in the relief effort (including Nice and Hickey), he explained ways to avoid having items like cigarettes and new clothing stolen in transit. To some, his method seemed deceitful and immoral. Hammy explained that the duty on cigarettes was very high (except in the U.S. Zone) and the value of cigarettes was outlandish. To get around this duty, he would "put in a pack or two and list the [item] on the customs slips as ETC." He also suggested marking boxes as "used clothes" when they were only very slightly worn, because thieves would break into boxes of new clothing. He signed a letter explaining this as follows: "Sincerely Hammy, Chairman, AOU Comm. Of Moral Lepers."[30]

Problems with Communications

Sometimes information about the American ornithologists' peers was even more important than the actual physical commodities being sent to them. When Nice wrote Mayr on January 5, 1946, she finally knew for certain that Lorenz was alive: "There have been so many deaths of fine ornithologists that I'm thankful he was spared." With so many people interested in the destiny of the Europeans, round-robin letters seemed the most efficient way to pass on news. For example, Mayr forwarded a long letter to Nice that he had received from Stresemann that contained information about other ornithologists, including a report of the death of ornithologist Jakob Schenk and information on three other colleagues who had survived. When Nice visited the Field Museum in Chicago she was able to show the letter from Stresemann and others to herpetologist Karl Schmidt (1890–1957) and expatriate German ornithologist Oscar Rudolph Neumann (1867–1946). In order for everyone who was interested to get the news, Nice suggested to Mayr that Science might publish some of the letters under "News from Abroad."[31]

During this time, Nice received a letter from Stresemann in which he praised the second part of her Song Sparrow monograph, which he had just received. He wrote that although it was a pity it arrived too late for the deceased Heinroth to review it, he was happy that "another genius . . . will read it." That genius was Konrad Lorenz. Stresemann explained how he found out for certain that Lorenz was alive: "Frau Heinroth went to see me two days ago on a dark stormy night to give me the wonderful news at once: Gretel Lorenz now again staying with her father-in-law at Altenberg, had a postcard written by her husband! He is a Russian prisoner, not wounded, and employed in a camp as a physician. Isn't that simply marvelous news? Please do spread it at once, and don't forget to inform Dr. Tinbergen and other friends abroad!"[32]

Konrad Lorenz and his family were always the recipients of Margaret's good thoughts and caring gestures. Although she could not physically help Konrad, she could send supplies to his family. Mayr explained that it had become possible to send CARE packages to Austria by 1946: "We certainly can send such packages to the Lorenz family."[33] Margarethe Lorenz wrote that the items Nice sent were very important to her and her children and "how thankful" they were for them. She proposed to "keep the durable things for the return of Konrad," though she had "not the least idea when" that would be. She added, "We had a card only today from him."[34] Nice did not write just to her good friends among the Europeans, but also to those with whom she had only a passing acquaintance. It is little wonder she became exhausted with the effort of responding to all who asked.

Nice finally took a vacation of sorts—more of a "busman's holiday." She and Constance left Chicago for a week to visit two state parks in Indiana (Indiana Dunes State Park and Pokagon State Park) and the

Kellogg Bird Sanctuary near Augusta, Michigan. Upon returning she was overwhelmed by stacks of mail containing reports about some of the specific help that they had provided already and asking for help that was still needed.[35]

Need for Professional Information

It was not just the necessities of life that were in short supply in Europe, but information on the latest research, which made life worth living for many of these scientists. Nice wrote to the president of the AOU, Hoyes Lloyd, "As you are well aware, many European ornithologists are suffering greatly from lack of food, clothing and all sorts of material goods. I am very happy that the A.O.U. has appointed a committee to assist our colleagues in these vital matters." However, she went on to say that they also had a different kind of hunger—for ornithological journals.[36]

As early as 1946, some scholarly materials were getting through to Europe. Although on April 3, 1946, Stresemann reported to Nice that mail to Germany could not be opened, the rules were soon relaxed, apparently, because a few days later he reported that the journal *Bird-Banding* had arrived. In the same letter he asked her for some hundreds of colored bird bands for Dr. Schüz. Nice hesitated to ask the acknowledged expert on bird banding, Frederick Lincoln, to send them, because she was certain he did not like her and might refuse her request for that reason. She asked Mayr about the advisability of approaching ornithologist Donald Sankey Farner as an intermediary. Farner, she assumed, would have a better chance of success with Lincoln, because she was convinced that Farner got along better with him than she did.[37] Mayr agreed: "It might be best to be diplomatic and get Farner to handle the matter of the colored bands. I shall certainly be glad to handle the shipping."[38]

If Nice had complained previously about the difficulty involved in shipping personal items to the Europeans, the financial and the physical costs of sending boxes of books, journals, and reprints to Europe were even more taxing: "I have mailed Stresemann six packages, several of them up to twenty-two pounds heavy, but I am glad to learn that you [Mayr] will want to send something too because we have had so many requests for packages that it begins to be quite difficult to make ends meet."[39] The red tape involved in sending these packages presented another layer of difficulty. After the defeat of Nazi Germany, the country was divided into four military occupation zones: France in the southwest, Britain in the northwest, the United States in the south, and the Soviet Union in the east. Different rules and costs applied when sending packages to different zones. Nice asked Mayr for information about mail between the different zones in Germany. She wanted to send the Song Sparrow volumes and reprints to ornithologist Dr. H. Laven, who was in the British Zone and had lost his entire library: "But we can send nothing to the British Zone. Nor can we send printed matter to the American Zone." She included the items in the box to Stresemann, but before she mailed them she asked whether Mayr knew if Stresemann would be able to forward them. Or, she wondered if it was better to just wait.[40]

The American ornithological community as a whole responded to their European colleagues' need for reprints. Mayr explained that the Americans had "long since started to fill the gaps in the files of the active French, Dutch, Danish, and Swedish workers." He had been able to get a number of reprints to Stresemann and had "sent another big book package to [ornithologist] Pappas."[41] As late as 1947, it remained difficult to get printed matter to certain parts of Europe. Alexander Wetmore (1886–1978), ornithologist and sixth secretary of the Smithsonian Institution, reported that the International Scientific Exchange was an improvement over the old ways of shipping. However, Nice found it to be very slow and noted that Tinbergen had complained that her second Song Sparrow volume had taken a year by that route.[42]

The uncertainty of mailing printed materials to European ornithologists continued to haunt Nice. She wrote a convincing letter to Lloyd indicating that the AOU had not done what it promised to do, which was to provide European ornithologists with needed journals. After voting by a large majority to appoint a committee that would consider providing ornithological journals to Europeans who lacked them, the society allowed the American Library Association (ALA) to take over the task. Nice was convinced the society had made a serious mistake. Since ornithology was a specialized field, the ALA, even with the best of intentions, was incapable of deciding which journals should be sent to which ornithologists. The AOU seemed to feel that it no longer had the responsibility for supplying the journals. Nice listed many reasons it should remain involved, but she found the most important reason to be the chance for the organization "to do a good deed both for ornithology and humanity."[43]

Doing good deeds "both for ornithology and humanity" had become a defining principle in Nice's life. The postwar years were focused on "humanity," and her own ornithological research was, of necessity, put on hold temporarily. Her tolerance originated in the respect she had for the work of her European colleagues, no matter their political affiliation or moral stance. She found it easier to attribute Lorenz's connection with the Third Reich to misunderstanding rather than intent. As the years passed, life improved for both the Germans and the Dutch. Stresemann was united with his wife, and Tinbergen was able to leave the Netherlands and visit Nice in the United States.[44]

Although the amount of time Nice spent on correspondence, sending packages to European colleagues, and writing reviews impinged on her own research time, she found the gratitude expressed by those she helped well worth the effort. In her autobiography, she wrote that over one thousand donors had sent over three thousand boxes of necessary supplies to fifteen countries: Germany, Austria, Hungary, Belgium, Poland, Finland, Bulgaria, Czechoslovakia, Yugoslavia, Italy, Romania, Greece, France, Holland, and England. Nice found "rich rewards . . . in the touching gratitude of the recipients" and also noted "firm friendships . . . formed between people who had never seen each other."[45]

Chapter 13

THE BEHAVIOR
OF THE SONG SPARROW
Problems and Solutions

Unlike the first volume, a population study of the Song Sparrow, the second was a more generalized work comparing the behavior of this species to that of other passerines (perching songbirds). Nice combined her experience with birds in Massachusetts and Oklahoma, her intensive study of Song Sparrows in the field in Ohio, and her observation of hand-raised birds in Austria and the United States to produce the second part of this monograph, on the behavior of the Song Sparrow. She documented the life of this bird so extensively that this publication became a model of what a life-history study should be. This work, as did the first, included numerous tables, appendices full of data, and an extensive bibliography reflecting Nice's mastery of the literature.

This second portion covering the bird's behavior was not published until 1943. Many factors delayed its completion, not the least of which was the difficulty Nice had in finding a young female Song Sparrow to study in captivity. The war in Europe was also a factor. It had interrupted communication with European colleagues, and her attempts to connect with them consumed many hours. In addition, the formerly pleasant task of reviewing books had turned into the "dreaded reviews." The deterioration of her health also made it difficult to conduct research. To make matters even worse, the financial returns of *The Watcher at the Nest* were disappointing, and money was definitely hard to come by.

However, the most serious delay in publication was caused by deciding on a theoretical basis for Song Sparrow behavior. Although Nice herself was knowledgeable about behavioral theories, she deferred to her male colleagues, Lorenz and Tinbergen, when it came to developing such a framework for her work. The framework was supposed to have emerged from a joint paper by Nice and Lorenz based on her time in Altenberg. It would have been titled "The Maturation of Some Activities in Young Redstarts and Serins." They had intended for Nice to write the observational section, while Lorenz would furnish the theoretical portions and sketches. However, Lorenz never found time to write his share of the article, and consequently, it was never published. When she sent him her portion, he returned it with comments that eventually provided her with the desired information, which she incorporated into chapters 3 and 4 of the second volume of her major Song Sparrow publication.[1]

Mayr's Advice

Ernst Mayr could always be depended on to provide Nice with excellent advice. When she sent him a preliminary version of the first six chapters for comments, he suggested that she forward them to Frank Ambrose Beach (1911–1988), then a curator at the American Museum of Natural History (AMNH) and a researcher in psychology and animal sexual behavior. Since Beach was an animal (comparative) psychologist rather than an ornithologist, his concerns differed from those of bird behaviorists. After reading through Beach's suggestions several times, Nice became convinced that it was impossible to suit both ornithologists and animal psychologists. Recognizing that the ideas appealing to the latter might be of little interest to the former, she eventually chose to select ornithologists as her primary audience. Nevertheless, she was unable to ignore the animal psychologists altogether. She assumed that if she followed Oskar Heinroth, Konrad Lorenz, Nikolaas Tinbergen, and Wallace Craig, she would be "in the best of company."[2] She had not achieved her goal of wooing the animal psychologists in this early draft. One of the statements Beach found objectionable was her assertion that "Heinroth and Lorenz say that when a bird shakes itself it is sometimes a 'sign of relief from tension.'" He warned, "Imputing human emotions to the bird is dangerous business." Nice strongly disagreed with his interpretation of her language; as she complained to Mayr, "I do not consider 'relief from tension' an exclusively human emotion." Beach also objected to her use of the words "antagonism" and "indignant." Although she was unable to find where in the text she had used "indignant," she agreed that if she had done so it was anthropomorphic. But, she asked Mayr, "What is the matter with 'antagonism'? What would one use?" There were several other objections that Nice questioned, although she agreed that some were useful.[3]

In March 1942 Nice sent Mayr her completed magnum opus on the behavior of the Song Sparrow for his comments. Recognizing the importance of having colleagues read her work before publication, she recalled that when she was working on her first large English-language study on the population of the Song Sparrow, Mayr and others who critiqued it "started me off on new tacks and I did a vast amount of rewriting."[4] Therefore, in spite of her disagreement with Beach, she tried to incorporate his criticisms into the first chapter of the behavior study. Because she wanted the final product to be as perfect as possible, she welcomed adverse comments. Consequently, she sent drafts of this to various scholars and anxiously awaited their verdicts.

Mayr, as the critic she probably most respected, was generally complimentary, calling it "awe inspiring," although his assessment of the first chapter was negative. He considered it "very poorly done" and advised her to "rewrite it completely." Mayr predicted that not doing so would seriously jeopardize the rest of the volume. He cautioned that by trying to incorporate Beach's suggestions, she had unsuccessfully mixed "two totally different things": the material she had personally observed, and the theoretical framework (*Fragestellung*) that incorporated the cause or causes of various bird behaviors. This muddling of topics would weaken the entire work, Mayr predicted. In discussing the *Fragestellung*, she had implied that the study of bird behavior was completely separate from the investigation of other animal behavior. The question of audience thus appeared again. Mayr insisted that she must decide whether she was writing for "the bird student only, or for the animal psychologist only, or for both." Although she explained to Mayr that she was writing mainly for ornithologists, he did not consider her attempt successful. Because she had included some statements that seemed to be mainly for animal psychologists, he assumed she was trying to write for both groups and therefore should add a section on the "status of bird psychology in general animal psychology." It was also important, he insisted, that she add an explanation of several behavioral terms for the ornithology student, and explain the difference between learning, conditioning, and maturation. Since Mayr was dubious about her competence to write an entire chapter on general animal psychology, he provided her with two alternatives: "Call attention to the hiatus between bird psychology of the Heinroth-Lorenz-Tinbergen school and the field of general animal psychology," or "let some animal psychologist, like Beach, write this section."[5]

Nice was well aware of the conflict between the European ethologists of the Heinroth-Lorenz-Tinbergen school and the majority of American comparative psychologists. The Europeans complained that the Americans tended to concentrate their research on a single species, the laboratory rat, and its behavior in a laboratory setting. Not only was this research not comparative, they complained, it focused almost entirely on learned behavior and tended to ignore instinct.[6] However, the AMNH in New York City employed a group of comparative psychologists whose approach differed from that of the majority of the Americans. They lamented the direction that behavioral studies in the United States had taken and were more sympathetic to the views of the European ethologists, although they did not wholeheartedly accept Lorenz's and Tinbergen's ideas. The Department of Experimental Biology at the AMNH was established by G. K. Noble in 1928 and attempted to integrate natural history and experimental biology in order to study the evolution of the neural and hormonal components of vertebrate social behavior. After Noble's death, in 1940, Frank Beach, whom Noble had hired to study the social behavior of mammals, became curator and reconstituted the unit as the Department of Animal Behavior. Beach hired animal psychologist T. C. Schneirla (1902–1968) as associate curator, and Schneirla became curator after Beach left to become a professor at Yale.[7]

Beach and Schneirla had proposed an agenda that was much friendlier to the European ethologists than to the American rat-running psychologists. Nevertheless, the AMNH biologists were unwilling to accept the European work uncritically. They were suspicious of Lorenz's notion that patterns of behavior were innate, rather than reasoning that some could be modified through learning. Although many of the AMNH animal behaviorists recognized the importance of Lorenz's and Tinbergen's contributions, some, like A. I. Rand, were very negative. In Rand's discussion of Lorenz's *Kumpan* paper, he agreed that the work had received favorable notice and promised to be influential. He then attempted to demolish some of Lorenz's key concepts, including that of the "releaser," his use of *Kumpan*, and the nature of imprinting. He discounted Lorenz's examples and scoffed at his need to find something "absolute and inflexible to which to cling." Nevertheless, other investigators, such as Daniel S. Lehrman, were generally positive about Lorenz's ideas. However, Lehrman too had difficulties with what he considered Lorenz's overbroad conclusions.[8]

Mayr recognized the complex nature of the responses to Lorenz's work and did not want Nice to accept them uncritically. It was for this reason he suggested that someone like Beach, who understood all the complexities, should write the section. Nice, of course, had already received Beach's comments, rejecting some and accepting others. Mayr clearly respected Beach's opinions. Nevertheless, after Mayr's rather harsh criticism of Nice, he softened his advice: "It [the chapter] could be improved without much effort."[9]

Mayr suggested that Nice might use her own experiences as a connecting link between bird psychology and general animal psychology. By describing her first encounters with the concepts and terminology of Lorenz, she could explain that she understood the disparagements of some of his American critics. Both Noble and Schneirla were convinced that Lorenz had overstated the dichotomy between innate and acquired characteristics and tended to believe that so-called innately organized behavior patterns were subject to modification. They were also convinced that his "one size fits all" writings on instinct did not take into consideration the differences between different types of animals.[10]

In addition to the problem regarding theory in the first chapter, Mayr noticed another major difficulty in the manuscript. Nice's consideration of sexual dimorphism and sexual selection ignored the recent work of the evolutionist Theodosius Dobzhansky (1900–1975) and others. Those studies indicated that one of the primary functions of distinctive male coloration and song was to serve as specific recognition signs to prevent the hybridization that occurs through mating with other species. Dobzhansky called recognition of these characters "biological isolation mechanisms." Mayr's other suggestions were more cosmetic. For example, he suggested moving the list of the birds and their life histories from the first chapter to an appendix to improve the homogeneity of the main text. He also suggested scattering the figures throughout the volume, and using the ones that had been published in *Bird-Lore* as ornamental illustrations.[11]

Nice gratefully responded to Mayr's criticisms and explained the steps she had taken to rectify the problems he had noted. By visiting local libraries and consulting with animal behaviorists apropos of his criticism of the first chapter, she tried to correct the difficulties. She agreed that it would not be too hard to "bridge the gap between the Lorenz-Tinbergen school and the other animal psychologists." To broaden her general perspective, she had read works by controversial animal psychologists Norman R. F. Maier (1900–1977) and his better-known student T. C. Schneirla. Schneirla became famous for his classic study on army ants. Nice promised Mayr she would read Dobzhansky when the new edition of his work came out.[12]

Nice sent a second draft to American animal psychologist Wallace Craig that included Mayr's recommendations. Craig returned the draft with some "good suggestions" that she found comforting because they were not radical. Since Beach had been notably critical of her earlier draft and she had benefited from his suggestions, she also wanted his opinion on this later, more complete version and sent it to him as well.[13] At Mayr's suggestion, Nice sent a draft to AOU president Joseph Hickey (1907–1993) for review, and he then provided twenty-seven pages of criticisms in addition to "some nice encouragements."[14]

Nice's Illness and Song Sparrow II

Making the changes was difficult and time consuming under any circumstances, but Nice's health problems added to the difficulty. Her doctors told her to stay in bed for a month to six weeks. Upon hearing of her illness, Mayr wrote, "The main thing now is to follow the doctor's orders and to see that your recovery is not jeopardized by the work on S.S. II." He assured her that although prospective readers would be anxious to see the manuscript in print, there was no immediate rush, especially "now that the printing prices have been frozen." He suggested that she could spend a little more time polishing the manuscript. "I am sure that S.S. II will be a classic for all times, and you might as well try to make it as nearly perfect as this can be done."[15]

Vol. 2, The Behavior of the Song Sparrow and Other Passerines

In the foreword, Nice recognized her fellow behaviorists and ornithologists who had provided her with important theoretical and methodological ideas; she also credited an international group of researchers for helping her develop her thinking and research practices. She singled out the Americans Francis Herrick and Wallace Craig; the Germans Oskar Heinroth and Konrad Lorenz [Austrian]; the Englishmen Henry Eliot Howard, Julian Huxley, and David Lack; and the Dutchman Niko Tinbergen as especially important.[16]

Francis Herrick, professor of zoology at Case Western Reserve University in Cleveland, Ohio, had developed techniques for observing the breeding behavior of wild birds using a blind and camera, and he had completed one of the few studies in the United States and England on the development of young birds. A pioneer in the use of photography to document bird behavior, Herrick was one of the American researchers Nice introduced to European behaviorists.[17] With photography he was able to document the chains of reflexes involved in care of the young. Herrick's detailed study of the development of the Black-billed Cuckoo as well as his work on pigeons provided Nice with procedural ideas.[18]

For purposes of comparison, it was important for Nice to have information on European birds. Oskar and Magdalena Heinroth's four-volume work on central European species supplied a wealth of information on the development of young birds in that part of the world.[19]

Nice credited three British men who combined ornithology, evolutionary biology, and behavior—Henry Eliot Howard, Julian Huxley, and David Lack—with providing her with vital information on territory and courtship. Howard, an amateur ornithologist in the best sense of the term, published, among other works, influential books on territory in bird life.[20] Before Julian Huxley became involved in the evolutionary ideas that characterized his later research, he was fascinated by ornithology stemming from a boyhood interest in bird-watching. His systematic observation of courtship behavior of waterbirds resulted in a 1914 paper on the Great Crested Grebe, which became a standard work in bird behavior.[21] The third Englishman Nice mentioned was ornithologist and evolutionary biologist David Lack. Rather than focus his attention on morphology and geographic distribution, Lack emphasized life-history studies and concentrated on the living bird, an approach that appealed to Nice. She cited many of his publications in her bibliography.

The Search for a Framework

EDWARD CHASE TOLMAN

Even before Nice published the first volume of Studies in the Life History of the Song Sparrow, she sought an interpretive framework for the behavior of her species. Until she finally settled on Lorenz's theoretical structure, she explored other possibilities. She first turned to behavioral psychologist Edward Chase Tolman (1886–1959) for help. Lorenz had advised her to read Tolman's 1932 book on the purposive behavior of animals and humans.[22] Interestingly, Tolman was one of the American comparative psychologists who concentrated on the behavior of the laboratory rat, even going so far as to dedicate his book to "M.N.A.," Mus norvegicus albinus, the white rat. He credited his understanding of the operation of ultimate drives to Wallace Craig, and it was Nice who had introduced Craig's work to Lorenz. In spite of Tolman's dedication to the white rat, Lorenz was sufficiently impressed by his work to recommend it to Nice.[23] She found it "the most helpful treatment" she had come across. So taken was Nice that she worked out "tentative outlines, tables and charts on Tolman's ideas" and sent them to Noble and Lorenz, requesting that Noble forward them to Mayr. Not having read Tolman, Mayr was able to comment only on Nice's application of his work. He found major problems, complaining that some of the behavioral "drives" she described overlapped, while others excluded each other. For example, he assumed "food-hunger and nest-hunger" excluded each other, whereas territory drive, "self assertion-hunger," and "pugnacity" overlapped completely. Mayr found that Nice had left out many points in her Tolman-based classification, although "maybe they actually do not belong in there." Among the "left out" items, according to Mayr, were such activities as bathing, preening of the feathers, and scratching. Mayr argued, "Would not the migratory impulse be mentioned somehow or other as well as the reaction to light and darkness, to rain, wind, and other meteorological factors? What about ecology in general. Isn't habitat selection a very definite drive"?[24]

In other words, Mayr was less than enthusiastic about Nice applying Tolman's ideas to Song Sparrows. As it turned out, though, once Lorenz had published his *Kumpan* paper, Nice had her interpretive framework.

KONRAD LORENZ AND *KUMPAN*

After she studied Konrad Lorenz's paper "Der Kumpan in der Umwelt des Vögels," which had appeared in 1935, Nice realized she had the solution for her explanatory framework.[25] Although she had recognized Lorenz's great talent before reading this paper, previously she had not seen him as establishing an entirely new theoretical basis for the understanding of bird behavior. However, after Nice reviewed this work for Bird-Banding, she was convinced that his monograph was "great" and "a most remarkable paper of fundamental importance."[26] His concepts of "releasers" and "companions," among other ideas, provided a new theoretical foundation for the study of bird behavior. This monograph established Lorenz's reputation as a world leader in the study of animal behavior. Even though Nice had praised this work in her review in Bird-Banding, it took her more time to apply it to her own Song Sparrow work.

All animal behaviorists did not agree with Lorenz's theory. David Lack, among others, criticized the concept of releasers as oversimplification. Although Tinbergen basically agreed with Lorenz's views, he preferred the term "signal," a more general term than "releaser." He used it to incorporate the functions of both Lorenz's "releaser" and what he called the "director." Tinbergen noted that although most signals have both functions, there are examples in which only one term applies.[27]

G. K. Noble, one of the early experimenters working with living birds and other vertebrates, was a prominent skeptic. Nice had claimed Noble as a "new friend" in 1934 when she met him at the Pittsburgh meeting of the Wilson Club.[28] Noble took issue with Lorenz's distinction between innate and learned behavior; Nice questioned why Noble objected to Lorenz's theory and asked him about his doubts.[29]

Although agreeing that Noble's questioning of certain Lorenzian concepts might have had some merit, Nice held that by demanding experimental evidence, he neglected to give Lorenz, the expert on avian behavior under natural circumstances, the credit he deserved. Undaunted by Noble's exalted position at the AMNH, she continued to probe him for additional explanations for his objections.[30] In an attempt to clarify the problem, Nice turned to Lorenz and asked him whether he had "proof" for his theory. "Of course we do have plenty of proof that releasers are responded to innately and not through training," responded Lorenz.[31] As she attempted to understand and develop her own theory, Nice continued to probe Noble to clarify his exact objections.[32]

Noble challenged both Lorenz's and Tinbergen's construction of the line between instinctive behavior and learning. He further questioned the two Europeans' assertions that visual images, including colors, were inherited and functioned as sign stimuli, or visual signals that released an innate reaction among other individuals of the same species.[33]

In a letter Nice received from Lorenz, it was apparent that he and Noble seriously disagreed. In response to Noble's accusation that no proper explanation for imprinting existed, Lorenz indignantly insisted that he did have "proof," and that his concept of releasers explained it. The proof, Lorenz insisted, was that imprinting and learning were two different processes, a distinction that he implied Noble had failed to recognize. In learning, he contended, a process of trial and error occurs, whereas in imprinting there is no "trial and error, no executing of the respective action during the time in which the imprinting process takes place."[34] Noble's mistake occurred, opined Lorenz, because he had not read closely and understood the *Kumpan* monograph. Lorenz stated that he "very expressly refused to generalize" from birds to other vertebrates: "It is irrelevant for my thesis if there are other types of courtship in fishes. So I do not think that Dr. Noble who is a great generaliser has much to worry about." Lorenz did, however, note the case of another vertebrate, the male of the turtle *Chrysemia picta* (now *Chrysemys picta*), courting a female; his description implied that his concept was indeed general: "The male gets into a position right head on to the female, facing it, and then begins excitedly to fan the female's head with the back of his forepaws." Like birds, the turtle "has got a real releasing structure for doing this. The claws of the forepaws are elongated and quite straight and the back of the hand is striped radially in green and yellow, each yellow stripe being in line with one straight claw." Lorenz objected to Noble's experiments because he considered them artificially contrived and their results thus unreliable.[35]

While accepting Lorenz's basic premises, Nice also took into account some of Noble's objections. These seemed to point mainly to the need for more experiments prior to generalizing. Nevertheless, the basic theoretical structure for her book was Lorenzian. In early drafts of her manuscript, Nice had assumed that readers would understand her use of "innate" and "learned" behavior and the way in which Lorenz and Tinbergen used the terms. Perhaps because of Noble's objections, Mayr insisted that she explicitly define these terms. In response to Mayr's demands, she explained that her views were similar to Lorenz's and clarified the ways in which she used "innate" and "learned" in explaining behavior. She defined behavior as partly "natively determined and partly modified by experience," and instinctive action as "an innate coordination of movement." By using these narrow definitions, she could support Lorenz's insistence that instincts were not modifiable. She agreed that animals could be conditioned to exhibit a certain motor reaction in response to a certain set of sensory stimuli, but they had to use the existing repertory of inherited motor mechanisms.[36]

Nice's Use of Lorenz's Concepts

In The Behavior of the Song Sparrow, Nice followed Mayr's suggestions and defined her use of various terms. She and Lorenz both described learning (as opposed to innate behavior) as "the adjustment of behavior through experience." Nice asserted that although learning can determine the "intensity" (or strength) of the release of a certain instinctive act, it will never change the form of the response.[37] Lorenz, when studying various types of learning, included one that had a strong innate element, "imprinting." As hatchlings, most birds do not instinctively recognize their own species but must be conditioned to do so. If a young bird first comes in contact with another individual, it may become "imprinted" on it rather than on its own species. The most famous example is Lorenz's work on Greylag geese. He found that when the geese encountered him before they saw other Greylags, and if he raised them from the moment of hatching, they would treat him like a parent bird. Imprinted goslings followed him around, and when they became adults they preferred to court him rather than other geese. From these experiments he posited that there were critical periods in a bird's life when a particular type of stimulus was necessary for normal development.[38] Therefore, a bird had to imprint on another of the same species in order to develop properly.

In her *Behavior of the Song Sparrow* publication, Nice summarized Lorenz's understanding of the many factors that worked together in order to produce a particular behavior. A case in point was improving an instinctive action through practice. This improvement could include maturation as well as practice. She and Lorenz agreed that the exercising of wings by young birds was not the act of learning to fly—it was just the premature appearance of an instinctive action. Nice observed that many birds flew well with no wing exercise at all. They assumed that the potentially improved skill that came from exercising the wings could also be due to "facilitation." The term "facilitation," as used in animal behavior studies, explains how the performance of a behavior by one animal increases the probability that another animal also innately engaged in that behavior will mimic the activity of the other animal or increase the intensity of that behavior (in this case the prelude to flying). To explain another aspect of the concept of facilitation, Nice quoted Craig's study of the sexual behavior of male doves raised in isolation. He had noted that when a dove first performed an instinctive act, it seemed surprised, hesitant, bewildered, or fearful; the act performed was merely mechanical. However, after the dove had additional experience with the same act, it was then performed with ease and the separate elements involved worked smoothly together; this improvement was called "facilitation."[39]

Nice described another piece of the puzzle that did not fit the criteria for instinct—learning, or imprinting. This activity was spatially directed, inherited movements known as taxes. Nice defined a taxis as an "inborn form of reaction, released by an external stimulus and directed in relation to an object."[40]

Three investigators, Lorenz, Tinbergen, and D. J. Kuenen, described how taxes and instinct were related but different. Lorenz and Tinbergen did this through a study of egg rolling in the Greylag goose, in which they investigated how a goose reacted to an egg that rolled out of the nest. When the goose sitting on its nest saw the errant egg, it extended its head toward it, fixed its eyes on it, stood up, and slowly moved to stand on the rim of the nest. It then bent its neck downward and forward so that the egg rested against the underside of its bill. As it moved its head and neck, the goose also performed side-to-side movements of its head that resulted in balancing the egg against the underside of the bill and rolling the egg back into the nest. These two distinct types of movement (the ventrally directed bending of the head and neck and the laterally balanced movements that kept the egg moving back toward the nest) were explained differently. The first type of motion (extending the neck) represented a typical instinctive action; that is, a rigidly stereotyped innate movement elicited by the goose seeing an egg or an egg-shaped object outside the nest. The second type of motion, the taxis component, kept the egg rolling in the direction of the nest. The taxis (side-to-side motion of the head elicited independently by contact) kept the egg balanced. These two activities worked together to restore the egg to the nest. Before the work on taxis by Lorenz and Tinbergen, Tinbergen and his student D. J. Kuenen had investigated what came to be called taxes in several birds, including the gaping behavior of baby birds.[41]

The Scope of Nice's Second Volume on the Behavior of the Song Sparrow

The melding of the theoretical positions already described with Nice's meticulous observations ensured that this study would become a model for future investigations of bird behavior. In order to illustrate the observational aspect of this work, a brief discussion of its content follows.

In the second of twenty-two chapters, Nice described the five stages of Song Sparrow development from a "blind almost cold-blooded, nearly naked creature weighing about a gram and a half" to the fifth stage of development, from the age of seventeen to about twenty-eight days, when the young birds became independent of their parents. Her subjects included both hand-raised and wild birds. As she described various behavioral patterns and their time of appearance, she compared the timing of developmental stages to those of certain passerine relatives of the Song Sparrow, such as Serins and Redstarts.[42]

In subsequent chapters, Nice correlated the five stages of development of the young Song Sparrow with six different types of activities engaged in by the bird (those concerned with nutrition, care of plumage and other motor coordination in situ, locomotion, escape reactions, social behavior, and vocalizations). She found that the first stage lasted about four days, and most of the activities were concerned with nutrition. The second stage, days five and six, involved the first appearance of new motor coordination, such as standing. The third stage, days seven, eight, and nine, was characterized by the rapid acquisition of motor activities. During the fourth stage, from ten to sixteen days, the birds left the nest, began to fly, and adopted a more solitary life in the fields and bushes; they also began to feed themselves, drink, and bathe. The fifth stage, from seventeen to twenty-eight days, was characterized by feeding independently. Nice carefully detailed the activities that appeared as the young bird matured, presenting tables with supporting data.

In chapter 4, Nice applied the Lorenzian theoretical scheme as she discussed innate and learned reactions. Nice noted that the activities described were innate modes of behavior, although some could not occur effectively without conditioning (behavior modification whereby a subject associates a desired behavior with a previously unrelated stimulus). She also stressed that learning was largely related to the object of the instinctive actions. For example, although picking up insects for food was innate, young Song Sparrows soon learned not to pick up large or bright-colored insects or, in a really unfortunate possible scenario, stink bugs.[43]

When Nice compared the course of development of different passerine birds, she noted the considerable difference in the timing of leaving the nest and other activities. She concluded there were two main considerations that influenced when the young birds left: the safety of the nest and the size of the bird. Birds that nested in less protected situations often left the nest before they could fly, and birds like crows that developed slowly spent more time in the nest. Song Sparrows and many other small passerine birds become independent at about four weeks of age.[44]

Nice discussed the activities of adult Song Sparrows and also compared them with those of other passerines in subsequent detailed chapters, including the following: "Song Sparrow Society in Fall and Winter," "Awakening and Roosting," "Song of the Adult Male Song Sparrow," "Song in Female Birds," "Development, Inheritance and Function of Song," "The Male and His Territory," "The Function of Territory," "The Male and His Mate," "Relations of the Pair to Each Other and Their Neighbors," "The Problem of Pair Formation," "The Nest," "The Eggs," "Defense of the Young," and "Innate and Learned Behavior in the Adult." The comprehensive nature of this work made it suitable as a model for other studies of avian behavior.

Reviews

World War II slowed down the incoming flow of periodical reviews of The Behavior of the Song Sparrow. This delay was especially evident in the publication of European reviews. Even before many reviews had appeared in journals, Nice expressed pleasure that this second volume was selling well "for so specialized and rather technical a volume." As is often the case even after the most careful proofreading, Nice found an error in the published work. She wrote Mayr that she had "just discovered a horrible error on p. 169." Instead of "Instinctive Behavior Patterns," the published text read "Patters." Nice asked Mayr to "insert an 'n' in the volumes sent out."[45]

Nearly all the reviews were positive. One of the early ones, written by ornithologist Herbert Friedman, who reviewed it for the Wilson Ornithological Society's journal, *The Wilson Bulletin*, praised the behavior volume highly. He reported that it was "a work of much wider interest and value than the first [population] part," though he thought that part was also "admirable." Friedman noted that Nice's publication presented more information than was yet available for any single species, and that the included data were also "more thoroughly analyzed, and more completely integrated with current knowledge and modern concepts of animal behavior" than in any other work. He found only one negative, questioning "the soundness of

[Nice's] judgment in so completely accepting Lorenz as a guide." Friedman ended the review by congratulating the author and the Linnaean Society "on the publication of the most searching study yet made of any wild bird."[46]

In his review in the *American Naturalist*, ornithologist Josselyn Van Tyne stated that Nice had made the Song Sparrow "perhaps the most thoroughly known wild bird in the world." The volume was "practically a monograph on bird behavior," because about 420 species of birds were considered. He also praised the organization, extensive bibliography, and indices. According to Van Tyne, one of the most important contributions in this work was its "tremendously stimulating effect on ornithological research of many kinds." The one negative mentioned was the "considerable number of minor errors, not all of which can be attributed to the printer."[47]

The review by Laidlaw Williams in *Bird-Banding* was basically descriptive without any critical judgments.[48] In contrast, in *The Auk*, Joseph Hickey offered a review that was not only descriptive but critically astute in assessing the publication's importance to both animal behavior and ornithology in general. He praised especially the chapters on song as a "landmark in bird watching." Hickey, like Van Tyne, mentioned typographical errors, but he attributed these to Nice's "long and critical illness" and to the fact that the Linnaean Society's editor, Dean Amadon, had been called to military service before the final proofs were available. He asserted that the errors did not detract from the readability of the volume or from its authority.[49]

After praising the volume by declaring that it "provided a stimulus and directive for present and future studies on bird life histories in this country" and that it was enriched by Nice's familiarity with foreign literature, the author of an unsigned review implied that she had relied too heavily on the theories and concepts of Howard, Lorenz, and Tinbergen. He or she also pointed out the numerous typographical errors, bad typesetting, and the "terse style of writing" that left "the reader in mid-air in certain circumstances." Nevertheless, this reviewer closed with the statement that these adverse criticisms were insignificant when one considered that the volume was a "milestone in ornithology which will long remain an excellent guide, text and reference for all ornithologists, whether they be professional or just observant housewives."[50]

A statement in a 1946 letter from Nice to Mayr probably refers to this unsigned review. She wrote Mayr that she was offended that a Tom Parks (she placed a question mark after his name), in the *Review of Biology* (rather than the *Quarterly Review of Biology*), had referred to her as a "housewife." She protested that she was "weary of the 'professionals' patronizing the housewife." Rather indignantly, she referred to her "excellent biological training in college and some 2½ years of graduate work" after her children grew out of babyhood. Nice added, "I had more time for research than did my husband, for instance, who taught to earn our living."[51]

Although some male "professional ornithologists" may have felt threatened by the extra time she had for research, most were supportive. They realized that her nonprofessional activities were important as well and praised her ability to produce first-rate research while caring for home and family. This respect for her research became evident when Nice was awarded the Brewster Medal of the AOU for this study, which marked it as "the most important work relating to the birds of the Western Hemisphere."[52]

Chapter 14

POSTWAR LIFE

Nice capped her most productive years of original research with the publication of the second volume on the Song Sparrow in 1943. Nonetheless she remained active by publishing small observational works, reviews, and previously unpublished research. She remained involved in ornithological societies and used her reputation to help European colleagues regain their old positions or locate new ones after the war. Her children became self-sufficient, which left her more time to spend on conservation efforts. She also spent the postwar years publicizing the second volume of her Song Sparrow research on behavior.

Publicizing SS II after the War

The second Song Sparrow volume appeared in 1943, while Europe and the United States were fully embroiled in World War II, clearly a terrible time to market a book. Consequently, in spite of the many encouraging reviews in the United States, sales were lower than anticipated in this country and practically nonexistent in Europe, where it was not reviewed and her colleagues were unfamiliar with it. In an attempt to rectify the situation, Nice produced a circular to publicize both Song Sparrow volumes. She sent a draft to Mayr, who approved it but warned that the publisher, the Linnaean Society of New York, would be slow to produce it. No longer an officer in the society, Mayr agreed to use his influence with the editor but pointed to the additional postwar problem of getting "paper or printers." It took him "about six weeks to get a simple one-page announcement printed, he explained."[1]

The circulars came out early in 1947, and the results pleased Nice: "What an excellent circular about SSI and II!" In a letter to Mayr, she wrote, "I think I had better get a supply of books for myself [the two Song Sparrow volumes] for the future, so I am enclosing a check for $29.00—$20 for 10 SSII; 9 for 6 SSI."[2] Intent on gaining European attention, she wrote Mayr that she was sending both Song Sparrow volumes to geneticist Hannes Laven (b. 1913) and only the second one to German ornithologist Ernst Schüz (1901–1991). She asked, "Shall I send SSII also to German ornithologists [Friedrich] Goethe [1911–2003] and [Gustav] Kramer [1910–1959]? What about Frau Heinroth?" (She referred to Oskar Heinroth's wife.) Mayr replied, "By all means send a copy of SS II to Kramer" because "he has been doing research full time on behavior work." Mayr hesitated about Goethe, explaining that despite earlier behavioral work, his economic situation might preclude future efforts.[3] Sending materials to Europe was expensive enough to warrant careful thought before posting materials that might not be used.

Postwar Research

With her work in the doldrums in the 1940s, Nice hesitated to agree to Mayr's invitation to contribute an article for a Festschrift honoring Stresemann. She had completed an unpublished study of the Carolina Wren during those years, so she floated the idea of using material she had included in that work, "Incubation Rhythm in Relation to Temperature," for the Festschrift. Noting that "Dr. [Josselyn] Van Tyne did not care for" a chart she had used, she proposed sending Mayr that chart for a second opinion. Perhaps because she had been away from active research for such a long time, her confidence level seemed low and she was not sure that her article merited inclusion in the Festschrift.[4]

Apparently Mayr sent Nice off on another path, for in about a month she sent him a different manuscript, "The Question of Sexual Dominance." The inspiration for this paper seemed to have come from Heinroth's article on the Rock Pigeon (*Columba livia*) that had recently appeared in the *Zeitschrift für Tierpsychologie*.[5] Heinroth repeated the common observation that just before the pigeon's eggs are laid, the male pecks his mate vigorously when she is away from the nest at the feeding trough, driving her away from the food. He, however, refuted the accepted view that this "driving" in the pigeon indicated that the male dominates his mate through fear. Heinroth tested that hypothesis by picking up the male and hiding him behind his back. He postulated that if the female feared the male, she would take advantage of the opportunity and eat. However, when her mate disappeared, she stopped eating and looked around for him. It seemed, he concluded, that when the male provided her a "breathing spell" in which to eat, she had no fear of him. At times she would caress him and "gently drive him from the nest." Heinroth concluded, as did Nice, that if the female pigeon, the classical example used to illustrate sexual dominance, was not afraid of her mate, "the hypothesis has lost its chief support."[6]

Of course, she sent a draft of her paper to Mayr, who proclaimed that it was fine but then proceeded with some "minor suggestions." These minor suggestions went to the heart of some of Nice's critics' complaints about her work. The first, but the least important, recommendation involved her tendency to word her statements "somewhat carelessly." Mayr proposed that this defect could easily be modified by consistency in word usage. For example, although in two instances (the first page and the summary) she had concluded that sexual dominance did not occur, in the body of the same paper she wrote that social and sexual dominance were two different phenomena. Mayr insisted that by including the second wording, she implied that she still accepted "sexual dominance as a valid biological phenomenon." He proposed a change in wording to clarify the situation.

In Mayr's second objection he noted her tendency to accept authority too readily. As a willing disciple of Lorenz and others, Nice often failed to explain that some of their ideas were controversial and simply used them to explain the behavior of her birds. Mayr wrote, "You imply that a phenomenon has such and such an explanation because Tinbergen or Lorenz or Heinroth had said so. There is some danger of similar criticism in the present paper. Your wording might be interpreted as indicating that there is no sexual dominance because Heinroth said so."[7] Nice appreciated the remarks, made the suggested changes, and resubmitted the paper. She agreed with Mayr that she was too prone to accept authority without explaining why. Although many American behaviorists were moving toward an ethological position, most continued to be unwilling to accept European ideas uncritically. A slightly later appraisal of Lorenz's theories by American behaviorist Daniel S. Lehrman can be found in a 1953 article in the *Quarterly Review of Biology*.[8]

The published paper represented an important contribution, because Nice confronted the ideas of Thorleif Schjelderup-Ebbe, the Norwegian biologist who introduced the idea of social dominance to behavior studies. In her Song Sparrow writings in the 1930s, Nice had accepted contemporary ideas of male dominance but later came to realize that these conclusions represented a male bias. By the time of the publication of the Festschrift (1949), she had concluded that male behavior was a signal of readiness to mate rather than an expression of dominance. Nice roundly rejected Schjelderup-Ebbe's view that male dominance was essential for the welfare of the world. She was convinced that gender biases colored his interpretations and caused him to confuse social and sexual dominance. The study of animal behavior was becoming less androcentric as female scientists such as Nice became more involved in the profession.[9]

Nice's Self-Evaluation

As she evaluated the significance of her own work, Nice was baffled and concerned as to why her original theories were "so completely over-looked, at least many of them." She asked Mayr whether he had any explanation as to why others did not consider her theoretical contributions: "Take, for instance the relationship of temperature and spring migration that I worked out convincingly in SS I with your help and that of Selig Hecht. So far as I know not a single person has tried it out with other species." She asked poignantly why she had not been able to stimulate researchers more with her writings. Perhaps, she mused, her publications were too condensed, for she herself found that "they take careful reading and study to work out techniques when I go back to them after a lapse of years."[10]

Mayr wrote that he did not have an answer to Nice's concern. Actually, he wrote, "Everybody must be reading them since we have sold out the entire edition of SSI and most of SSII." He added, "You will hardly find another life history study that doesn't quote you." Mayr proposed that since many of the ideas were embedded in a complete book, "people . . . seem to forget about [individual] items contained" within. He suggested that she might avoid the problem if she published her findings piecemeal with titles appropriate to the subject she wanted to emphasize.[11] Although Nice published extensively in journals, most but not all of her articles stressed fieldwork rather than theoretical conclusions. Gender may have had a significant role in the acceptance or rejection of theoretical papers by women in different fields, but Nice's output of published articles on theoretical subjects in ornithological journals was similar to that of most of her male colleagues, and there is no evidence that she submitted articles that were rejected. However, neither is there evidence that she submitted papers to behavioral journals that might have found a problem with theoretical papers by a woman without a PhD.

Nice's paper on sexual dominance raised some interesting responses. Stresemann wrote, "I believe all good observers of bird behavior will agree with what you say, save some exceptional cases as exemplified by the Muscovy Duck, for instance. May this teach a lesson to all husbands!"[12] The lesson to be taught to husbands was that Song Sparrow females were dominant over males during the breeding season and that this pattern was widespread in monogamous birds.[13]

Recent research provides some up-to-date ideas on dominance, flowing from the ideas of Heinroth, Stresemann, and Nice. When the ornithologist Susan Smith presented the 2000 Margaret Morse Nice Lecture, she described how her own research on a population of Rufous-collared Sparrows provided her first experience with a social system dominated by females. While engaging in a literature search, she found that female dominance was widespread among monogamous birds, but the reports of it were often placed inconspicuously at the end of papers. However, when she encountered a paper by Nice titled "The Question of Sexual Dominance," she found female dominance prominently discussed and dedicated her own paper on this general pattern in monogamous birds to Nice.

Apparently, when Stresemann referred to the Muscovy Duck as an exception, he was referring to its courting behavior. He probably did not apply what was known about Muscovy anatomy to explain sexual dominance. Later ornithologists explained how vaginal anatomy contributed to female choice. In the male Muscovy, the penis can be up to forty centimeters in length—about half its body length. This structural arrangement enables the male Muscovy to copulate with an unwilling female. However, recent research has suggested that the female has evolved in such a way as to prevent pregnancies from an undesirable male. The male duck's penis is spiral shaped and twists in a counterclockwise direction so that the sperm will target the oviduct on the left-hand side of the female. In most birds only the left ovary is functional, but a recent study on ducks indicates that in the female Muscovy, the vagina twists in a clockwise direction. This arrangement seems to make successful copulation more difficult for the male. Even though the male's long, flexible penis helps him force copulation, the adaptation of the female's complex vaginal anatomy allows her to take control over which sperm fertilizes the egg. When a female wants to mate with a chosen partner, she makes conception more likely by relaxing the muscles around the entrance to the vagina.[14]

Ornithologist Amelia Laskey, who corresponded with Nice, noted in 1950 that after she reread Nice's paper on sexual dominance she concluded that there were no instances of sexual dominance of the male among wild or domestic birds that she had observed. She was perplexed by Stresemann's mention of the Muscovy Duck and "others," for she had no information about sexual dominance in this duck. Another of Nice's women correspondents, amateur ornithologist Ruth Thomas, wrote that she thoroughly appreciated the reprint of "The Question of Sexual Dominance," and that "it boils down to a definition of dominance, doesn't it?"[15] Nice, and through her, Laskey and Thomas, did not make the connection of anatomy to female dominance.

This changing view of dominance between genders in ornithology went along with that in other scientific disciplines, especially primatology. In the 1970s, women made up about 50 percent of the PhDs in primatology, and by 2001 around 80 percent. However, before women became dominant in the field, sexual selection emphasized competition between males for females. Males were thought to woo passive females and compete with other males to establish territory boundaries, thus pushing the less dominant out of the rivalry. It was thought that the female role was to be sexually available to males according to the males' dominance rank and to be good mothers to the infants. Although there is some variation in dominance patterns among different species, historian of science Londa Schiebinger notes that early primatologists did not consider female-to-female competition important. She argues that the failure of male scientists to accept the existence of this competition skewed ideas about sexual selection, as did ignoring the interactions between males and females that suggested sex was not only for reproduction. As the number of female primatologists increased, the perception of the role of the supposedly passive female changed. Females were now observed to be active participants, and in some species, leaders.[16]

Purple Martins

After her paper on sexual dominance was completed, Nice began to work on a thesis on Purple Martins that had been begun by Josselyn Van Tyne's student Robert S. Allen (1913–1943), who had been killed in New Guinea during the war. She applied her tables on the Song Sparrow to birds that

Allen had studied. He had collected Purple Martin migratory arrival dates
for six years. Charting the dates against mean temperature, he had concluded only that "the first arrivals coincided with the appearance of a warm
wave during the end of March or early part of April." Nice found that by
using his dates and weather records, she could work out "a beautiful table
like III in SSI and a chart like Chart VII."[17] Employing Allen's data and
listing him as the posthumous first author, she produced a fifty-nine-page
paper that not only was a tribute to his work but included some of her own
interpretations.[18]

Konrad Lorenz in 1949

Nice's loyalty to her colleagues remained exceptional. Her relationship
with Konrad Lorenz was especially important even after the end of the war.
She felt she owed a debt of gratitude to him for hosting her during her long
visit in the summer of 1938 and was almost reverential in her acceptance of
his ideas. It was difficult for her to believe that he may have shown a dark
side during the war.

Lorenz and his wife wrote quite different letters to Nice describing
their postwar situation. A letter from Lorenz in May 1949 provided additional information about his state of mind at that time. He explained that
he suffered "quite a beautiful nervous breakdown" during January and
February of that year, caused by overwork. Trying to finish his paper for a
symposium in Cambridge, England, on time, he lived on too much black
coffee, Sympathol (a dietary supplement for anxiety disorders), and strych-
nine (for his "failing blood pressure"). He reported that although he "did
not run in circles yelping," he "quite simply was not able to form one written
sentence."

When his "mental powers were at their lowest," Lorenz encountered "a
very unpleasant obstacle" to his "re-installation at the Vienna University."
The old accusations surfaced when "some dear friend, I have a shrewd suspicion who it was, accused me (of course anonymously!) of having done god
knows what politically during the time of my professorship at Königsberg."
That professorship was in 1941, when it was claimed that he had obtained
the position through friends in high places. However, Lorenz enthusiasti-
cally reported that he had been cleared of the charges and that his life was
improving. His letter ended on an upbeat note. He reported that the Academy of Science was supporting his zoological station at Altenberg and that

the English playwright and novelist John Boynton Priestley (1894–1984) was giving him the royalties from his plays performed in Austria for the purchase of equipment and animal food.[19] Gretel Lorenz's letter was more pessimistic. She reported that in order to earn money, Konrad was working on a popular book on animals, and that both of them were very nervous. Although they had enough food (Gretel had given up her medical practice to work on the farm), they did not have money for the children's schooling or for clothes. She asked Margaret to determine whether there was any hope for a grant from the Rockefeller Institute.[20]

Nice informed Mayr that the Lorenzes were going to England for a month for an animal behavior conference and would visit the Priestleys and ornithologist Peter Scott (1909–1989). Gretel Lorenz had written Nice that what her husband really wanted was to give a lecture tour in the United States. Nice explored possible ways this tour might be arranged. However, when she contacted American ecologist W. Clyde Allee (1885–1955), she found that he had "no bright ideas except that he'd [Lorenz] be assured of a $50 lecture in Chicago." Nice also reported to Mayr that Allee suggested Mayr might think of a plan for support.[21] Mayr's response was not positive and reflected not only the continued suspicion in the United States of former Nazis but also the lack of interest among American zoologists in animal psychology: "Konrad Lorenz, with his very un-American approach to science, might not be much of a success as a lecturer." This reality had been brought home to Mayr when he had attempted to locate a professorship in the United States for Niko Tinbergen and found little interest among the Americans. What this meant was that any tour of the United States would have to be arranged by the psychologists, or so Mayr thought. Less than enthusiastic, Mayr also noted that arranging a lecture tour for a foreign scientist "is almost a full-time job, as I know from my experiences with arranging Tinbergen's tour" (1946–1947). Mayr also did not know who would be willing to become Lorenz's lecture manager, because he (Mayr) did not have the time or inclination to do it himself.[22]

Mayr recalled the time-consuming nature of the Tinbergen tour. To make it feasible for him to come, Mayr first had to arrange for invitations to lecture at various institutions. This task proved to be arduous. As he told Tinbergen, it was "not entirely hopeless but the colleges usually do not pay very much more than the expenses of the lecture." He assumed that the best arrangement would be for Tinbergen to give "a sort of a course" at a college. After spending an inordinate amount of time on the problem, Mayr arranged for him to give a course in New York City under the joint auspices of the American Museum of Natural History and Columbia University, for $400. In addition, he arranged for a lecture at Yale University that would pay "either fifty or one hundred dollars." By finding other lectures, he hoped to find another $200. As he explained to Tinbergen, "This should be ample income to take care of all traveling and other expenses during your stay in the United States. The housing situation is pretty terrible and you may have to be satisfied to stay with us in Tenafly during the time you spend in the New York region."[23] It is not surprising that Mayr was unwilling to take on another European visitor, especially one whose reputation had been tarnished. It is unclear how much Mayr himself resented Lorenz's position during the war and how much he recognized the difficulty in persuading his colleagues to accept him.

Nice's indignant response to Mayr stressed her respect for the European point of view and her extreme loyalty to Lorenz: "It is too bad that most American zoologists and psychologists are so blind and stupid about animal behavior. I fear that nothing can be done for Dr. Lorenz in this country. Dr. Allee wrote to the Rockefeller Institute and never got an answer."[24]

Nonetheless Nice continued to try to find a way to get Lorenz to the United States in January 1950. She contacted scientist Paul Weiss, formerly of Austria and now in the United States, for his advice. Although Weiss wrote that he would like to see Lorenz come, he did not "see the way clear."[25] Mayr had an additional reason for not strongly supporting a visit by Lorenz. Repeating some of his previous objections, such as "I am not quite sure that he is the kind of speaker who would go well with American audiences," he added another: "Also, I don't know if Lorenz has anything new to offer. His older work is very well known to students of animal behavior in this country, and copies of his films have been shown to audiences in many American cities and universities."[26] Mayr implied the obsolescence of some of the ethological ideas of one of the subject's founders and suggested that they were being replaced by a different view of animal behavior.

Lorenz continued to pressure his friends, including Mayr, to arrange this trip. In a letter to Nice, Mayr explained that he had delayed his answer to Lorenz because he did not "know quite what to tell him." Since he would see Lorenz during the summer of 1950, he promised to then "discuss the matter with him in more detail."[27]

A Different Kind of Animal Behavior Study

The difficulty swirling around Lorenz's visit to the United States reflected changes in emphasis in studies of animal behavior during the late 1940s. Some of these alterations involved issues that linked animal behavior's early history with that of other field sciences. In particular, tensions between field sciences and laboratory sciences that had begun in about 1890 were again visible during Nice's ornithological career. Over time, the field sciences had lost status relative to the laboratory sciences, which garnered more research money and took advantage of statistical methods. As laboratory technology improved, scientific experiments could be done in well-equipped laboratories anywhere in the world. Confidence was enhanced if similar results were obtained from the same experiment done in California and Paris. Moreover, laboratories were created for a single purpose—doing science—and relied on a credentialed research population of trained staff who were there for one purpose—to do science. By contrast, the field sciences demanded a specific place for their practice, but, as Kohler explained, this space had to be shared with "hunters, fishers, poachers, trappers, surveyors, tramps, madmen, shamans, loggers, prospectors, bird watchers, bandits, vacationers, herbalists, cowboys, students, con men, true and false prophets, and green terrorists."[28] Laboratory experiments were tightly controlled and seemed to give repeatable results, unlike the messy, often variable field observations. Since working with a small part of an organism could provide consistent, reproducible results and create confidence, Kohler noted that this assurance meant that early-nineteenth-century field biologists were "sometimes made to feel that they do not live in the best neighborhood, so to speak."[29] Similarly, historian of biology Paul Farber concluded that such an emphasis on experimental science was not fair to natural history. He proposed that the latter had a history that was just as interesting and complex as that of the experimental sciences.[30] Most historians of biology would probably agree that there was some kind of shift (perhaps the perception of a conflict) that occurred between natural history studies, behavioral studies, and experimental biology in the late nineteenth century and escalated in the twentieth century, although they differ in the weight they give to the balance of authority in this relationship.[31]

Although detailed laboratory results on some small part of an organism were useful, field data provided contextual information that was often essential as well. By the mid-twentieth century, however, some theoreticians were again realizing that there was a symbiotic relationship between field data and laboratory data and that the boundary between field and laboratory was permeable.[32] Kohler's argument for the overlapping of the laboratory-field border as a "mixed practice" can be seen in Nice's old friend Ernst Mayr's evolutionary biogeography.[33]

Nice's career thus coincided with a period of changing standards and status in natural history and biology. Her initial interest in birds was spawned when the field sciences stressed the collection, preparation, and identification of specimens and the deposition of them in a museum. Many of her colleagues were collectors who provided museums with series of study specimens (e.g., skins, skulls, shells) for academic zoologists who used calipers and color charts to determine taxonomic relationships. At the same time, the field of laboratory biology had developed, with a focus on physiological processes, and for Nice these seemed less interesting because they did not highlight animal behavior. At midcentury biologists began to recognize that a synthesis was needed of these skills and outlooks coming from natural history and physiology, and there was renewed interest in finding ways to integrate them.

During her early years, Nice had helped shape yet another dimension in natural history, namely ethology. She became part of a movement dominated by European animal behaviorists or animal psychologists who saw the importance of studying the living animal in its natural environment. In an effort to supplement field observations, she created controlled experiments to study animal behavior systematically. This program involved learning to keep birds in captivity, and she helped persuade American ornithologists of the importance of this approach. As the second quarter of the twentieth century progressed, many of the European methods became acceptable, complementing but not displacing older natural history.

After the Second World War, both traditional museum taxonomic studies and the imported European ethological approach began a gradual process of modification. As new technologies were introduced, taxonomists modified the ways in which species relationships were deduced. Calipers and color charts were replaced by electrophoresis and paper chromatography to determine relationships. New laboratories were built complete with elaborate apparatus to examine relationships on the molecular level. These, too, contributed to that loss of status as molecular biology occupied a higher place in the hierarchy of biological investigations. Margaret Nice's most productive period came during a time when the boundaries between field and lab sciences were not fixed, and her reputation was built on methods, clearly respected in Europe, that were perceived as innovative.

The ethology of Lorenz had also evolved after World War II. Mayr's hesitation to push his colleagues to find money to bring Lorenz to the United States for lectures may be a recognition that he was no longer the cult figure he had been previously. Bird behaviorist Douglas W. Mock believes that little of Lorenz's "theory" has stood the test of time and that today's behavioral ecology "is the synthesis of classical ethology, theoretical/mathematical modeling, natural history, and a great deal of experimental rigor."[34]

Many of the changes in ethology that occurred during Nice's later years and continue to the present day have been made possible because of advances in technology. Moreover, many of the Lorenzian generalities have been supplanted by tighter theoretical structures based on new data. Each time period tends to have its own characteristic idea that is in vogue. The new approach usually builds upon its predecessor.[35]

Later Research

Nice considered the period from 1951 to 1955 her "second bird life."[36] She worked on a major project with Constance during that time, a study of the stages of behavior development in precocial species, which are fairly independent at birth, as compared with altricial species, which still require substantial parental care. Precocial birds have the ability to move about shortly after hatching, while altricial birds are helpless; they are nest bound, blind, and naked.

PRECOCIAL BIRDS

There are different degrees of precociality. At one end of the spectrum are birds such as the megapodes (e.g., Brush Turkey, Australian Malleefowl), whose chicks are totally independent of their parents when they hatch; they are feathered and able to fly. Somewhat less independent are ducklings and shorebird chicks, which follow their parents but can find their own food. The young of game birds are even more dependent; they follow their parents, who indicate forage items. The most dependent of the precocial birds are those such as rails and grebes that follow their parents shortly after hatching; the parents not only show them food but also feed them.

Semialtricial birds are covered with down, are incapable of leaving the nest, and are fed by their parents. Some of these birds, such as hawks and herons, hatch with their eyes open, although hatchling owls have their eyes closed. Fully altricial birds hatch with little or no down and with eyes closed; they are incapable of leaving the nest and must be fed by the parents. All birds belonging to the order Passeriformes, which includes the majority of species, are altricial; these include the perching birds such as Song Sparrows.

Although Nice's earlier experience had been with altricial birds, she studied precocial species during the summers of 1951 through 1954, when she and Constance were invited by the director of the Delta Waterfowl Research Station in Manitoba to be "visiting investigators." These summer activities resulted in a major work, "The Development of Behavior in Precocial Birds." The *Transactions of the Linnaean Society of New York* devoted an entire issue to this study in 1962.[37] This work evolved from Nice's past research on the early development of precocial chicks and moved to a broader consideration of the development of behavior in vertebrates. Although emphasizing the class Aves and stressing precocial birds, the first chapters included a brief survey of parental care throughout the vertebrates, a summary of some aspects of behavior development in the vertebrate classes, and a discussion and comparison of stages in behavior development in an altricial bird, a mammal, and a precocial bird. Nice also included a classification of birds according to maturity at hatching. After this sweeping, theoretical introduction, Nice moved to the specific results of her study at the Delta Research Station. By applying her knowledge beyond a few species of birds, Nice showed that she had developed into a mature scientist.

INCUBATION PERIODS OF BIRDS

A second important project—investigating the sources of published errors on the incubation periods of birds—involved library rather than field research. Nice described this project to Stresemann, writing that it was proving to be a much larger and more complex project than she had imagined. After a visit to her amateur bird-watching friends Doris and Murray Speirs in Pickering, Ontario, and their excellent library, she was "shocked" to find that the incubation periods in their new bird books varied greatly from the well-established ones. After she reported her findings to Joseph Hickey, he suggested that she write them up for The Auk. Thinking this project would take only about two weeks, she agreed. She was uninterested in a long project because she was involved in her study of precocial birds. Since 1931, after Heinroth had sent her his classic paper on the subject (published in 1922), she had been aware of the problems surrounding the determination of the length of incubation periods.[38]

This study began Nice's only foray into the history of science. In a letter to Stresemann, she wrote, "It has been fascinating consulting the old books in the Field Museum." She then regaled him with a list of the authors she had consulted, "with very little success in my special quest." She began her search with Aristotle and proceeded chronologically through the history of ornithology, searching for observations and estimates of incubation periods.[39]

Suspecting that many of the incubation periods described by nineteenth- and early-twentieth-century ornithologists were erroneous, Nice asked her colleagues for their opinions. Approaching the problem as a mystery to be solved, she reported tracing the "too short incubation periods of Falconidae to Aristotle."[40] She followed errors in American bird books from Charles E. Bendire (1892) to Franklin Lorenzo Burns (1915) to William Harry Bergtold (1917). Regrettably, the only earlier American book she had located that recorded many incubation figures was by T. G. Gentry (1876, 1882).[41] She discounted his results because "his figures were so ridiculously short (from 8 to 10 days for small birds to 21 for the Great Horned Owl and Red-tailed Hawk) that no one had bothered to quote him."[42] Once Nice had determined that Bendire was the most reliable source for incubation periods in the United States, her next step was to ascertain where Bendire got his data. She discounted the idea that he had made observations himself and presumed that he had imported the incubation periods from his native Germany and applied them to American birds. Other ornithologists or collectors referred to by Heinroth included the Scottish naturalist William Evans, who recorded the incubation period of his own hatchlings as well as quoting 251 periods from the literature.[43] Although Evans pointed out some of the most fantastic errors in the sources, Nice discovered that his list may have had the unanticipated consequence of perpetuating guesses and estimates that were subsequently quoted by careless compilers.

After Nice read Friedrich Tiedemann's multivolume work on birds in which he cited ninety-nine incubation periods, she came closer to a solution.[44] Although most of the times were far too short to be correct and the sources were undocumented, Tiedemann cited a statement by Aristotle that incubation in hens lasted twenty-five days in winter and only eighteen in summer. While tracing this source, she found the key to many of the mistakes by later ornithologists who had taken the words of the great "biologist" of antiquity as a "truth" that did not require verification. In the *Historia animalium*, Aristotle explained different lengths of incubation periods: "The eagle incubates for about thirty days. The incubation period is about the same with other large birds, such as the goose and the bustard. With middle-sized birds, it lasts about twenty days, as with the kite and the hawk."[45] Nice was triumphant as she explained that Aristotle's numbers were "the original too-short incubation periods for the birds of prey!" Apparently, Aristotle had analogized that incubation in large birds would follow the pattern of the domestic goose, whereas incubation in midsized birds would match that of the domestic hen. This analogy clearly did not work, and attempting to assign incubation periods based on bird size had been a failure.

Nice found it difficult to believe that Aristotle's mistakes had been transmitted for twenty-two centuries and were still found in nineteenth- and twentieth-century ornithological publications. Was it possible, she wondered, that the nineteenth-century ornithologists had arrived independently at the same conclusion as Aristotle? Using her language skills, Nice checked the works of the great naturalists and compilers from the first century C.E. to the eighteenth century and found that they had all quoted Aristotle's incubation periods and omitted the qualifying "about" found in the original when citing him.

Although she found the succession clear from Aristotle to Buffon, she was interested in the post-Buffon publications. She found that two Germans, Johann Matthäus Bechstein (1757–1822) and A. J. Naumann (1795–1803), had published sets of books that included the incubation periods of all the birds they studied according to the size of each species. These books were very popular and were reissued and translated along with all of their incorrect incubation periods. It was these books that Evans had used, and although he had pointed out the errors in the earlier literature, as already mentioned, the fact that they were printed caused careless compilers to perpetuate the mistakes.[46]

Nice's work from 1951 to 1955 resulted in four papers, the last of which summarized the problem of the mistaken incubation periods. She wrote:

> Three kinds of people have been concerned with incubation
> periods: Guessers, Copyists, and Investigators. History of statements
> on incubation periods has been largely a copying of assumptions
> by such important people as Aristotle, Bechstein, Naumann, and
> Bendire. Sixty years ago ornithologists in the Old World were set on
> the right path by the first great investigator in this field—Evans—
> and 30 years later they were again stimulated by the second great
> investigator—Heinroth. In the New World, however, we were led
> astray by a great "Guesser"—Bendire—and many of us still believe
> him. For the most part the 2300 years during which men have
> recorded their thoughts on incubation periods of birds make a sad
> story of the blind leading the blind.[47]

Before actually submitting this paper for publication, she queried Stresemann on several points.[48]

This particular project, so different from Nice's previous research, provides an excellent example of the maturation of her thought throughout
the years. No longer able to do actual field research, she used her grasp of
ornithology to critique the works of others. She drew on critical faculties
long developed through reviewing articles by her peers to assess the work
of her predecessors. After marketing her work on the Song Sparrow after it
was published in 1943, Nice showed her mastery of the literature on territoriality in her publication in the Stresemann Festschrift. During the time in
her life when she might have been expected to wind down her research, she
embarked on two quite different projects—her works on precocial birds
and incubation periods. At a stage when many scientists would only have
modified previous research, Nice showed her willingness to try two very
different types of investigation.

Chapter 15

THE LAST YEARS

Although Nice knew that aging was inevitable, she maintained her fascination with bird behavior until the end of her life. Even as the study of animal behavior moved away from Lorenz-Tinbergen ethology, and classic taxonomy veered from its concentration on geographic distribution, she managed to keep up with the literature of the newer emphases by continuing to write reviews, although in decreasing numbers. Her letter-writing output, always spectacular, continued even as her handwriting became shaky and difficult to read. During the time Nice was involved with her late-life research, family, friends, and their problems became increasingly important to her.

Family Concerns

One of Margaret's family concerns involved her youngest daughter, Janet, who had married a German man, Henry Fredericks. Fredericks was having little luck in his attempt to become an American citizen. That he was married to an American did not seem to matter. Although the company he worked for engaged an attorney experienced in immigration problems, he offered Fredericks scant hope. Nice's solution was to seek help from her adviser and friend Mayr. Since Mayr had his own citizenship problems, now presumably "finally ironed out," Nice hoped his personal experience and his knowledge of other German immigrants' experiences might be useful for Fredericks. She asked whether he knew of other Germans who had come to the United States after Pearl Harbor and were in a similar situation.[1] Mayr replied by describing his own eight-year struggle, which "finally came to a happy ending" when he and his wife, Gretel, "were naturalized last week." He commiserated with Henry's struggles, explaining that "now is about the worst imaginable time to try for naturalization since the McCarran Law has become valid on Sept. 23." This law, the Internal Security Act of 1950, was named after Pat McCarran, a Democrat from Nevada, and is also known as the Subversive Activities Control Act. Passed over President Harry S. Truman's veto, this McCarthy-era law established the Subversive Activities Control Board to investigate those it suspected of engaging in subversive activities or those who had in any way supported either a Fascist or Communist dictatorship. This same law revoked the passport of the African American singer and actor Paul Robeson. Any person who had any connection at all with a totalitarian power was disqualified for citizenship. Mayr suggested that Henry wait until the McCarran Law had been modified by the next Congress. Then Janet, as an American citizen, could take the initiative rather than Henry. "This is how two local cases were brought to a happy ending."[2] Although in the 1950s Margaret's relatives, friends, and colleagues often asked for her help and advice and praised her accomplishments in letters and publications, she did not receive any official awards or honors until 1952.

Margaret Nice Ornithological Club

In January 1952, the Margaret Nice Ornithological Club for women only was founded in Toronto, Canada. The only other ornithological club in Toronto until this year, the Toronto Ornithological Club, was a male-only organization. The unfairness of this situation was brought to the attention of Nice's friend Doris Huestis Speirs when her husband, Murray, proposed to take their Hungarian guest Miklos Udvardy to the club meeting. When Udvardy asked whether the ladies were coming, Murray Speirs explained that the Toronto Ornithological Club was for men only. Udvardy answered, "Is this the fourteenth century?" The seed planted by Udvardy germinated during a luncheon of four women bird enthusiasts who discussed forming a women's ornithological club. They organized the club and affiliated with the Federation of Ontario Naturalists. All agreed that the club should be named after "its patron saint, Margaret Morse Nice."

Pleased with the honor, Margaret wrote that she was "very proud and happy" over the founding of her club. Although she did not feel that she "deserved such honor," she hoped the club would help "earnest students" of birds who happened to be female. She recalled her own bitterness at being excluded from the Wheaton Club in Columbus. "It would have helped me immensely to have been able to tell the men what I was finding." Nice recalled how Althea Sherman had inspired her both by her writings and through her friendship. "She was a true pioneer in life history studies. I am realizing this more than ever when I compare her absolute accuracy—even to the minute in some cases—with incubation periods, to the shocking carelessness of most men in this field."[3]

The founding of this club illustrates Nice's importance to women in ornithology. Although much of her actual work was with men, she carried on a vibrant correspondence with women ornithologists. After Nice's death, this organization, led by Speirs, published her autobiography. In a letter to Nice's brother Edward S. Morse, Speirs described how Nice had inspired her. This description can be extrapolated to other women ornithologists.

> She was one of the most helpful friends that ever blessed my experience—I was a young amateur when we met at an AOU meeting in Washington, D.C. (1938, was it?) and she a most distinguished and already famous ornithologist. Yet she questioned me on my research with evidently a sincere and even keen interest, as though I could really contribute to her knowledge of bird behaviour by my observations. Her simplicity, her deep humility and sense of awe and wonder were evidences of her greatness.[4]

Honorary Degree

A second honor came to Nice three years after the formation of the club. In spite of all her accomplishments, she had never received official recognition from her alma mater, Mount Holyoke College. This situation changed on February 3, 1955, when Mount Holyoke zoologist and ecologist Ann Haven Morgan (1882–1966) wrote Holyoke alumna Dorothea Smeltzer Schleuning that Nice's "unique and important work in ornithology" had not been recognized by the college, and "it would seem helpful to Mount Holyoke to join in giving tribute to her even though late in doing so."[5] To support her view, Morgan established that experts in Nice's field—W. C. Allee, George M. Sutton, and others—had praised her work and that Mount Holyoke had been negligent in not honoring her. In nominating Nice for an honorary degree, her supporters quoted a footnote in Principles of Animal Ecology, edited in 1949 by Allee, in which he wrote, "Initiated students will recognize as do we, our indebtedness to the competent scholarship of Margaret Morse Nice." In the same application, her supporters also quoted Sutton,

Margaret Morse Nice receiving an honorary degree from Mount Holyoke College. *Courtesy Mount Holyoke College Archives and Special Collections.*

by then curator of birds and professor of zoology at the University of Oklahoma, who wrote, "Margaret Nice has made the outstanding contribution of the present quarter century to ornithological thinking in America." Not surprisingly, Ernst Mayr, who was then Alexander Agassiz Professor of Zoology at Harvard, praised her work extravagantly: "Mrs. Nice's studies on territory in bird life, on bird song, and on the incubation period of birds, are classics in their field." He concluded, "If you were to ask any young American ornithologist who more than anyone else is responsible for the new widespread biological study of birds in America, I am certain you will get the answer, Mrs. Nice. I do not know of any other American ornithologist as deserving of an honor as is she."[6]

In a letter to Mayr, Nice explained that she was puzzled as to "who had stirred them [Mount Holyoke] up—although I was told at College that the zoology department had been urging it for years." Clearly pleased when she found it was Mayr who had pushed the nomination, she noted, "It is especially welcome, coming from Mount Holyoke to which I owe so much." In his citation, Holyoke's first male president, Roswell G. Ham, "quoted you [Mayr] and George Sutton and this made me very happy."[7]

Probably in 1969, the Wilson Ornithological Society established the Margaret Morse Nice Awards, to go to amateurs "like their namesake." She suspected that Sutton was the "generous and thoughtful donor," but he denied it, writing that "my abiding belief in honesty forces me to say that I did not start the Margaret Morse Nice Awards—though I wish I had."[8]

Nice and Sutton

Nice had a special relationship with well-known ornithologist and bird painter George Miksch Sutton. Because they had both spent time in Oklahoma and worked on Oklahoma birds, they developed a friendship based on this common interest. They carried on an extensive correspondence during Nice's later years.

Sutton first became interested in birds when he was five years old. By the time he was sixteen, he had published articles in several ornithological journals, including *Bird-Lore*. As a young man, Sutton met the bird artist Louis Agassiz Fuertes, who gave him advice on drawing birds. He spent part of several summers with Fuertes. Although the Sutton family moved often, they ended up in Bethany, West Virginia, where both parents taught at the college there. As seemed to be his pattern, George's father soon lost this job. However, his mother, tired of moving their family, insisted that they stay in Bethany, where George attended college. During the summer of 1918 he worked at the Carnegie Museum in Pittsburgh, where, along with other duties, he was in charge of the egg collection. During this time he began his frequent expeditions to both study the habits of birds and hone his skills at painting them. He returned to Bethany College in the fall of 1918 and was due to receive his bachelor's degree in 1919. However, the degree was not granted until 1923 because he was expelled for leading a student revolt against mandatory ROTC training.

From 1925 to 1929 Sutton served as Pennsylvania state ornithologist and wrote *An Introduction to the Birds of Pennsylvania* (1928), his first book. He left Pennsylvania for Ithaca, New York, where he earned a doctorate at Cornell University in 1932. After he received this degree, Sutton remained there as curator of the Louis Agassiz Fuertes Memorial Collection of Birds. During the Second World War he joined the U.S. Army Air Corps, where he tested Arctic survival gear. After the end of the war, he worked at the University of Michigan in a makeshift position with split duties until 1952, when he accepted a position as a zoology professor at the University of Oklahoma, where he remained for the rest of his life. Although Sutton officially retired in 1968, he remained as emeritus professor and curator of birds at the Stovall Museum of Science and History. During his lifetime, he wrote thirteen books, eighteen monographs and museum publications, and 201 journal articles. He illustrated at least eighteen books.[9]

Since Nice had left Oklahoma before Sutton arrived, it is not altogether clear when they first met, although it was most likely at an ornithological society meeting. On his first trip to Oklahoma, in 1932, Sutton drew on knowledge gained from Nice's *Birds of Oklahoma*.[10] They had definitely met by 1938, the year Sutton made his first collecting trip to Mexico. On his return he found that his drawing of the Wilson's Warbler that had adorned the cover of the *Wilson Bulletin* had been removed from the first (1938) issue of the journal. Although Sutton did not complain, "there was a firestorm of protest from Wilson members, including the president, Margaret Morse Nice."[11] While Sutton was in the Army Air Corps he wrote, "Mrs. Nice writes me further about the Oklahoma book [her two books on the birds of Oklahoma]. I was quite serious when I told her I would take over and do the third edition as soon as possible after the war."[12] Sutton used her book as a source for his *Oklahoma Birds* (1967) and sent Nice a copy of his list of Oklahoma species for her comments before the book was published. In May 1966 she congratulated him on his list of birds. "I was greatly impressed by your 'official' list of the species you accredit to Oklahoma. What a wonderful list it is." She proceeded to ask a series of questions and looked forward to the appearance of the book.[13] Because he had been on one of several trips to the Arctic region to study and paint birds, Sutton's reply to Nice's letter was delayed until August 1966. He explained the reasons for his decisions to include or exclude certain birds on his list. He assured Nice that he would send her a copy as soon as it appeared, and that it was in the hands of the editors. "And I do hope you will review it for *Bird-banding*. No one could be better qualified than you for this assignment and the fact that you have always liked Oklahoma and Oklahoma people is an important point in favor of your doing it." Sutton's letter was written in a style that made it obvious that he and Nice had long been friends, casually referring to the death of their colleague in Tulsa, Edith Force Kassig (1890–1966), and noting the activities of other Tulsa people. Assuming that Nice would be interested, he even shared the activities of his graduate students.[14]

Sutton endured numerous delays in the publication of his book, some of which were his doing and others of which were the responsibility of the University of Oklahoma Press and its editor, Savoie Lottinville. Nice had expected Sutton to send her a review copy directly, and when she received a letter from the review editor of *Bird-Banding* asking her to review the book, she seemed somewhat miffed that Sutton had not yet sent her a copy. He apologetically explained, "Everything moves so swiftly here *when it does move*, that I can't keep track of it. I've been waiting for months for the book to 'come out'; when I inquired about review copies, I was given to understand that one had already been sent you for *Bird-Banding*; so I've supposed that you already had one. If your copy doesn't come, let me know right away." The book arrived and Nice reviewed it, appending a copy to her letter to Sutton on June 19, which he acknowledged on July 4.[15]

A series of letters between Nice and Sutton discussed the disposition of archival materials relating to Oklahoma birds. This correspondence resulted from a request from Emma Messerly of Bartlesville, Oklahoma, regarding the work of the bird observer A. J. B. Kirn. Sutton was dismayed because Messerly was certain that the University of Oklahoma held some Kirn material in the notebooks that Nice had sent him when he came to the university in 1952. Although he was able to locate most of the material, including Nice's own work, he could not find the Kirn material. Although it turned out that Nice had not sent this information, it sparked both of their interests in archiving bird material. Sutton was relieved that he had not misplaced the Kirn material: "I greatly dislike losing things, especially such things as notebooks, important letters, etc." However, this futile search sparked a discussion of where Nice should keep her Oklahoma material. Sutton wrote that he would urge her to send everything related to Oklahoma birds to him, "if only we had a fire-proof building in which to keep such material. I have my valuable bird collection and extensive library in a large room whose walls and ceiling are of transite, but the whole building's superstructure is wood and would go up like tinder were a real fire to take hold."[16]

An experience Sutton had on October 9, 1963, partially explains his fear of fire. One morning he walked into the storeroom of the bird range and accidentally knocked a bottle of carbon disulfide off its shelf. The bottle shattered and the carbon disulfide fumes were ignited by a nearby water heater. Sutton fought the blaze himself until the fire department arrived. By this time his hands were burned and he had breathed in toxic fumes. Although the fire damaged him, it did little damage to the bird range. However, it further convinced Sutton of the need for a more fireproof place to store rare specimens and archives.[17]

Sutton concluded in his letter to Nice that if she did not have a fireproof storage place for the Oklahoma material in Chicago, sending it to Oklahoma "might be the best thing." They both eventually agreed that the archives would be better off in Oklahoma. In October 1969, Nice was still slowly "collecting the Oklahoma material" for Sutton. However, she sent "all the Song Sparrow and other Ohio records, as well as the Massachusetts ones to Cornell."[18] James Tate of Cornell came to Chicago and picked up "a vast amount of ornithological" material and took it to the archives in Ithaca, where archive director Finch was delighted to receive it.[19]

By January 31, 1970, Nice had still not sent the materials to Oklahoma because she had forgotten the name of the librarian. Sutton supplied the name of the library director, Arthur McAnally, but suggested that she send the materials to the science librarian, T. H. Milby.[20] Nice sent a box of Oklahoma bird material to Sutton, not to the library.[21]

Margaret Morse Nice at eighty-seven. *Courtesy Kenneth Boyer Collection.*

Slowing Down

As Margaret grew older, she was unable to continue the frantic pace that characterized her early years. Although she no longer kept up with her correspondence to the degree that she had previously, she still wrote an impressive number of letters. Her interest in things ornithological never lapsed. Although the Mayr correspondence definitely flagged in the 1960s, they still kept in touch. In a handwritten letter to him, Nice recalled that the last time they had met was at the international congress in 1962, when he was president. When he wrote a "friendly letter" to her in January 1969, it "warmed her heart." She wrote, "How many honors have come to you. We are proud of you." She vicariously went along on his travels, for her own years of attending meetings had ended in 1964. She still had the urge to travel, but "age is slowing both of us [Margaret and Blaine] down very much. We stay at home most of the time and our output of work is small." She found it a pity that they could not "whiz around the world and see strange birds and beasts and countries."[22]

Although traveling to meetings was no longer feasible, in 1969 Nice was still writing "a moderate number of reviews for *Bird-Banding*." Complaining that "old age is catching up with me," the eighty-five-year-old Nice sought to "outwit it" by averaging between forty and sixty reviews a year. "I still like to have my say—my chance to praise or blame." However, writing reviews was not as satisfying as it had been earlier in her life. Nice was unhappy with the new "technical ethological ideas." She informed Mayr that his old student Jack Hailman had become review editor of *Bird-Banding*. However, his "zeal and new ideas" displeased her. "I try to curb some of his fancy new ideas by right of seniority and having been the inventor of our kind of reviews 36 years ago." Although she had never met him, they had corresponded for many years. She liked him as a person more than she approved of his ideas. "I'm not in sympathy with his technical ethological ideas."[23]

The Search for a Publisher

Another project occupied Nice's later years—writing her autobiography. After completing a preliminary draft, she searched for a publisher. Originally, she was optimistic, but as different publishers rejected the manuscript she became discouraged. She initially sent it to the University of Oklahoma Press. Before she sent the manuscript, she considered drastically editing it, because "it is far too long for the present age of hurry and worry." She decided it was best to keep only what she considered to be her most important contributions. These included her "adventures" in the study of the birds of Oklahoma, and the Song Sparrow work. Probably "these two subjects should be emphasized and much of the rest omitted." Before she mailed a letter to Sutton explaining her intention to cut extraneous material, she received a letter from Edward Shaw, the third director of the University of Oklahoma Press, who wanted "to see the mss, despite its great length."[24]

Although Sutton assumed Shaw would be in favor of shortening the book, he said he would "hate to see any part that you consider important removed." The solution he suggested to Nice was for her to designate the parts that she herself felt "to be comparatively unimportant," but to include all the material when she sent the manuscript to Shaw. Although he emphasized that it was important to include all parts germane to a central theme, the best way to decide on a central theme would be to submit everything. "One might say that life-story itself is a central theme, but you will understand me when I say that it should be more than that; it should be the story of a life aimed at, or centered in, habitat preservation; conservation, education, etc. Once this central theme is established, the value of certain parts of the whole can be judged accordingly."[25]

Nice followed Sutton's advice and sent the manuscript to Shaw, with disappointing results. "I had hoped that Mr. Shaw would consult you [Sutton] about my autobiography. But he doesn't even seem to have looked at it himself. He sent it back in 2 weeks, saying that his 'readers' were 'unable to forecast it for a considerable or even a break-even sale.'"[26] Only slightly disillusioned, Nice vowed to explore other university presses. She next sent the manuscript to Cornell University Press, but she was again discouraged when editor Charles Santoro replied: "Finding a qualified reader for your manuscript proved more difficult than we anticipated. We do not expect to have a report in hand in the course of the next few weeks and shall write to you again as soon as we receive it."[27]

The report finally came back to Nice with four pages of comments from the reader. She found some cause for optimism. "This man praised portions of my ms and criticized other portions. He made helpful suggestions as to condensing and enlivening the text." Most gratifying was a line from the editor: "Should you undertake such a revision, we should be pleased to consider it."[28]

Nice immediately and optimistically set about cutting and revising the manuscript, but this effort failed to result in publication in spite of positive recommendations from her ornithological friends. It was not until after Nice's death that the autobiography was finally published.

Barbara did not mention in her memoir that she had helped her mother edit the autobiography. However, in a letter to Sutton, Margaret wrote: "The critic of this chapter was my daughter Barbara. I do not know whether you ever met her. She is a brilliant, lovely person, wife of a professor at Howard University, mother of three fine sons."[29] Margaret's late-life praise of Barbara casts some doubts on Barbara's fear that she was the unappreciated child.

Reminiscence and Regrets

Writing on a holiday card decorated with a blue jay and holly, Margaret reminisced to Mayr about her friends and their accomplishments. "Dr. Stresemann wrote me a lovely letter in answer to my congratulatory one on his 80th birthday. Konrad and Gretel have just been here; Konrad told me that Dr. Stresemann had had a mild coronary (before his birthday) and had given up smoking. Konrad thinks his health is going now to be excellent. How very much I owe to you, to Dr. Stresemann and to Konrad."[30]

The accomplishments of her seven grandchildren made Margaret proud: "One has a Ph.D. in physics, another almost has his in history, and a third is well on the way in economics. Two have been in the Peace Corps— Turkey and Bolivia. Three have married and all our grand-daughters are lovely girls."[31]

Although Nice had traveled to Europe several times, she had always wanted to go to Africa to see its spectacular birds. When she found that Mayr was planning a trip to that continent, she congratulated him for not putting off "travel till too late as so many people do," she being one of the "many people" who put off traveling.[32]

Margaret's health had its ups and downs. She suffered from high blood pressure from 1967 to 1969, and during these years travel was not an option. When a "satisfactory regime of drugs" controlled her blood pressure, she no longer felt able to travel. Nevertheless, at age eighty-seven she wrote Mayr that she hoped to resume her "ornithological duties" again. These duties were confined mostly to writing reviews and corresponding with colleagues.

Margaret's physical limitations became more apparent in her handwritten letter to Mayr in May 1971. She apologized for her delay in answering his Christmas letter, explaining that she had fallen on the pavement and broken her right hip. Although it was "skillfully repaired," she was still far from her "normal vigorous self." Although Blaine had previously broken his hip on December 26, 1967, he and Constance were her caretakers, and Constance took over the housekeeping, "serving delicious meals three times a day." Blaine took her outside each pleasant day, where she was able to walk with her walker. "Before long I hope to graduate to my cane, but that is still a little risky."[33] Constance had never found a satisfying profession and lived with her parents, and at this time she was a substitute teacher in the public schools.

Nice's Last Days

In spite of her optimistic appraisal of her own situation, Nice seems never to have recovered from the last accident. Blaine, who had been her caregiver, died January 18, 1974, in Chicago.[34] Her letter writing to friends had almost disappeared by 1974. On July 24, 1974, Dale Pontius, a Chicago neighbor, wrote in a letter to Nice's Columbus Audubon Society friend Edward S. Thomas that he had learned of Margaret's death. Although he did not know exactly when she died (it was June 26, 1974), he assumed it was when he was away on a canoe trip to northern Minnesota. During his last visit he knew that her death was imminent: "I saw her briefly, sitting at the front door in a wheel-chair with her nurse in early June." She was "almost lifeless, with little power of recognition or communication. I had no feeling, then of being comprehended in anything I said." However, just as he was about to leave she rallied and spoke "a couple of words thanking us for stopping in." In the few months since the death of Dr. Nice, she had declined abruptly. Pontius lamented, "The death of Dr. and Mrs. Nice within a period of a few months ends a solid link in Chicago with Columbus and with the world of interest in birds and the out-of-doors." Although they had long been friends, there were long periods when they did not see each other. Nevertheless, "there was always the knowledge that these links existed, and they seemed a part of something final in what life in Chicago meant over the last 24 years."[35]

CONCLUSION

In 1993 Margaret Rossiter wrote an article titled "The Matilda Effect in Science," which expanded on sociologist of science Robert Merton's article "The Matthew Effect in Science." The latter referred to Matthew 13:12: "For to him who has will more be given, and he will have abundance; but from him who has not, even what he has will be taken away." Merton used this verse to describe contributors to science who were missing from the major narratives in the history of the discipline. Rossiter found it to be especially relevant in explaining the absence of women in scientific narratives. She coined the term "Matilda Effect" after late-nineteenth-century suffragist Matilda J. Gage, who recognized this phenomenon.[1]

Although Margaret Nice does not quite fit into Rossiter's Matilda Effect because she came to be recognized by her colleagues and by some historians of science, including Richard W. Burkhardt Jr., Gregg Mitman, and Mark V. Barrow Jr., she is still missing from most accounts of the history of ornithology and animal behavior. Nice's career, along with that of many other women scientists, followed a path that differed from that of most male scientists. This is not to say that all male scientists followed identical professional paths, for some encountered the same anonymity as women and were victims of the Matthew Effect. Also, like men's career paths, those of women differed from each other, but women generally had different cultural concerns and obstacles to deal with than did men.

Many characteristics conspired to make Nice the scientist she became. She had natural ability on her side. But intelligence, while important for success in science, did not ensure it, especially for women. It was often overridden by the cultural expectations of the late nineteenth and early twentieth centuries, which discouraged intelligent women who were interested in science from pursuing their goals. Nice was fortunate in this respect, for her early experiences and educational opportunities inspired a commitment to nature that endured throughout her life. Even when it was difficult or uncomfortable to investigate the natural world, she found ways to do so. Lacking a PhD, which had become the standard academic credential, she taught herself basic techniques, studied the literature in order to become familiar with what others were doing, attended academic meetings, and volunteered to help other investigators with their projects and, in turn, was not shy in asking for help with hers.

Ambition, in a positive sense, was an important motivator for Nice. The title of her autobiography, *Research Is a Passion with Me*, indicates how important it was for her to make her mark on the world by adding to the corpus of basic knowledge about nature. She chose to do this by learning more about her beloved birds—their development, habits, and relationship to the rest of the natural world. This goal proved difficult in the years when her children were young and fieldwork was challenging. During these years she took a temporary detour from her career as a budding naturalist to study her own children's acquisition of language. The fields of human psychology and animal psychology proved not to be so different, as Nice found out in her later studies. Development, important in all species, always intrigued Nice. Curiosity, the question of both why and how animals behaved as they did, characterized Nice from her earliest days into her maturity as a scientist.

Intelligence, ambition, and curiosity, while essential characteristics of Nice as a scientist, would not have made her successful if it had not been for her excellent organizational abilities and her successful multitasking. Caring for her family, doing field research, writing up research for publication, producing hundreds of reviews, attending professional meetings and giving papers, and collaborating with colleagues would never have happened if she had not learned to harness household duties in such a way as to open the time and space necessary for her research and related occupations.

Nice had personality features that influenced the dynamics of her interpersonal relationship with peers. One of the most important was generosity. Although she wanted credit for her ideas, it was never at the expense of others. She willingly shared data and methodology. Magnanimous with her time, she worked unselfishly with her colleagues, especially with aspiring women ornithologists. While working full time on her own projects, she encouraged and advised other women on ways to continue their research. Perhaps because she depended so much on her own mentorship by male scientists, she wanted to help other women who did not have the same opportunities. Through helping others, Nice reciprocated the assistance she had received as a neophyte from established ornithologists, animal behaviorists, and evolutionary biologists. Without their help she might have remained an aspiring but not very productive amateur all her life. Ernst Mayr, especially, became a lifelong mentor, confidant, critic, and supporter. Perhaps because of her language background at Mount Holyoke, she was fascinated by the contributions of the European ornithologists and behaviorists and they, in turn, supported her research. The support of Stresemann for the German-language production of Nice's Song Sparrow research led to Mayr's backing of the two-volume English work. Nice repaid those Europeans who had supported her with unwavering loyalty during and after World War II. Warranted or not, she could not believe that Konrad Lorenz had unfortunate intentions with his science and was his lifelong ally.

It was not just women whom Nice helped. When openings arose to assist anyone in need, she returned the favors done for her by assisting others. Moreover, her generosity expanded beyond mentorship. For example, she arranged for needed clothing and food items to be sent to European scientists affected by World War II and completed the thesis begun by Josselyn Van Tyne's student Robert S. Allen, who was killed in New Guinea during the war.

The relationship between Nice's family life and her science was complex. Her decision to marry and have children highlights a problem that women scientists face if they make that same decision. She clearly loved her family and used her organizational skills to fit their needs with hers. However, as she arranged her busy scientific life she sometimes left her children feeling neglected, at least according to her daughter Barbara. The assistance and understanding of her husband, Blaine, seems to have made this conflict between work and family somewhat less onerous. Unfortunately, little information about how Blaine viewed this situation is available, but we do know that he helped around the house and with the girls so that Margaret could do her work. To add to the complexity of her life, Margaret had a strong social conscience. Many times her support involved conservation and preservation, and that, too, required time and attention.

Moreover, she was a strong opponent of unfair politicians, especially during the McCarthy era. When she perceived injustice she made it a priority in her busy life to oppose what she considered unfair targeting of innocent people. When many Americans were afraid of the communist USSR, Nice wrote that "Capitalists are terrified of Communism" and "we conveniently forget that it was practiced by the Early Christians—for it means sharing their money bags."

The life and career of Margaret Morse Nice illustrates the special problems faced by women scientists. In Nice we see a talented, ambitious, and creative woman who worked constantly to improve her skills. Her original plan to earn advanced degrees and devote her life to science had to be modified after she married and had a family. The practical thing for her to do would have been to give up her scientific ambitions and live the life of an intelligent dilettante, as her mother had done. Unwilling to do this, she tried to accomplish it all through self-study and working with colleagues, a path that few women took. Choices faced by women were heavily influenced by cultural forces. Typically it was the woman, not the man, who had to give up career aspirations when she married, as was the case with Nice. Moreover, finding well-paid employment as a woman, let alone as a wife, was very difficult indeed. Nice's decision was a practical one when she elected to follow where Blaine's job took him. This was especially necessary because Nice did not finish her PhD degree.

During Nice's time many professional organizations, while open to women, afforded them an inferior status. Nice showed that these and other handicaps could be overcome, but it involved working very hard and putting in long hours. That her hard work succeeded is clear from the comments of her colleagues. An especially important example can be found in the *Columbus (OH) Dispatch* in an interview with her mentor Stresemann, who was visiting the United States to study the Rothschild collection of birds at the American Museum of Natural History in New York. The story was headlined "German Ornithologist Reveals Columbus Woman as World Authority on Sparrows." In the interview Stresemann stated:

> Mrs. Nice has done something that is unprecedented in Science. . . .
> She has given the world the most complete study of one species
> of bird that has ever been made—the common song sparrow—a
> bird that is considered by ornithologists as the standard of the

feathered family. All of her research has been done at home, in
the space of a few acres around her home in the Olentangy River
bottoms. . . . The behaviorism of song sparrows is entirely a new
thought in ornithology, and it is Mrs. Nice who has given it its best
development.[2]

Stresemann was just one of many colleagues who praised her successful
career. He recognized that she had not received the accolades she deserved
from the public, pointing out that "probably 800 people in Columbus know
that Mrs. Nice is the foremost authority in the world on the song sparrow,
but all over the world she is known to the leading scientists."[3]

There are many lessons to be learned from Nice's life and the uneven,
but persistent path she followed. This path perhaps presages the possibility of a humane science shared by both men and women that can bring
together the multiple aspects of their lives.

NOTES

PREFACE

1. Ogilvie, *Women in Science.*
2. Ogilvie and Harvey, *Biographical Dictionary of Women in Science.*
3. Ogilvie and Choquette, *Dame Full of Vim and Vigor*; Ogilvie, *Marie Curie*; Ogilvie, *Searching the Stars.*

INTRODUCTION

1. Konrad Lorenz, quoted in Morse Nice, *Research Is a Passion with Me* (1979), ix.
2. Trautman, "In Memoriam," 438.
3. Ibid. Quoted by Trautman from a letter received from Ernst Mayr (italics in the original).
4. Morse Nice, *Development of Behavior in Precocial Birds* (1962).
5. Morse Nice, "Problems of Incubation Periods" (1954).
6. Morse Nice, "Incubation Periods throughout the Ages" (1954).
7. Thompson, *My Life*, 1.
8. Ogilvie, *Searching the Stars.*
9. Neeley, *Mary Somerville.*
10. Harvey, *"Almost a Man of Genius."*
11. Barrow, *Passion for Birds*; Burkhardt, *Patterns of Behavior.*
12. Mitman and Burkhardt, "Struggling for Identity."
13. Kohlstedt, *Teaching Children Science.*
14. Strasser, "Collecting Nature."
15. Trautman, "In Memoriam," 430–41.
16. Rossiter, *Women Scientists in America*; Dahlberg, "'Strong Sympathy and Fellowship'"; Ainley, "Field Work and Family"; Bonta, "Margaret Morse Nice"; Dunlap, *Birds in the Bushes*; Gibbons and Strom, *Neighbors to the Birds*, 179–81, 249, 278, 334–35; Kastner, *World of Watchers*, 145–55.

Chapter 1. **FAMILY BACKGROUND AND CHILDHOOD**

1. Morse Nice, *Research Is a Passion with Me*, 323–24; J. Allen, *Seven Years' Retrospect.*
2. Morse Nice, *Research Is a Passion with Me*, 1; biographical note, Anson Daniel Morse Papers, Amherst College Archives and Special Collections.

3. Morse Nice, *Research Is a Passion with Me*, 5.

4. Thompson, *My Life*.

5. Ibid.

6. Morse Nice, *Research Is a Passion with Me*, 4.

7. Ibid.

8. Barrow, *Passion for Birds*, 11–12.

9. Kohlstedt, *Teaching Children Science*, 1.

10. Morse Nice, *Research Is a Passion with Me*, 4, 5.

11. Ogilvie and Harvey, *Biographical Dictionary of Women in Science*, 2, 1407; Wright, *Friendship of Nature*, 5; Wright, *Birdcraft*.

12. Harvey, *"Almost a Man of Genius."*

13. Wright, *Friendship of Nature*, 3–20.

14. Morse Nice, *Research Is a Passion with Me*, 5, 7; Clark, *Birds of Amherst and Vicinity*; Grant, *Our Common Birds*.

15. Thompson, *My Life*, 24.

16. Morse Nice, *Research Is a Passion with Me*, 8.

17. Ibid., 9.

18. Ogilvie and Harvey, *Biographical Dictionary of Women in Science*, 2, 897; Welker, "Miller, Olive Thorne," 2, 543–45.

19. Morse Nice, *Research Is a Passion with Me*, 9.

20. Ibid., 10.

21. Ibid., 11.

22. Ibid., 10, 11.

23. Ibid., 12; Schjelderup-Ebbe, "Beiträge zur Socialpsychologie."

24. Morse Nice, *Research Is a Passion with Me*, 13–14.

25. Ibid., 13.

26. Rensing, "Women 'Waking Up,'" 97; Popenoe and Johnson, *Applied Eugenics*, 378–84.

27. Morse Nice, *Research Is a Passion with Me*, 14.

28. Ibid.

29. Ibid., 15.

Chapter 2. **ADVENTURES IN SELF-RELIANCE**

1. Levin, *Defining Women's Scientific Enterprise*.

2. Ibid., 88.

3. Ibid.

4. Ibid., 101–7.

5. Morse Nice, *Research Is a Passion with Me*, 16 (italics added).

6. "Courses Taken," Margaret Morse Papers, Mount Holyoke College Archives and Special Collections, LD 7096.6, box 1, folder 1.

7. Morse Nice, *Research Is a Passion with Me*, 17.

8. Ibid., 18; Clark, *Birds of Amherst and Vicinity*, 2nd ed.

9. Morse Nice, *Research Is a Passion with Me*, 18.

10. Ibid., 18–20.

11. Ibid., 20.

12. "Courses Taken," Margaret Morse Papers, Mount Holyoke College Archives and Special Collections.

13. Morse Nice, *Research Is a Passion with Me*, 20.

14. Mignon Talbot, "*Podokesaurus holyokensis*"; Ogilvie and Harvey, *Biographical Dictionary of Women in Science*, 2, 1263.

15. Ogilvie, Harvey, and Rossiter, *Biographical Dictionary of Women in Science*, 2, 1342.

16. Ibid., 2, 1263.

17. Kohlstedt, *Teaching Children Science*, 20–22, 27.

18. Ogilvie and Harvey, *Biographical Dictionary of Women in Science*, 1, 258–59.

19. Morse Nice, *Research Is a Passion with Me*, 21.

20. Ibid., 22.

21. Ibid., 23.

22. Ibid.

23. Ibid., 23–25.

24. "Jonas Clark Biography," Clark University, Archives and Special Collections, accessed December 11, 2017, http://www.clarku.edu/research/archives/archives/JC_bio.cfm.

25. Morse Nice, *Research Is a Passion with Me*, 28.

26. Kohlstedt, *Teaching Children Science*, 71.

27. Hodge, *Nature Study and Life*; Morse Nice, *Research Is a Passion with Me*, 26–27.

28. Morse Nice, *Research Is a Passion with Me*, 26.

29. Ibid.

30. Ibid., 29.

31. Thompson, *My Life*, 28.

32. Morse Nice, *Research Is a Passion with Me*, 33.

33. Unknown newspaper article, 1909. Photocopy, Margaret Morse Papers, Mount Holyoke College Archives and Special Collections.

34. Morse Nice, *Research Is a Passion with Me*, 33–34.

35. Ibid., 34–35.

36. Ibid., 35–36.

37. Ibid.

38. Third class letter, April 1913, class of 1905, Margaret Morse Papers, Mount Holyoke College Archives and Special Collections.

Chapter 3. **MOVE TO OKLAHOMA**

1. Morse Nice, *Research Is a Passion with Me*, 33.

2. Ibid., 37.

3. Levy, *University of Oklahoma*, 7.

4. Ibid., 16.

5. Ibid., 91–92.

6. Ibid., 38; Morse Nice to John C. Johnson Jr., September 27, 1952, Margaret Morse Nice Collection, Western History Collections, University of Oklahoma Libraries, box 1, folder 2. The Western History Collections are hereafter cited as WHC and the University of Oklahoma Libraries as OU.

7. Fourth class letter, June 1919, class of 1905, Margaret Morse Papers, Mount Holyoke College Archives and Special Collections, LD 7096.6, box 1, folder 1.

8. Morse Nice, *Research Is a Passion with Me*, 39; G. W. Stevens to Morse Nice, February 27, 1915, Morse Nice Collection, WHC, OU, box 2, folder 1.

9. Fourth class letter, Margaret Morse Papers, Mount Holyoke College Archives and Special Collections.

10. Darwin, "Biographical Sketch of an Infant."

11. Browne, *Charles Darwin*, 441.

12. Harvey, "Darwin's 'Angels.'"

13. Darwin, "Letter of Mr. Charles Darwin," 6–8.

14. Preyer, "Dr. Preyer's Observations," 44–48.

15. Shinn, *Biography of a Baby*, 1–2.

16. Ibid., 19.

17. Moore, "Mental Development of a Child."

18. Darwin, *On the Origin of Species*, 449.

19. To see the problems with evolutionary psychology and its broader applications to the origin of language, see Chomsky, *Language and Problems of Knowledge*, 167; Scott-Phillips, "Evolutionary Psychology."

20. Morse Nice, "Development of a Child's Vocabulary" (1915), 35.

21. Ibid., 63.

22. Morse Nice, "Speech Development of a Child" (1917).

23. Marjorie Duncan Nice, manuscript, July 1916–November 1917, three and a half to five years old. Diary handwritten by Margaret Morse Nice, Norman, OK, 1916–1917. History of Science Collections, OU.

24. Ibid.

25. Morse Nice, "Speech Development of a Little Girl" (1925).

26. Morse Nice, "Ambidexterity and Delayed Speech Development" (1918).

27. Morse Nice, "Child Who Would Not Talk" (1925), 105, 138, 140; Blanton and Blanton, *Speech Training for Children*.

28. Morse Nice, "Child Who Would Not Talk" (1925), 106.

29. Morse Nice, "Child's Vocabularies" (1927), 317, 343.

30. Morse Nice, "Child's Attainment of the Sentence" (1933); Morse Nice, "Length of Sentences" (1925).

31. Morse Nice, "Child's Imagination" (1919), 201.

32. Morse Nice, "Child and Nature" (1921), 22–23.

33. Morse Nice, "Speech of a Left-Handed Child" (1915), 117.

34. Morse Nice, "Ambidexterity and Delayed Speech Development" (1918).

35. Curie, *Madame Curie*, 163.

36. Lutkehaus, *Margaret Mead*, 64.

37. Morse Nice, *Research Is a Passion with Me*, 39.

38. Thompson, *My Life*, 4.

39. Ibid., 5.

40. Ibid.

41. Ibid., 9–10.

42. Ibid., 10.

43. Ibid., 11–12.

44. Ibid.

45. Ibid., 12–13.

46. Michael S. Thompson to Marilyn B. Ogilvie, November 16, 2010. In the author's possession.

47. Bix, "'Chicks Who Fix.'"

48. Thompson, *My Life*, 24–25.

49. Ibid., 25–29.

50. Morse Nice, *Research Is a Passion with Me*, 41.

51. Ibid. (italics in the original).

52. Ibid.

53. Ibid.

Chapter 4. **THE MAKING OF A CAREER**

1. Morse Nice, *Research Is a Passion with Me*, 42; "No Closed Season on Doves in State," *Daily Oklahoman* (Oklahoma City, OK), August 13, 1919.

2. Morse Nice, *Research Is a Passion with Me*, 42, 44.

3. Ibid., 40.

4. Morse Nice to Ralph C. Hardie, January 26, 1921, Morse Nice Collection, WHC, OU, box 2, folder 6. It is unknown whether Nice's letter inspired Hardie to vote as she hoped.

5. Morse Nice, *Research Is a Passion with Me*, 43.

6. Ibid.

7. Rossiter, *Women Scientists in America*, 129–34.

8. Barrow, *Passion for Birds*, 43.

9. Birkhead, Wimpenny, and Montgomerie, *Ten Thousand Birds*.

10. Merchant, "George Bird Grinnell's Audubon Society," 5.

11. Ibid., 6.

12. Morse Nice, "Some Experiences with Mourning Doves" (1921).

13. Morse Nice, *Research Is a Passion with Me*, 44; Morse Nice, "Some Weights of Mourning Doves" (1929).

14. Morse Nice, "Study of the Nesting of Mourning Doves," Part 1 (1922); Part 2, (1923), 50.

15. Morse Nice, "Study of the Nesting of Mourning Doves," Part 1 (1922), 457.

16. Morse Nice, *Research Is a Passion with Me*, 45. See chapter 3 for a discussion of the zoology professor's mistaken idea that Song Sparrows did not live in Oklahoma.

17. Morse Nice and Nice, "Christmas Census from Norman" (1920); Morse Nice, *Research Is a Passion with Me*, 45.

18. Morse Nice, *Research Is a Passion with Me*, 46.

19. Nice and Morse Nice, "Roadside Census" (1921), 113.

20. Ibid.

21. Barrow, *Passion for Birds*, 46–47.

22. Morse Nice, *Research Is a Passion with Me*, 47.

23. Ibid.

24. Ibid., 47–48.

25. Ibid., 48.

26. Pycior, Slack, and Abir-Am, *Creative Couples in the Sciences*; Kofalk, *No Woman Tenderfoot*.

27. Sherman, *Birds of an Iowa Dooryard*.

28. Sherman to Morse Nice, March 26, 1921, folder 2993, Margaret Morse Nice Papers, Division of Rare and Manuscript Collections, Cornell University Library. Hereafter cited as Nice Papers, Cornell, with box and folder numbers.

29. Sherman to Morse Nice, December 30, 1921, Nice Papers, Cornell, box 1, folder 2992. For the Nice/Sherman relationship, see also Morse Nice, "Some Letters of Althea Sherman" (1952).

30. Sherman to Morse Nice, August 9, 1922, Nice Papers, Cornell, box 1, folder 2993.

31. Sherman to Morse Nice, November 10, 1922, Nice Papers, Cornell, box 1, folder 2993.

32. Sherman to Morse Nice, March 27, 1923, Nice Papers, Cornell, box 1, folder 2993.

33. Morse Nice, "Some Letters of Althea Sherman" (1952).

34. Ibid., 54.

35. Ibid., 55.

36. Ibid.

37. Ibid.

38. Morse Nice, *Research Is a Passion with Me*, 50–51; Morse Nice notes, undated, Morse Nice Collection, WHC, OU, box 2, folder 1. In Nice's notes in this same folder, she analyzes the early bird lists and notes errors; Morse Nice to John C. Johnson Jr., September 27, 1952, Morse Nice Collection, WHC, OU, box 2, folder 1.

39. Morse Nice to John C. Johnson, September 27, 1952, Morse Nice Collection, WHC; Morse Nice, *Research Is a Passion with Me*, 50–51.

40. Morse Nice, *Research Is a Passion with Me*, 52; Bailey, *Handbook of Birds*; Chapman and Reed, *Color Key to North American Birds*; Reed, *Land Birds East of the Rockies*; Reed, *Water Birds East of the Rockies*.

41. Morse Nice, *Research Is a Passion with Me*, 54 (italics in the original).

42. Ibid., 56; Nice and Morse Nice, "Summer Birds of Oklahoma," September 1929, Morse Nice Collection, WHC, OU, box 2, BY2FF2.

43. Nice notebook, camping trip 1920, Morse Nice Collection, WHC, OU, box 3; Morse Nice, *Research Is a Passion with Me*, 56.

44. Questionnaire, September 22, 1920, Morse Nice Collection, WHC, OU, box 2, folder 8.

45. Morse Nice, *Research Is a Passion with Me*, 56–57.

46. Ibid., 59.

47. "Summer Birds of Oklahoma," handwritten note by Nice on cover, Morse Nice Collection, WHC, OU, box 2, folder 8 (italics in the original).

48. Morse Nice, *Research Is a Passion with Me*, 59.

49. Ibid., 60–61.

50. Ibid., 61.

51. Ibid.

52. Ibid.

53. Ibid., 61–62; Sherman to Morse Nice, December 30, 1921, Nice Papers, Cornell, box 1, folder 2993.

54. Morse Nice, *Research Is a Passion with Me*, 62–63.

55. Ibid., 63–64.

56. Ibid., 66.

Chapter 5. **THE BIRDS OF OKLAHOMA**

1. Morse Nice, *Research Is a Passion with Me*, 68–71.

2. Morse Nice, "Study of the Nesting of Mourning Doves," Part 1 (1922); Part 2 (1923).

3. Morse Nice, "Study of the Nesting of Mourning Doves," Part 1 (1922), 458–65.

4. Ibid., 465–70.

5. Ibid., 470–74.

6. Morse Nice, "Study of the Nesting of Mourning Doves," Part 2 (1923), 37.

7. Ibid., 43.

8. Ibid., 44–49.

9. Morse Nice, *Research Is a Passion with Me*, 72.

10. Ibid., 72–73.

11. Ibid., 74.

12. Ibid.

13. Ogilvie, *Marie Curie*, 39–40.

14. Morse Nice and Nice, *The Birds of Oklahoma* (1924).

15. Ibid. The photographs from Plate I include Figure 1, "Boulders in the Wichita Mountains. Home of the Rock Wren and Rock Sparrow"; and Figure 2, "A Stream in the Arbuckle Mountains. Frequented by the Louisiana Water Thrush." Plate II includes Figure 1, "Yellow Pines in Pushmataha County. Abode of the Pine Warbler, Chipping Sparrow and Wood Thrush"; and Figure 2, "A Mesa in Cimarron County. Haunt of the Pinyon and Woodhouse Jays and Canyon Towhee."

16. In descriptions of the contents of this work, ideas are often attributed to just Margaret Nice. This has been done with the realization that although Blaine no doubt agreed with Margaret's sentiments, the method of expressing the ideas was hers.

17. Morse Nice and Nice, *The Birds of Oklahoma* (1924), 3.

18. Ibid., 4–5.

19. Ibid., 5–6.

20. Ibid., 6.

21. Ibid., 8–10.

22. Ibid., 10–12.

23. Ibid., 12–14.

24. Ibid., 14–17.

25. Ibid., 18–101.

26. Morse Nice, *Research Is a Passion with Me*, 74–75.

27. Alexander Wetmore to Morse Nice, April 18, 1925, Morse Nice Collection, WHC, OU, box 2, folder 1.

28. Ibid.; Morse Nice, *Research Is a Passion with Me*, 74–75.

29. Morse Nice, *Research Is a Passion with Me*, 74–75; Grinnell, "Editorial Notes and News," *The Condor* 26 (May–June 1924): 115.

30. Morse Nice, *Research Is a Passion with Me*, 75.

31. Ibid., 78; Ogilvie and Choquette, *Dame Full of Vim and Vigor*, 4.

32. Morse Nice, *Research Is a Passion with Me*, 79.

33. Ibid., 79–80.

34. Ibid., 82.

35. Ibid., 83.

36. Ibid., 89.

37. Thompson, *My Life*, 34.

38. Morse Nice, *Research Is a Passion with Me*, 89–90.

39. Ibid., 90.

40. Thompson, *My Life*, 35.

41. Morse Nice, *Research Is a Passion with Me*, 91.

42. Thompson, *My Life*, 35–36.

43. Podolsky, *Pneumonia before Antibiotics*, 4–8.

44. U.S. Department of Commerce, Bureau of the Census, *Mortality Statistics 1927: Twenty-Eighth Annual Report* (Washington, DC: Government Printing Office, 1929), https://www.cdc.gov/nchs/data/vsushistorical/mortstatsh_1927.pdf.

45. Thompson, *My Life*, 36.

46. Ibid., 37.

47. Morse Nice, *Research Is a Passion with Me*, 91.

Chapter 6. **A SECOND EDITION OF *THE BIRDS OF OKLAHOMA* AND THE BEGINNING OF A NEW PROJECT**

1. Morse Nice, *Watcher at the Nest* (1939), 2–3.

2. Morse Nice, *Research Is a Passion with Me*, 101.

3. Ibid., 100.

4. Ibid., 101.

5. Ibid., 102.

6. Ibid., 103.

7. Ibid., 106.

8. Ibid.

9. Keller, *Feeling for the Organism*, 197–98.

10. Keller, *Reflections on Gender and Science*, 173–74.

11. Morse Nice, *Research Is a Passion with Me*, 107–8.

12. Ibid., 108.

13. Rossiter, *Women Scientists in America*, 275–76.

14. Quotation from Rossiter, *Women Scientists in America*, 276.

15. Morse Nice, *Research Is a Passion with Me*, 108–9.

16. Heinroth, "Die Beziechungen."

17. Haffer, *Ornithology, Evolution, and Philosophy*, 51. See Haffer for general biographical information on Mayr.

18. Morse Nice to Ernst Mayr, November 9, 1931, Ernst Mayr Collection, Harvard University Archives, Pusey Library, box 1, folder 12. Hereafter cited as Mayr Collection, Harvard.

19. Morse Nice to Mayr, March 5, 1932, Mayr Collection, Harvard, box 1, folder 12.

20. Mayr to Morse Nice, March 7, 1932, Mayr Collection, Harvard, box 1, folder 12.

21. Morse Nice to Mayr, March 29, 1932, Mayr Collection, Harvard, box 1, folder 12.

22. Morse Nice, *Research Is a Passion with Me*, 113–14.

23. Ibid., 115.

24. Morse Nice to Mayr, March 29, 1932, Mayr Collection, Harvard, box 1, folder 12.

25. Morse Nice to Mayr, March 5, 1932, Mayr Collection, Harvard, box 1, folder 12.

26. Mayr to Morse Nice, March 7, 1932, Mayr Collection, Harvard, box 1, folder 12.

27. Morse Nice to Mayr, April 20, 1932, Mayr Collection, Harvard, box 1, folder 12.

28. Morse Nice, *Research Is a Passion with Me*, 116.

29. Thompson, *My Life*, 42–43.

30. Ibid., 118–19.

31. Morse Nice to Mayr, November 1, 1932, Mayr Collection, Harvard, box 1, folder 12.

32. Ibid.

33. Morse Nice to Mayr, January 13, 1933 (incorrectly reads 1932), Mayr Collection, Harvard, box 1, folder 12.

34. Morse Nice to Mayr, November 1, 1932, Mayr Collection, Harvard, box 1, folder 12.

35. Morse Nice, *Research Is a Passion with Me*, 125–26.

36. Ibid.

37. Morse Nice to Joseph Grinnell, December 21, 1932, Mayr Collection, Harvard, box 1, folder 12.

38. Ibid.

39. Morse Nice to Mayr, January 16, 1933, Mayr Collection, Harvard, box 1, folder 12.

40. Mayr to Morse Nice, January 13, 1933, Mayr Collection, Harvard, box 1, folder 12.

41. Morse Nice to Mayr, January 18, 1933, Mayr Collection, Harvard, box 1, folder 12.

42. Mayr to Morse Nice, October 17, 1934, Mayr Collection, Harvard, box 1, folder 28.

43. Morse Nice to Mayr, November 17, 1934, Mayr Collection, Harvard, box 1, folder 28.

44. Morse Nice to Mayr, February 18, 1936, Mayr Collection, Harvard, box 1; Mayr, "Bernard Altum."

Chapter 7. **PUBLISHING THE SONG SPARROW RESEARCH**

1. Morse Nice, *Research Is a Passion with Me*, 120–23.

2. Morse Nice to Mayr, November 1, 1932, Mayr Collection, Harvard, box 1, folder 12.

3. Morse Nice to Mayr, March 22, 1932, Mayr Collection, Harvard, box 1, folder 12.

4. Morse Nice, *Research Is a Passion with Me*, 121.

5. Morse Nice to Mayr, April 6, 1933, Mayr Collection, Harvard, box 1, folder 12.

6. Morse Nice to Mayr, June 2, 1933, Mayr Collection, Harvard, box 1, folder 12.

7. Morse Nice to Mayr, May 8, 1933, Mayr Collection, Harvard, box 1, folder 12.

8. Morse Nice, *Zur Naturgeschichte*, Part 1 (1933); Part 2 (1934).

9. Morse Nice, *Zur Naturgeschichte*, Part 1 (1933), 552–57.

10. Ibid., 558–62. Burkitt, in "Study of the Robin," and Butts, in "Study of the Chickadee," described the pioneering use of colored celluloid bands.

11. Birkhead, Wimpenny, and Montogomerie, *Ten Thousand Birds*. Includes information on the history of bird banding as well as descriptions of the use of this technique.

12. Nice used her tools in the following ways:

BANDING RECORD

The banding record for each bird consisted of the band number, field number, colored band scheme, date, hour, measurements, state of molt, and any relevant additional information.

CARD CATALOG

Additional information was recorded on a card and included a summary of the most relevant data for each bird. The original card for a bird included the data from the banding record, such as sex, field number, and year of first nesting. Each card thus included a summary of the most relevant data for each bird. For males, the cards included weights and other measurements taken each time the bird was captured; it was also specified whether it was a permanent resident or only a summer visitor. If the bird was just a summer resident, Nice recorded the dates of the bird's arrival and departure. The cards also included the dates of when and where the male claimed territory in the spring, when he began singing in the fall, and when his mate arrived. The cards for females were similar but included the K number (a unique, easy-to-read field number given to female birds), the number of the mate, and the number of eggs laid. If ancestry was known, that too was included. The advantage of the card catalog in addition to the banding record list was the convenience of updating the record with each capture.

KEY TABLES

Nice also kept track of the birds by using two series of tables, one for males and the other for females. She listed the males in order by their field number. The years, beginning with 1929, were represented by vertical columns and divided into four seasons. She designated the period during which she was "acquainted" with each bird by a horizontal line: blue for the permanent residents and red for the summer transients. Females were listed by their K numbers, but their mates' numbers were also recorded each year.

DAILY RECORD

Nice recorded each day's observations in the field so that they could be transferred to permanent records. She kept a record of all the different species she encountered in what she called the "Roll Book." However, for the Song Sparrow she reserved a special place in the book for each nesting pair. When she had positively identified a bird by its band or by a known song, she underlined its designation in her record, and if it was trapped she underlined it twice. She also noted the sex and whether the bird was singing. She found this procedure useful in recording the beginning and end of song production for each individual. It also served as an index to the more complete notes in her large field notebook.

FIELD NOTEBOOK

Nice carried a large notebook "in a school satchel along with a sack of bait and [her] Game Protector's badge." In addition to a daily record, it contained a detailed chronicle of activities and included previously prepared material that she would need in her daily observations, such as a map of the Upper Interpont that showed each pair's banding scheme in color on its territory. Inside the back cover she recorded possible banding combinations in color by either the bird's field number or the abbreviated banding number if it did not have a field number. This record served as a guide for future banding schemes and could be accessed in the field. The field book also included daily summaries of the most important events for each day.

MAPS

The last two parts of Nice's record-keeping program involved mimeographed maps of Interpont. She used crayons to color nonmigratory residents in blue, summer residents in red, winter residents in brown, and birds of unknown status in pencil. When the Song Sparrows arrived in the spring, she filled in a new map nearly every day.

NEST RECORD

During the nesting season Nice carried sheets of lined paper divided into ten or twelve columns folded inside her field notebook. The vertical columns were devoted to pairs in the order in which she found the nest, and the horizontal lines represented the day. Thus, by looking at a page she was able to glimpse a brief account of the nesting activities of ten or twelve pairs for over three weeks.

13. Selous, "Observational Diary"; Burkhardt, *Patterns of Behavior*, 82.
14. Howard, *British Warblers*; Burkhardt, *Patterns of Behavior*, 93.

15. A. Allen, "Red-Winged Blackbird."

16. Morse Nice, *Research Is a Passion with Me*, 149–50.

17. Kluijver, "Bijdrage tot de Biologie"; Nice, "Review of Bijdrage tot de Biologie."

18. Morse Nice, *Research Is a Passion with Me*, 124–25.

19. Howard, *Territory in Bird Life*; Morse Nice, "Theory of Territorialism" (1933), 90.

20. Morse Nice, "Theory of Territorialism" (1933), 97.

Chapter 8. **A POPULATION STUDY OF THE SONG SPARROW**

1. Morse Nice to Mayr, February 23, 1934, Mayr Collection, Harvard, box 1, folder 28.

2. Morse Nice, *Research Is a Passion with Me*, 128.

3. Ibid., 128–29.

4. Ibid., 129.

5. Ibid., 135.

6. Boakes, *From Darwin to Behaviourism*, 8; Mill, *System of Logic*.

7. Darwin, *On the Origin of Species*; Darwin, *Descent of Man*; Darwin, *Expression of the Emotions*.

8. Darwin, quoted in Boakes, *From Darwin to Behaviourism*, 1.

9. Boakes, *From Darwin to Behaviourism*, 2–8; Daston, "British Responses to Psycho-Physiology."

10. Boakes, *From Darwin to Behaviourism*, 8–16; Bain, *Senses and the Intellect*; Bain, *Emotions and the Will*. Lorraine Daston ("British Responses to Psycho-Physiology") also writes of the movement of psychology away from its home in philosophy and toward the natural sciences. She suggests that this transfer required moving away from the traditional Cartesian mind-matter dualism and led to many problems. Although some psychological phenomena such as reflexes and other types of involuntary behavior could easily be assimilated into the materialistic, mechanistic, and reductionist model favored by the natural sciences in that period, other phenomena such as volition, aesthetics, and even consciousness itself were difficult to explain in terms of the reductionist model; the notions that could be examined only through the individual's consciousness were subjective, not objective. See also "Alexander Bain (1818–1903)," The Victorian Web, updated June 14, 2012, http://www.victorianweb.org/science/psych/bain. htm; Dr. C. George Boeree, "Psychology: The Beginnings," http://webspace. ship.edu/cgboer/psychbeginnings.html; Spencer, *Principles of Psychology*, 1st and 2nd ed.

11. Boakes, *From Darwin to Behaviourism*, 11, 22. The Spencer-Bain principle arose in the context of voluntary action. Bain assumed that physical events and mental events occurred in parallel and that psychology's task should be to study subjective experience (see note 10) and discover its relation to the workings of the brain.

12. Ibid., 14–16.

13. Ibid., 15–22.

14. Ibid., 51–52.

15. Ibid., 52–57.

16. Burkhardt, *Patterns of Behavior*, 127–28, 132, 134.

17. Uexküll's ideas were counter to mainstream ideas in biology. He was unconvinced by Darwin's theory of evolution. His goal was to lay the foundations for the integration of biology and epistemology. He considered biology, not physics, to be the basis of science and made subjectivity rather than objectivity the basis of biology. Each organism has its unique *Umwelt* (the system consisting of an animal together with its entire environment). Thus reality is subjective, created through the experience of each subject. Objective reality does not exist.

18. For a description of Uexküll's work on the behavior of the tick, see Rüting, "History and Signficance"; and Uexküll and Kriszat, *Streifzüge durch die Umwelten*. See also Kull, *Jakob von Uexküll's Theories of Life*, 7–27.

19. Burkhardt, *Patterns of Behavior*, 157–58.

20. Ibid., 164–65.

21. Ibid., 168. See note 17 to see how Uexküll's ideas influenced Lorenz's *Kumpan*.

22. Ibid., 167–68, 171.

23. Ibid., 170.

24. Ibid.,188, 192–93.

25. Ibid., 197–98.

26. Ibid., 197.

27. Ibid.

28. Ibid., 203–9; Mitman and Burkhardt, "Struggling for Identity," 182.

29. Morse Nice, *Research Is a Passion with Me*, 134–35.

30. Ibid., 137.

31. Morse Nice to Mayr, November 17, 1934, Mayr Collection, Harvard, box 1, folder 28.

32. Morse Nice to Mayr, January 22, 1936, Mayr Collection, Harvard, box 1, folder 45.

33. Mayr to Morse Nice, January 27, 1936, Mayr Collection, Harvard, box 1, folder 45.

34. Morse Nice to Mayr, January 30, 1936, Mayr Collection, Harvard, box 1, folder 45.

35. Mayr to Morse Nice, February 4, 1936, Mayr Collection, Harvard, box 1, folder 45.

36. Morse Nice to Mayr, February 6, 1936, Mayr Collection, Harvard, box 1, folder 45.

37. Mayr to Morse Nice, February 15, 1936, Mayr Collection, Harvard, box 1, folder 45.

38. Morse Nice to Mayr, June 25, 1936, Mayr Collection, Harvard, box 1, folder 45.

39. Morse Nice to Mayr, April 15, 1937, Mayr Collection, Harvard, box 1, folder 45.

40. Mayr to Morse Nice, April 26, 1937, Mayr Collection, Harvard, box 1, folder 45.

41. Morse Nice, *Research Is a Passion with Me*, 159–60; Morse Nice, *Studies in the Life History of the Song Sparrow, I, A Population Study of the Song Sparrow and Other Passerines* (1937), hereafter cited as *Population Study of the Song Sparrow*; Delacour, Review of *A Population Study of the Song Sparrow*.

42. Morse Nice to Mayr, October 4, 1937, Mayr Collection, Harvard, box 1, folder 45.

43. Morse Nice, *Population Study of the Song Sparrow* (1937), 2, 6, 214.

44. Ibid., 214.

45. Ibid., 8–12, 210.

46. Ibid., 10–12.

47. Ibid.

48. Ibid., 210.

49. Ibid., 15–16.

50. Ibid., 16.

51. Ibid., 84.

52. Ibid., 211, 84–86.

53. Howard, *Territory in Bird Life*, 90.

54. Hutchinson, *Introduction to Population Ecology*.

55. Morse Nice, *Population Study of the Song Sparrow* (1937), 18–21.

56. Morse Nice to Mayr, November 11, 1937, Mayr Collection, Harvard, box 1, folder 45. In this letter Nice quotes McCabe's comment to her on the population study; Delacour, Review of *A Population Study of the Song Sparrow*.

57. Leopold, Review of "Studies in the Life History," 126.

58. For general discussions of the process of professionalization, see Cooter and Pumfrey, "Separate Spheres and Public Places"; Farber, *Discovering Birds*; Thackray, "Natural Knowledge in Cultural Context"; Reingold, "Definitions and Speculations."

59. Morse Nice to Mayr, September 2, 1937, Mayr Collection, Harvard, box 1, folder 45.

60. Errington, *Wilson Bulletin*, 308; G. M. A., "Review of Studies in the Life History"; Hicks, Review of *Studies in the Life History*.

61. Morse Nice to Mayr, July 13, 1935, Mayr Collection, Harvard, box 1, folder 45.

62. Morse Nice, *Research Is a Passion with Me*, 149.

Chapter 9. **THE WINDY CITY**

1. Morse Nice, *Research Is a Passion with Me*, 153.

2. Morse Nice to Mayr, September 15, 1936, Mayr Collection, Harvard, box 1, folder 45.

3. Morse Nice, *Research Is a Passion with Me*, 151.

4. Ibid.; Morse Nice to Mayr, September 15, 1936, Mayr Collection, Harvard, box 1, folder 45.

5. Morse Nice, *Research Is a Passion with Me*, 153–54.

6. Thompson, *My Life*, 1.

7. Ibid., 40–41.

8. Ibid., 1.

9. Ibid., 51.

10. Morse Nice to Mayr, September 15, 1936, Mayr Collection, Harvard, box 1, folder 45.

11. Morse Nice, *Research Is a Passion with Me*, 155.

12. Thompson, *My Life*, 50–52.

13. Morse Nice, *Research Is a Passion with Me*, 156.

14. Barrow, *Passion for Birds*, 166. Harland Ballard was a school administrator from Lenox, Massachusetts, who established a new kind of natural history association aimed primarily at young people. The movement accelerated rapidly after Ballard established his first chapter in 1884 and included chapters all over the United States. The nature-study movement, which had similar goals, including providing children with firsthand exposure to the natural world, began to eclipse Barrow's original organizations by the turn of the twentieth century.

15. Barrow, *Passion for Birds*, 198.

16. Morse Nice, *Research Is a Passion with Me*, 157–58.

17. Ibid., 158.

18. Ibid., 158–59.

19. Thompson, *My Life*, 55.

20. Morse Nice, *Research Is a Passion with Me*, 160–61.

21. Morse Nice, *Watcher at the Nest* (1939), 58–61.

22. Ibid., i.

23. Morse Nice, *Research Is a Passion with Me*, 161.

24. Morse Nice, *Watcher at the Nest* (1939), 5.

25. Ibid., 5–7.

26. Morse Nice, *Research Is a Passion with Me*, 203.

27. Mayr to Morse Nice, November 10, 1937, Mayr Collection, Harvard, box 1, folder 45; Morse Nice to Mayr, November 11, 1937, Mayr Collection, Harvard, box 1, folder 45.

28. Thompson, *My Life*, 61–63.

29. Ibid., 68–69.

30. Ibid., iii.

Chapter 10. **PREPARING FOR SONG SPARROW, VOLUME TWO**

1. Morse Nice, *Research Is a Passion with Me*, 164.

2. Ibid.

3. Lorenz to Morse Nice, September 13, 1937, Nice Papers, Cornell, box 1, folder 4.

4. Morse Nice, *Research Is a Passion with Me*, 172–73.

5. Ibid.; Lorenz to Morse Nice, September 13, 1937, Nice Papers, Cornell, box 1, folder 4.

6. Morse Nice to Mayr, no date, 1937, Mayr Collection, Harvard, box 1, folder 45.

7. Morse Nice, *Research Is a Passion with Me*, 164–71.

8. Ibid., 173–74.

9. Ibid., 175–76.

10. Ibid., 177–80.

11. Ibid., 190.

12. Lorenz to Morse Nice, July 18, 1938, Nice Papers, Cornell, box 1, folder 5.

13. Morse Nice, *Research Is a Passion with Me*, 193.

14. Ibid., 194–95.

15. Morse Nice to Lorenz, October 5, 1938, Nice Papers, Cornell, box 1, folder 5.

16. Morse Nice, *Research Is a Passion with Me*, 197–99.

17. Ibid., 199.

18. Ibid., 201.

19. Morse Nice to Mayr, June 15, 1939, Mayr Collection, Harvard, box 2, folder 64.

20. Morse Nice, *Research Is a Passion with Me*, 207.

21. Morse Nice to Mayr, June 15, 1939, Mayr Collection, Harvard, box 2, folder 64.

22. Morse Nice, *Research Is a Passion with Me*, 209.

23. Ibid., 210.

24. Mitman, *Reel Nature*, 8. For information on Marey, see Braun, *Picturing Time*.

25. Muybridge began experimenting in 1872 and perfected his method between 1878 and 1884. "Eadweard Muybridge," Biography.com, updated April 7, 2017, www.biography.com/people/eadweard-muybridge-9419513.

26. Mitman, *Reel Nature*, 9. See Mitman's discussion of the relationship between solely entertaining films and animal films that were entertaining, as well as the relationship between fact and fiction in animal films (9–11).

27. Morse Nice, *Research Is a Passion with Me*, 212; "History: Early Milestones," Cornell Lab of Ornithology, accessed December 15, 2017, http://macaulaylibrary. org/history/early-milestones.

28. "History: Early Milestones."

29. Morse Nice, *Research Is a Passion with Me*, 211.

30. Ibid., 212.

31. *Wilson Bulletin* 51 (September 1939): 188.

32. Morse Nice, *Research Is a Passion with Me*, 212.

33. Ibid., 213.

34. Ibid., 219.

35. Ibid., 239.

36. Tinbergen to Morse Nice, July 28, 1938, Nice Papers, Cornell, box 1, folder 5.

37. Morse Nice, *Research Is a Passion with Me*, 197.

38. Nice to Lorenz, October 5, 1938, Nice Papers, Cornell, box 1, folder 5.

39. Lorenz to Morse Nice, November 9, 1938, Nice Papers, Cornell, box 1, folder 5.

40. Morse Nice, *Research Is a Passion with Me*, 197.

41. Lorenz to Morse Nice, February 14, 1939, Nice Papers, Cornell, box 1, folder 6.

Chapter 11. **"DEAR EDITOR"**

1. Morse Nice, *Research Is a Passion with Me*, 238.

2. Ibid., 253.

3. Morse Nice, "Birds of an Hungarian Lake" (1940); "Fall on Interpont" (1944); "Adventures at a Feeding Shelf" (1945); "Seven Baby Birds in Altenberg" (1945, 1946); "Golden Orioles" (1940).

4. Morse Nice to the editor of the *Chicago Sun*, February 25, 1945, Nice Papers, Cornell, box 1, folder 8.

5. Morse Nice to Harold Ickes, April 3, 1945, Nice Papers, Cornell, box 1, folder 8.

6. Morse Nice to the editor of *Coronet*, May 1, 1945, Nice Papers, Cornell, box 1, folder 8.

7. Morse Nice to the editor of the *Chicago Sun*, July 5, 1945, Nice Papers, Cornell, box 1, folder 8.

8. Morse Nice to Adlai Stevenson, April 16, 1949, Nice Papers, Cornell, box 1, folder 17.

9. Morse Nice to Mayr, April 7, 1946, Mayr Collection, Harvard, box 4, folder 156.

10. Morse Nice to Lawrence, April 1, 1946, Nice Papers, Cornell, box 1, folder 9; S. Kip Farrington Jr., "Quacker Comeback," *Reader's Digest*, February 1946, 18–20, abstracted from *Maclean's* magazine, October 15, 1945.

11. Morse Nice to the editors of *Life* magazine, April 1, 1947, Nice Papers, Cornell, box 1, folder 11; Burnham, *Struggle for the World*.

12. The General Semantics movement was proposed by Alfred Korzybski in his book *Science and Sanity: An Introduction to Non-Aristotelian Systems and General Semantics*. For a summary of General Semantics, see Alfred Korzybski, "General Semantics."

13. Morse Nice to Barrows Dunham, December 14, 1947, Nice Papers, Cornell, box 1, folder 13.

14. Morse Nice and Janet Nice to President Harry S. Truman, June 28, 1948, Nice Papers, Cornell, box 1, folder 14 (signed by both Margaret and Janet Nice).

15. Morse Nice to editors of *Life* magazine, October 23, 1948, Nice Papers, Cornell, box 1, folder 15; Vogt, *Road to Survival*; Osborn, *Our Plundered Planet*.

16. Morse Nice to Henry L. Luce, November 18, 1948, Nice Papers, Cornell, box 1, folder 15.

17. Morse Nice to editors of *Chicago Sun-Times*, March 6, 1949, Nice Papers, Cornell, box 1, folder 16.

18. Morse Nice to Martin H. Kennelly, March 19, 1949, Nice Papers, Cornell, box 1, folder 17.

Chapter 12. **EUROPEAN ETHOLOGISTS, ORNITHOLOGISTS, AND THE WAR**

1. Burkhardt, *Patterns of Behavior*, 242.

2. Ibid., 231–32. For additional information, see the following: Tuchman, "Institutions and Disciplines"; Deichmann, *Biologen unter Hitler*; Beyerchen, "What We Now Know"; Macrakis, *Surviving the Swastika*.

3. Harwood, "German Science and Technology," 135.

4. Michael Ruse, "Vienna," *Chronicle of Higher Education*, accessed November 23, 2013, http://chronicle.com/blogs/brainstorm/vienna/21519.

5. Michael Ruse, "Konrad Lorenz," *Chronicle of Higher Education*, accessed July 15, 2014, http://chronicle.com/blogs/brainstorm/konrad-lorenz/21616.

6. Burkhardt, *Patterns of Behavior*, 237–39. Many Austrians praised the *Anschluss* (the union of Germany and Austria) not so much as an endorsement of Nazi principles but as a rejection of the state of the Austrian economy, blaming the entrenched Jesuits for their woes.

7. Lorenz to Morse Nice, September 13, 1937, Nice Papers, Cornell, box 1, folder 4.

8. Lorenz to Stresemann, quoted in Burkhardt, *Patterns of Behavior*, 238.

9. Burkhardt, *Patterns of Behavior*, 244–46; E. R. Jaensch, quoted from "Der Hüh-nerhof als Forschungs-und Aufklärungsmittel in menschlichen Rassenfragen," *Zeitschrift für Tierpsychologie* 2 (1938–1939): 252, in Burkhardt, *Patterns of Behavior*, 244.

10. Burkhardt, *Patterns of Behavior*, 253.

11. Ibid., 259.

12. [Edwin G. Conklin], "The Future of America"; Ogilvie, "Inbreeding, Eugenics, and Helen Dean King," 476, 488–91; additional sources may be found on pages 503–7 of the Ogilvie paper. Also see Kevles, *In the Name of Genetics*.

13. Burkhardt, *Patterns of Behavior*, 235.

14. Ibid., 267–68.

15. Ibid., 269–74; Lorenz, "Die Angeborenen"; Lorenz, "Durch Domestikation."

16. Burkhardt, *Patterns of Behavior*, 227–28; Tinbergen, "Objectivist Study."

17. Burkhardt, *Patterns of Behavior*, 229–30.

18. Morse Nice, *Research Is a Passion with Me*, 220–30.

19. Morse Nice to Mayr, December 1, 1945, Mayr Collection, Harvard, box 3, folder 137.

20. Morse Nice to Mayr, June 30, 1946, Mayr Collection, Harvard, box 4, folder 137.

21. Mayr to Morse Nice, July 3, 1946, Mayr Collection, Harvard, box 4, folder 156.

22. Morse Nice to Mayr, December 1, 1945, Mayr Collection, Harvard, box 3, folder 137.

23. Ibid.

24. Mayr to Morse Nice, December 21, 1945, Mayr Collection, Harvard, box 3, folder 137.

25. Tinbergen to Morse Nice, January 4, 1946, Nice Papers, Cornell, box 1, folder 9.

26. Stresemann to Morse Nice, June 6, 1946, Nice Papers, Cornell, box 1, folder 10.

27. McGavran, *Mice in the Freezer*, 119.

28. F. Hamerstrom to Gustav Kramer, November 9, 1947, quoted in McGavran, *Mice in the Freezer*, 125.

29. Morse Nice, *Research Is a Passion with Me*, 248–49.

30. Hamerstrom-Fisher correspondence, June 13, 1947, Nice Papers, Cornell, box 1, folder 11.

31. Morse Nice to Mayr, January 5, 1946, Mayr Collection, Harvard, box 3, folder 137.

32. Stresemann to Morse Nice, February 4, 1946, Nice Papers, Cornell, box 1, folder 9.

33. Mayr to Morse Nice, June 12, 1946, Mayr Collection, Harvard, box 4, folder 156.

34. Margarethe Lorenz to Morse Nice, August 21, 1946, Nice Papers, Cornell, box 1, folder 10.

35. Morse Nice to Mayr, June 18, 1947, Mayr Collection, Harvard, box 5, folder 214.

36. Ibid.

37. Morse Nice to Mayr, April 7, 1946, Mayr Collection, Harvard, box 4, folder 156.

38. Mayr to Morse Nice, April 16, 1946, Mayr Collection, Harvard, box 4, folder 156.

39. Morse Nice to Mayr, June 2, 1946, Mayr Collection, Harvard, box 4, folder 156.

40. Morse Nice to Mayr, June 15, 1946, Mayr Collection, Harvard, box 4, folder 156.

41. Mayr to Morse Nice, July 3, 1946, Mayr Collection, Harvard, box 4, folder 156.

42. Morse Nice to Mayr, March 21, 1947, Mayr Collection, Harvard, box 4, folder 174; Morse Nice to Mayr, January 4, 1947, Mayr Collection, Harvard, box 4, folder 193.

43. Morse Nice to Hoyes Lloyd, April 17, 1947, Mayr Collection, Harvard, box 4, folder 193.

44. Morse Nice to Mayr, January 4, 1947, Mayr Collection, Harvard, box 4, folder 174.

45. Morse Nice, *Research Is a Passion with Me*, 252.

Chapter 13. **THE BEHAVIOR OF THE SONG SPARROW**

1. Morse Nice, *Studies in the Life History of the Song Sparrow, II, The Behavior of the Song Sparrow and other Passerines*, 3. Originally published as vol. 6 of the *Transactions of the Linnaean Society of New York*, 1943. Hereafter cited as *Behavior of the Song Sparrow*.

2. Morse Nice to Mayr, February 25, 1940, Mayr Collection, Harvard, box 2, folder 83.

3. Ibid.

4. Mayr to Morse Nice, March 26, 1942, Mayr Collection, Harvard, box 2, folder 83.

5. Mayr to Morse Nice, March 17, 1942, Mayr Collection, Harvard, box 2, folder 83.

6. Burkhardt, *Patterns of Behavior*, 361–62. Douglas Mock mused in an e-mail to the author on August 16, 2014, that the "zombie false dichotomy" between instinct and learning that has been around for centuries was the "primary obstacle to the scientific establishment of animal behavior as a legitimate research topic." Mock recognized the "intellectual tenacity that scientists bring to their supposedly objective work" and noted the "vast supply of pattern-seeking and what psychologists call 'confirmation bias' built into scientists' cognitive machinery, such that once scientists become convinced of something it is exceedingly hard to shift gears."

7. Burkhardt, *Patterns of Behavior*, 362–63.

8. Ibid., 366–68.

9. Mayr to Morse Nice, March 17, 1942, Mayr Collection, Harvard, box 2, folder 83.

10. Ibid.; Burkhardt, *Patterns of Behavior*, 365.

11. Mayr to Morse Nice, March 17, 1942, Mayr Collection, Harvard, box 2, folder 83.

12. Morse Nice to Mayr, March 26, 1942, Mayr Collection, Harvard, box 2, folder 83.

13. Ibid.

14. Morse Nice to Mayr, May 19, 1942, Mayr Collection, Harvard, box 2, folder 83.

15. Mayr to Morse Nice, May 25, 1942, Mayr Collection, Harvard, box 2, folder 83.

16. Morse Nice, *Behavior of the Song Sparrow*, 1, 4.

17. Herrick, *Home Life of Wild Birds*; Morse Nice, *Behavior of the Song Sparrow*, 4.

18. Herrick, "Life and Behavior of the Cuckoo."

19. Heinroth, *Die Vögel Mitteleuropas.*

20. Howard, *Territory in Bird Life.*

21. Julian Huxley, "Courtship Habits."

22. Tolman, *Purposive Behavior in Animals and Men*; Burkhardt, *Patterns of Behavior,* 48, 57, 172, 362.

23. Morse Nice to Mayr, January 26, 1935, Mayr Collection, Harvard, box 1, folder 28.

24. Mayr to Morse Nice, February 6, 1935, Mayr Collection, Harvard, box 1, folder 28.

25. Lorenz, "Der Kumpan in der Umwelt des Vogels."

26. Morse Nice, Review of "The Kumpan" (1935); Burkhardt, *Patterns of Behavior,* 172; Mitman and Burkhardt, "Struggling for Identity," 182–83; Morse Nice, "My Debt to Konrad Lorenz" (1963).

27. Morse Nice, *Behavior of the Song Sparrow*, 10–11; see also Lehrman, "Critique of Konrad Lorenz's Theory," 338–40; Tinbergen and Kuenen, "Über die auslösenden."

28. Morse Nice, *Research Is a Passion with Me*, 140.

29. Noble objected to Lorenz's assumption that newly hatched birds had an instinctive knowledge of certain objects that appeared before them. A mammalian example might be a very young monkey fearing snakes despite having no experience of snakes. Nice was not satisfied by this explanation, for she claimed that the experiments Noble constructed to refute Lorenz's claims often did not demonstrate what he intended.

30. Mitman and Burkhardt, "Struggling for Identity," 183–84; Morse Nice to Noble, November 13, 1938, Nice Papers, Cornell, box 1, folder 5. For example, Nice asked Noble whether his problem was that he suspected Lorenz had overgeneralized by presuming that striking colors and structures served as releasers of instinctive behavior in all species.

31. Lorenz to Morse Nice, February 14, 1939, Nice Papers, Cornell, box 1, folder 6; Lorenz to Morse Nice, December 3, 1936, Nice Papers, Cornell, box 1, folder 3.

32. Nice asked Noble whether he was positing that what Lorenz claimed was inborn should be considered learned "until proved otherwise." If this was his objection, Nice agreed that Lorenz's ideas should be the subject of further careful experiments. But she still did not clearly understand his objection to "releasers." She asked whether he also objected to Tinbergen's use of "signals," a modification of the releaser construct. Morse Nice to Noble, November 12, 1940, Nice Papers, Cornell, box 1, folder 7.

33. Mitman, *Reel Nature*, 69. The manner in which Tinbergen and Noble explained the way that the red patch on the lower mandible of the Herring Gull functioned illustrates their disagreement. Tinbergen explained it as a sign stimulus that directed the innate reaction of newly hatched birds to peck at their parents' bills

for food. Noble, however, posited that the red patch served as a social releaser and was a stimulus that triggered the pecking response through training.

34. Lorenz to Morse Nice, December 3, 1936, Nice Papers, Cornell, box 1, folder 3.

35. Mitman, *Reel Nature*, 69.

36. Morse Nice, *Behavior of the Song Sparrow*, 2, 7.

37. Ibid.

38. Ibid., 9; Burkhardt, *Patterns of Behavior*, 17.

39. Morse Nice, *Behavior of the Song Sparrow*, 8.

40. Ibid., 8–9.

41. Ibid., 9.

42. Ibid., 12–34.

43. Ibid., 35–59, 60–68.

44. Ibid., 69–74; see appendix for the listing of chapters and their inclusions.

45. Morse Nice to Mayr, February 27, 1944, Mayr Collection, Harvard, box 3, folder 102.

46. Friedman, Review of *Behavior of the Song Sparrow*.

47. Van Tyne, Review of *Behavior of the Song Sparrow*.

48. Williams, Review of *Behavior of the Song Sparrow*.

49. Hickey, Review of *Behavior of the Song Sparrow*.

50. Anonymous, Review of *Behavior of the Song Sparrow*.

51. Morse Nice to Mayr, June 15, 1946, Mayr Collection, Harvard, box 4, folder 156.

52. Morse Nice, *Research Is a Passion with Me*, 239.

Chapter 14. **POSTWAR LIFE**

1. Mayr to Morse Nice, July 3, 1946, Mayr Collection, Harvard, box 4, folder 11.

2. Morse Nice to Mayr, March 17, 1947, Mayr Collection, Harvard, box 4, folder 48.

3. Mayr to Morse Nice, March 21, 1947, Mayr Collection, Harvard, box 4, folder 48.

4. Morse Nice to Mayr, January 1, 1949, Mayr Collection, Harvard, box 6, folder 27.

5. Morse Nice to Mayr, February 16, 1949, Mayr Collection, Harvard, box 6, folder 27; Heinroth and Heinroth, "Verhalten der Felsentaube."

6. Morse Nice, "Question of Sexual Dominance" (1949).

7. Mayr to Morse Nice, February 24, 1949, Mayr Collection, Harvard, box 6, folder 27.

8. Morse Nice to Mayr, February 27, 1949, Mayr Collection, Harvard, box 6, folder 27; Lehrman, "Critique of Konrad Lorenz's Theory."

9. Mitman and Burkhardt, "Struggling for Identity," 186; Morse Nice, "Question of Sexual Dominance" (1949), 158–61. Douglas Mock, in an e-mail to the author on August 16, 2014, described his experience in the Department of Ecology and Behavioral Biology at the University of Minnesota and suggested that although biology might have become less androcentric, sexism was certainly alive and well in about 1973. He described an incident in which a feminist from another academic unit brushed aside the "standard defense of science departments" with "equality will have been reached when female mediocrity marches alongside

male mediocrity!" A professor in the department completely missed the subtlety of her statement. He said, "Ethology doesn't have any of those problems . . . consider how well respected Esther Cullen is." This example is very telling, as Cullen, who did classic work in Tinbergen's Oxford group on the behavior of kittiwakes for cliff-nesting, published "one big-splash paper . . . and then . . . no career."

10. Morse Nice to Mayr, February 27, 1949, Mayr Collection, Harvard, box 6, folder 27.

11. Mayr to Morse Nice, March 14, 1949, Mayr Collection, Harvard, box 6, folder 27.

12. Stresemann to Morse Nice, January 4, 1950, Nice Papers, Cornell, box 1, folder 10.

13. Nice indicated that what appeared to be sexual dominance was actually social dominance.

14. Smith, "Henpecked Males"; Smith, "Ducks Fight the Battle of the Sexes."

15. Amelia Laskey to Morse Nice, March 27, 1950; Ruth Thomas to Morse Nice, May 3, 1950, Nice Papers, Cornell box 2, folder 1.

16. Schiebinger, *Has Feminism Changed Science?* For more extensive information on primates and feminism, see Haraway, *Primate Visions*; and Hrdy, *Woman That Never Evolved.*

17. Morse Nice *Population Study of the Song Sparrow* (1937), Table III: "First Arrival of the Breeding Male Song Sparrows on Interpont," 46; Chart VII: "Average Mean Temperature of Last Ten Days of February and First Date of Arrival of Male Song Sparrows," 47.

18. Allen and Morse Nice, "Study of the Breeding Biology" (1952).

19. Lorenz to Morse Nice, May 19, 1941, Nice Papers, Cornell, box 1, folder 17.

20. Morse Nice to Mayr, April 26, 1949, Mayr Collection, Harvard, box 6, folder 309.

21. Morse Nice to Mayr, July 3, 1949, Mayr Collection, Harvard, box 6, folder 309.

22. Mayr to Morse Nice, August 31, 1949, Mayr Collection, Harvard, box 6, folder 309.

23. Mayr to Tinbergen, January 25, 1946, Mayr Collection, Harvard, box 3, folder 141; for more on Mayr's perspective, see Burkhardt, *Patterns of Behavior*, 37.

24. Morse Nice to Mayr, September 21, 1949, Mayr Collection, Harvard, box 7, folder 328.

25. Morse Nice to Mayr, January 26, 1950, Mayr Collection, Harvard, box 7, folder 328.

26. Ibid.

27. Mayr to Morse Nice, February 16, 1950, Mayr Collection, Harvard, Box 7, folder 328.

28. Kohler, *Landscapes and Labscapes.*

29. Ibid.

30. Farber, "Transformation of Natural History."

31. G. Allen, *Life Science in the Twentieth Century*; G. Allen, "Teaching and Research"; Maienschein, Rainger, and Benson, "Were American Morphologists in Revolt?"; G. Allen, "Naturalists and Experimentalists"; G. Allen, "Transformation of a Science."

32. Ibid.

33. Kohler, *Landscapes and Labscapes*, 566.

34. Douglas W. Mock, e-mail to author, August 16, 2014. In another e-mail from Mock to the author, on August 17, 2014, Mock took issue with thinking that much of what Nice and Lorenz considered theoretical was within the current scientific use of theory. The definition of "theory" as used by scientists today differs from that under which Nice and Lorenz operated. Whereas they would define theory as a generalized explanation for a phenomenon, modern ethologists consider theory to be more formal and "decidedly more mathematical" than the work Nice was doing. It must be remembered that Lorenz, operating in the early days of European ethology, was attempting to create a respected scientific discipline out of what most people considered a hobby. Consequently, his explanations, like Nice's, were provisional explanations. Concepts in the classical lexicon (redirected behavior, displacement behavior, misfiring, water-closet models, etc.) could be considered the theories of their day.

35. In the case of ethology, one of the current ideas is that of behavioral syndromes, referring to interindividual variation. Whereas some birds tend to be bold, others are timid—in other words, individual animals have different personalities. It appears that individuals that are more aggressive with predators are generally more aggressive in feeding and mating contexts. Since Darwinian natural selection is fundamentally a reproductive race, more-aggressive animals would be predicted to prevail over their more-timid relatives and produce more offspring. If this occurrence can be quantified over the lifetime of an animal, additional support for natural selection can be accrued. This study requires that the animals be individually monitored and, in the case of birds, can be done only by marking individuals. Research suggested by the concept of behavioral syndromes in birds requires colored bands such as those pioneered by Nice in her studies.

36. Morse Nice, *Research Is a Passion with Me*, 253.

37. Morse Nice, *Development of Behavior in Precocial Birds* (1962).

38. Morse Nice, *Research Is a Passion with Me*, 254; Heinroth, "Die Beziechhungen."

39. Morse Nice to Stresemann, February 16, 1952, Nice Collection, Cornell, box 2, folder 5. Some of the authors whose incubation periods she included after Aristotle were Pliny the Elder, Konrad von Megenberg (1309–1374), Konrad Gesner (1516–1565), Francis Willoughby (1635–1672), John Ray (1628–1705), Giovanni Zinanni (1692–1753), Eleazar Albin (1690–1742), George Edwards (1694–1773), Jacob Theodor Klein (1685–1759), Johann Leonhard Frisch (1666–1743), Thomas Pennant (1726–1798), Georges-Louis Leclerc, Comte de Buffon (1707–1788), and John Latham (1740–1837); Morse Nice, *Research Is a Passion with Me*, 255–56.

40. Morse Nice to Speirs, January 30, 1952, Nice Papers, Cornell, box 2, folder 5.

41. Gentry, *Life-Histories*; Gentry, *Nests and Eggs*.

42. Morse Nice, *Research Is a Passion with Me*, 255.

43. Evans, "On the Periods Occupied by Birds.

44. Tiedemann, *Anatomie und Naturgeschichte der Vögel.*

45. Aristotle, *Historia animalium,* book 6, chap. 6, quoted in Morse Nice, *Research Is a Passion with Me,* 255.

46. Morse Nice, *Research Is a Passion with Me,* 256.

47. Morse Nice, "Incubation Periods throughout the Ages" (1954).

48. Morse Nice to Stresemann, March 3, 1953, Nice Papers, Cornell, box 2, folder 5. A sample query from Nice to Stresemann was "Can you tell me where Vökie was and when he reported that Golden Eagles in captivity incubated 44–45 days? Heinroth quoted this in 1922 but I can find nothing about Vökie." She also reported that she was "puzzled about Johnstone" (Jonstonus, *History of the Wonderful Things*). She complained that the version of his book was such "a hodge-podge of fables that she "can't understand why so many ornithologists cited him." This letter contained additional questions to Stresemann similar to the ones above.

Chapter 15. **THE LAST YEARS**

1. Morse Nice to Mayr, November 18, 1950, Mayr Collection, Harvard, box 7, folder 367.

2. Mayr to Morse Nice, November 24, 1950, Mayr Collection, Harvard, box 7, folder 367.

3. Doris Huestis Speirs to Edward S. Morse, January 31, 1975, in Morse Nice, *Research Is a Passion with Me,* 267–71; Morse Nice to Speirs, January 26, 1952, Nice Papers, Cornell, box 2, folder 5.

4. Speirs to Morse, January 31, 1975, in Morse Nice, *Research Is a Passion with Me,* 267–71.

5. College memorandum, February 3, 1955, Margaret Morse Papers, Mount Holyoke College Archives and Special Collections.

6. Nomination for an honorary degree, 1955, Margaret Morse Papers, Mount Holyoke College Archives and Special Collections.

7. Morse Nice to Mayr, June 26, 1955, Mayr Collection, Harvard, box 3, folder 594.

8. Morse Nice to Sutton, August 8, 1969, Morse Nice Collection, WHC, OU, box 2, folder 1.

9. Jackson, *George Miksch Sutton.*

10. Ibid., 111.

11. Ibid., 81.

12. Ibid., 114.

13. Morse Nice to Sutton, no date, 1966, Morse Nice Collection, WHC, OU, box 2, folder 1.

14. Sutton to Morse Nice, August 29, 1966, Morse Nice Collection, WHC, OU, box 2, folder 1.

15. Sutton to Morse Nice, March 28, 1967; Morse Nice to Sutton, May 28, 1967; Sutton to Morse Nice, May 30, 1967; Morse Nice to Sutton, June 19, 1967; Sutton to Morse Nice, July 4, 1967, Morse Nice Collection, WHC, OU, box 2, folder 1.

16. Sutton to Morse Nice, February 29, 1968; Morse Nice to Sutton, March 4, 1968; Sutton to Morse Nice, March 6, 1968; Morse Nice to Sutton, July 27, 1969; Morse Nice to Sutton, October 24, 1969, Morse Nice Collection, WHC, OU, box 2, folder 1.

17. Jackson, *George Miksch Sutton*, 121–22.

18. Morse Nice to Sutton, October 24, 1969, Morse Nice Collection, WHC, OU, box 2, folder 1.

19. Morse Nice to Sutton, April 27, 1970; Morse Nice to Sutton, January 31, 1970; Sutton to Morse Nice, February 4, 1970, Morse Nice Collection, WHC, OU, box 2 folder 1.

20. Sutton to Morse Nice, May 22, 1970, Morse Nice Collection, WHC, OU, box 2, folder 1.

21. Morse Nice to Mayr, January 13, 1969; Morse Nice to Mayr, December 7, 1970; Morse Nice to Mayr, January 15, 1970, Mayr Collection, Harvard, box 18, folder 1.

22. Morse Nice to Mayr, January 13, 1969, Mayr Collection, Harvard, box 18, folder 1.

23. Morse Nice to Sutton, January 31, 1970, Morse Nice Collection, WHC, OU, box 2, folder 1.

24. Sutton to Morse Nice, February 4, 1970, Morse Nice Collection, WHC, OU, box 2, folder 1.

25. Ibid.

26. Morse Nice to Sutton, September 8, 1970, Morse Nice Collection, WHC, OU, box 2, folder 1.

27. Morse Nice to Sutton, November 20, 1970, Morse Nice Collection, WHC, OU, box 2, folder 1.

28. Ibid.

29. Mayr to Morse Nice, December 7, 1970, Mayr Collection, Harvard, box 18, folder 1060.

30. Morse Nice to Mayr, January 15, 1970, Mayr Collection, Harvard, box 18, folder 1060.

31. Morse Nice to Mayr, January 13, 1969, Mayr Collection, Harvard, box 18, folder 1060.

32. Morse Nice to Mayr, May 28, 1971, Mayr Collection, Harvard, box 19, folder 1112.

33. Ibid.

34. Ken Boyer, e-mail to author, January 16, 2012.

35. Dale Pontius to Edward Sinclair Thomas, July 24, 1974, Ohio Historical Society, series 3, box 4, folder 10.

CONCLUSION

1. Rossiter, "Matilda Effect in Science."

2. "German Ornithologist Reveals Columbus Woman as World Authority on Sparrows," *Columbus (OH) Dispatch*, February 1, 1936.

3. Ibid.

WORKS BY
MARGARET MORSE NICE

Publications are divided into "books and articles" and "reviews" sections. Books and articles are listed by year and alphabetically within years, and reviews are listed chronologically by year and within years.

BOOKS AND ARTICLES

1910
"Food of the Bob-White." *Journal of Economic Entomology* 3 (June 1910): 295–313.

1915
"The Development of a Child's Vocabulary in Relation to Environment." *Pedagogical Seminary* 22 (March 1915): 35–64.
"The Speech of a Left-Handed Child." *Psychological Clinic* 9 (June 1915): 115–17.

1916
"The Stories We Tell to Children." *University of Oklahoma Magazine*, April 1916.

CIRCA 1916
"Three Poems: The South Canadian in January; In Central Oklahoma; A Warbler in September." In *The Living Wilderness*. Washington, DC: Wilderness Society.

1917
"Marjorie Duncan Nice; July 1916 to Nov. 1917; Three and a Half to Five Years Old." Norman, OK, 1916–1917. History of Science Collections, University of Oklahoma. [This penciled manuscript or diary is a record of conversations between Nice and her second daughter, Marjorie. Nice transcribed Marjorie's words.]
"The Speech Development of a Child from Eighteen Months to Six Years." *Pedagogical Seminary* 24 (June 1917): 204–43.

1918
"Ambidexterity and Delayed Speech Development." *Pedagogical Seminary* 25 (June 1918): 141–62.

1919
"A Child's Imagination." *Pedagogical Seminary* 26 (June 1919): 173–201.

1920

"Concerning All Day Conversations." *Pedagogical Seminary* 27 (June 1920): 166–77.

Nice, L. B., and Nice, M. M. "Christmas Census from Norman." *Bird-Lore* 22 (1920): 41–42.

1921

"The Brown-Headed Nuthatch in Oklahoma." *The Condor* 23 (July 1921): 131.

"A Child and Nature." *Pedagogical Seminary* 28 (March 1921): 22–39.

"Late Nesting of Mourning Doves." *Proceedings of the Oklahoma Academy of Science* 1 (1921): 57.

"Nests of Mourning Doves with Three Young." *The Condor* 23 (September 1921): 145–47.

"Oklahoma's Unsuspected Riches." *Oklahoma Farmer-Stockman*, January 25, 1921.

"Our Greatest Food Loss—Shall We Have Cats or Birds?" *Proceedings of the Oklahoma Academy of Science* 1 (July 1921): 48.

"Some Bird Observations during a Mild Winter in Central Oklahoma." *Bird-Lore* 23 (December 1921): 302.

"Some Experiences with Mourning Doves in Captivity." *Proceedings of the Oklahoma Academy of Science* 1 (1921): 57–65.

Summer Birds on the University Campus." *University of Oklahoma Magazine*, May 1921, 10.

"A White Cowbird." *Wilson Bulletin* 33 (September 1921): 45–46.

Nice, M. M., and Nice, L. B. "The Roadside Census." *Wilson Bulletin* 33 (September 1921): 113–23.

1922

"A Child That Would Not Talk." *Proceedings of the Oklahoma Academy of Science* 2 (October 1, 1922): 108–11.

"Goldfinch Building Her Nest in September." *Oölogist* 39 (March 1922): 48.

"Notes from Lyme, Connecticut." *The Auk* 39 (January 1922): 117.

"The Short-Billed Marsh Wren in Amherst, Massachusetts." *The Auk* 39 (January 1922): 115.

"Some New Birds for Oklahoma." *The Condor* 24 (September 1922): 181.

"A Study of the Nesting of Mourning Doves, Part 1." *The Auk* 39 (1922): 457–74. [See 1923 for part 2.]

"A Third Christmas Bird Census." *Proceedings of the Oklahoma Academy of Science* 2 (October 1922): 31–32.

Nice, M. M., and Nice, L. B. "Further Roadside Census in Oklahoma." *Wilson Bulletin* 34 (December 1922): 238–39.

1923

"Nesting Records from 1920–1922 from Norman, Oklahoma." *Proceedings of the Oklahoma Academy of Science* 3 (October 1, 1923): 61–67.

"A Study of the Nesting of Mourning Doves, Part 2." *The Auk* 40 (January 1923): 37–58.

"What Is a Game Bird?" *Daily Oklahoman* (Oklahoma City, OK), 1923.

Nice, M. M., George F. Miller, and Margaret D. Miller. "A Boy's Vocabulary at Eighteen Months." *Proceedings of the Oklahoma Academy of Science* 3 (October 1, 1923): 140–44.

1924

"Extension Range of the Robin and Arkansas Kingbird in Oklahoma." *The Auk* 41 (October 1924): 565–68.

"Observations on Shore Birds in Central Oklahoma, in 1924." *Wilson Bulletin* 37 (December 1925): 199–203.

"The Red-Backed Sandpiper and Hudsonian Godwit in Oklahoma." *The Auk* 41 (October 1924): 600.

"The Speech Development of a Little Girl." *Proceedings of the Oklahoma Academy of Science* 4 (1924): 147–68.

"The Western House Wren Nesting in Central Oklahoma." *Wilson Bulletin* 36 (1924):137–38.

Nice, M. M., and L. B. Nice. *The Birds of Oklahoma.* University of Oklahoma Bulletin, New Series, No. 20. University Studies No. 2860: 1–122.

———. "Christmas Bird Census from Norman, Oklahoma." *Bird-Lore* 26 (February 1924): 48.

1925

"Bird Study and the Children." *Mount Holyoke Alumnae Quarterly* (July 1925) in *Bulletin of the Massachusetts Audubon Society* 9 (October 1925): 4–5.

"Changes in Bird Life in Amherst, Massachusetts, in Twenty-Five Years." *The Auk* 42 (1925): 594.

"A Child Who Would Not Talk." *Pedagogical Seminary and Journal of Genetic Psychology* 32, no. 1 (1925): 105–43.

"Length of Sentences as a Criterion of a Child's Progress in Speech." *Journal of Educational Psychology* 16 (September 1925): 370–79.

"Un enfant amoureux de la nature." *L'Educateur,* September 19, 1925, 270–72. [Published in Lausanne; a review and partial translation by Alice Desoendres of Nice's article "A Child and Nature" that appeared in *Pedagogical Seminary* in March 1921.]

Nice, M. M., and Constance Nice. "Christmas Census from Amherst, Massachusetts." *Bird-Lore* 27 (January–February 1925): 26.

Nice, M. M., and L. B. Nice. "Some Bird Observations in Cleveland County in 1924." *Proceedings of the Oklahoma Academy of Science* 5 (1925): 104–7.

1926

"Behavior of Blackburnian, Myrtle, and Black-Throated Blue Warblers, with Young." *Wilson Bulletin* 38 (June 1926): 82–83.

"A Child's Vocabularies from Fifteen Months to Three Years, Part 2." *Proceedings of the Oklahoma Academy of Science* 6 (1926): 317–33.

"Hawks of Oklahoma." *Outdoor Oklahoman* 2 (October 1926): 14–15.

"Letter on Hawks and Owls." *Sunday Oklahoman* (Oklahoma City, OK), June 13, 1926.

"The Mourning Dove." *Outdoor Oklahoman* 2 (August 1926): 6.

"Nesting of Mourning Doves during September 1925 in Norman, Oklahoma." *The Auk* 43 (January 1926): 94–95.

"On the Size of Vocabularies." *American Speech* 2 (October 1926): 1–7.

"A Study of a Nesting of Magnolia Warblers (*Dendroica magnolia*)." *Wilson Bulletin* 38 (December 1926): 185–99.

Nice, M. M., and L. B. Nice. "Christmas Bird Census." *Bird-Lore* 28 (February 1926): 48–49.

1927

"Bewick's Wren." *Sunday Oklahoman* (Oklahoma City, OK), March 20, 1927.

"The Cardinal." *Sunday Oklahoman* (Oklahoma City, OK), March 13, 1927.

Daily Oklahoman (Oklahoma City, OK), March 27; April 3, 10, 17, 24; May 1, 15, 22, 29; June 5, 12, 1927 [articles on various birds].

"Evening Bath of a Flock of Scissor-Tailed Flycatchers." *Wilson Bulletin* 49 (June 1927): 107–8.

"Experiences with Cardinals at a Feeding Station in Oklahoma." *The Condor* 29 (March 1927): 101–3.

"Further Note on the Singing of the Magnolia Warbler." *Wilson Bulletin* 39 (December 1927): 236–37.

"Pileated Woodpeckers Wintering in Cleveland County, Oklahoma." *The Auk* 44 (January 1927): 103.

"Seasonal Fluctuations in Bird Life in Central Oklahoma." *The Condor* 29 (May 1927): 144–49.

"September Nesting of Mourning Doves in Norman in 1925." *Proceedings of the Oklahoma Academy of Science* 6 (January 1927): 79–80.

"Some New Nesting Records in Cleveland County in 1925 and 1926: The Bird Life of a Forty Acre Tract in Central Oklahoma." *Proceedings of the Oklahoma Academy of Science* 7 (1927): 72–74.

Sunday Oklahoman (Oklahoma City, OK), June 19, 1927, through August 1927 [articles on various birds].

Nice, M. M., and L. B. Nice. "Christmas Bird Census from Norman, Oklahoma." *Bird-Lore* 29 (February 1927): 46.

1928

"Late Nesting of Indigo Buntings and Field Sparrows in Southeastern Ohio." *The Auk* 45 (January 1928): 102.

"Magnolia Warblers in Pelham, Massachusetts." *Wilson Bulletin* 40 (December 1928): 252–53.

"The Morning Twilight Song of the Crested Flycatcher." *Wilson Bulletin* 40 (December 1928): 255.

"Song Sparrows and Their Territories." *Proceedings of the Ohio Academy of Science* 8 (pt. 7): 386.

Nice, M. M., and L. B. Nice. "Christmas Census from Columbus, Ohio." *Bird-Lore* 30 (February 1928): 52.

1929

"Domestic Pigeons Nest Hunting on a Mountain Top." *The Auk* 46 (October 1929): 543–44.

"The Fortunes of a Pair of Bell Vireos." *The Condor* 31 (January 1929): 13–18.

"The Harris Sparrow in Central Oklahoma." *The Condor* 31 (March 1929): 57–61.

Letter on "Just One Baby." *Birth Control Review,* May 1929.

"Some Cowbird Experience in Columbus, Ohio." *Wilson Bulletin* 41 (March 1929): 42.

"Some Observations on the Nesting of a Pair of Yellow-Crowned Night Herons." *The Auk* 46 (April 1929): 170–76.

"Some Weights of Mourning Doves in Captivity." *The Auk* 46 (April 1929): 233–34.

"Vocal Performances of the Rock Sparrow in Oklahoma." *The Condor* 31 (November 1929): 248–49.

Nice, M. M., and L. B. Nice. "Christmas Bird Census from Columbus, Ohio." *Bird-Lore* 31 (February 1929): 48.

1930

Biological Abstracts 4–5 (1930, 1931) [seven abstracts under Aves].

"Do Birds Usually Change Mates for the Second Brood?" *Bird-Banding* 1 (April 1930): 70–72.

"Experiences with Song Sparrows in 1929." *Wilson Bulletin* 42 (September 1930): 219–20.

"Five Song Sparrows Raised with a Cowbird." *The Auk* 47 (July 1930): 419–20.

"Observations at a Nest of Myrtle Warblers." *Wilson Bulletin* 42 (March 1930): 60–61.

"Song Sparrows and Second Mates." *Oölogist* 47 (August 1930): 95.

"Spring Arrivals of Song Sparrows in 1930." *Bird-Banding* 1 (July 1930): 140.

"A Study of a Nesting of Black-Throated Blue Warblers." *The Auk* 47 (July 1930): 338–45.

"The Technique of Studying Nesting Song Sparrows." *Bird-Banding* 1 (October 1930): 178–81.

Nice, M. M., and L. B. Nice. "Christmas Bird Census from Columbus, Ohio." *Bird-Lore* 32 (February 1930): 48.

1931

"Bad Habits of the Pheasant." *Iowa Bird-Life* 1 (June 1931): 25.

The Birds of Oklahoma. Rev. ed. Norman: University of Oklahoma Press, 1931.

"Egg-Laying Record of a Captive Mourning Dove." *The Condor* 33 (July 1931): 148–50.

"Eight-Mile Censuses in 1927." *The Condor* 31 (March 1931): 29.

"Five Little Migrant Shrikes." *Wilson Bulletin* 43 (June 1931): 149–50.

"Nesting Success of a Song Sparrow Population in 1930." *Ohio Journal of Science* 31 (July 1931): 261–62.

"Notes on the Twilight Songs of the Scissor-Tailed and Crested Flycatchers." *The Auk* 4 (January 1931): 123–25.

"Returns of Song Sparrows in 1931." *Bird-Banding* 2 (July 1931): 89–98.

"A Study of Two Nests of the Ovenbird." *The Auk* 48 (April 1931): 215–28.

1932

"An Analysis of the Conversation of Children and Adults." *Child Development* 3 (September 1932): 240–46.

"Bissonnette's Experiments on the Modification of the Sexual Cycle in Starlings." *Bird-Banding* 3 (April 1932): 79–80.

"The Cowbird as Bait for the Capture of Its Foster Parents." *The Auk* 50 (January 1932): 120.

"Female Quail 'Bobwhiting.'" *The Auk* 50 (January 1932): 97.

"Habits of the Blackburnian Warbler in Pelham, Massachusetts." *The Auk* 49 (January 1932): 92–93.

"Measurements of White-Throated and Other Sparrows to Determine Sex." *Bird-Banding* 3 (January 1932): 30–31.

"Observations on the Nesting of the Blue-Gray Gnatcatcher." *The Condor* 34 (January 1932): 18–22.

"Observations on Two Nests of the Black-Throated Green Warbler." *Ohio Journal of Science* 32 (July 1932): 321.

"The Song Sparrow Breeding Season of 1931." *Bird-Banding* 3 (April 1932): 45–50.

Nice, L. B., and M. M. Nice. "A Study of Two Nests of the Black-Throated Green Warbler. Part 1." *Bird-Banding* 3 (1932): 30–31.

———. "A Study of Two Nests of the Black-Throated Green Warbler. Part 2. Chronicle of the August Nest." *Bird-Banding* 3 (1932): 157–72.

1933

"Birds in October." Radio talk given over station WOSU, October 6, 1933. Transcript in Mount Holyoke Archives.

"A Child's Attainment of the Sentence." *Pedagogical Seminary and Journal of Genetic Psychology* 42 (1933): 216–24.

"Experiments with the Terragraph on the Activities of Nesting Birds by Josef Bussmann." *Bird-Banding* 4 (January 1933): 33–40. [Translated from German by Nice.]

"From Ohio to New Mexico." Radio talk given over station WOSU, October 1933. Transcript in Mount Holyoke Archives.

"Locating Returned Song Sparrows Banded as Nestlings." *Bird-Banding* 4 (January 1933): 33–40.

"Methods of Capturing Birds at the Ornithological Station of Castel Fusano, Italy by Francesco Chigi." *Bird-Banding* 4 (April 1933): 59–67. [Translated from Italian by Nice.]

"Migratory Behavior in Song Sparrows." *The Condor* 35 (November 1933): 219–24.

"Nesting Success during Three Seasons in a Song Sparrow Population." *Bird-Banding* 4 (July 1933): 119–31.

"Relations between the Sexes in Song Sparrows." *Wilson Bulletin* 45 (June 1933): 51–59.

"Robins and Carolina Chickadees Remating." *Bird-Banding* 4 (July 1933): 157.

"Some Ornithological Experiences in Europe." *Bird-Banding* 4 (July 1933): 147–54.

"Summer Birds of Pelham., Massachusetts." *Bulletin of the Massachusetts Audubon Society* 17 (November 1933): 13–15.

"The Theory of Territorialism and Its Development." *Fifty Years' Progress of American Ornithology, 1883–1933* (1933): 89–100.

"Winter Range of Tufted Titmice." *Wilson Bulletin* 45 (June 1933): 87.

Zur Naturgeschichte des Singammers: Eine biologische Untersuchung mit Hilfe des Beringungsverfahrens. Part 1, Translated from the English manuscript by H. Desselberger. *Journal für Ornithologie* 81 (October 1933): 552–95. Part 2, *Journal für Ornithologie* 82 (January 1934): 1–96. [Translated by H. Desselberger from the English manuscript by Morse Nice.]

1934

"Dutch Studies on Nesting Birds." *Wilson Bulletin* 46 (June 1934): 130–32.

"A Hawk Census from Arizona to Massachusetts." *Wilson Bulletin* 46 (June 1934): 93–95.

"Les oixeaux et le 'cantonnement.'" *Alauda* 6 (September 1934): 275–97. [By Margaret M. Nice, translated by Georges de Vògüè and Henri Jouard.]

"The Opportunity of Bird Banding." *Bird-Banding* 5 (April 1934): 64–69.

"Poems: A Warbler in September in Central Oklahoma in January." *Oklahoma Live-Stock News*, December 7 and 14, 1933; February 2, 1934.

"Song Sparrows and Territory." *The Condor* 36 (March–April 1934): 49–57.

"Territory and Mating with the Song-Sparrow." *Proceedings of the Eighth International Ornithological Congress, Oxford* (1934): 324–38.

Zur Naturgeschichte des Singammers: Eine biologische Untersuchung mit Hilfe des Beringungsverfahrens. Part 1, *Journal für Ornithologie* 81 (October 1933): 552–95. Part 2, *Journal für Ornithologie* 82 (January 1934): 1–96. [Translated by H. Desselberger from the English manuscript by Morse Nice.]

1935

"American Egret and Anhinga Nesting in Oklahoma." *The Auk* 55 (January 1935): 121–22.

"Edmund Selous—an Appreciation," *Bird-Banding* 6 (July 1935): 90–96.

"The Eighth International Ornithological Congress." Reprinted from *Bird-Banding* 6 (January 1935): 29–31.

"The Fieldfare and Other Norwegian Birds." *Bird-Lore* 37 (March–April 1935): 112–13.

Letter to *Columbus (OH) Dispatch*, February 28, 1935.

"The Pole Trap in Belgium." *Bird-Lore* 37 (July 1935): 285.

"Some Experiences with Banded Cowbirds." *Inland Bird-Banding News* 7 (June 1935): 1.

"Some Observations on the Behavior of Starlings and Grackles in Relation to Light." *The Auk* 52 (January 1935): 91–92.

"Storks in Trees." *Wilson Bulletin* 47 (December 1935): 270–71.

Nice, M. M., and L. B. Nice. "Erythrocytes and Hemoglobin in the Blood of Some American Birds." *Wilson Bulletin* 47 (June 1935): 120–24.

1936

"Late Nesting of Myrtle and Black-Throated Green Warblers in Pelham, Massachusetts." *The Auk* 53 (January 1936): 89.

"The Nest in the Rose Hedge." *Bird-Lore* 38 (September 1936): 337–43.

"Uno and Una Return." *Bird-Lore* 38 (November–December 1936): 421–28.

"The Way of a Song Sparrow." *Bird-Lore* 38 (July 1936): 257–64.

"The White Stork as a Subject of Research." *Bird-Banding* 7 (July 1936): 99–107. [By Ernst Schüz, translated from German by Nice.]

1937

"Curious Ways of the Cowbird." *Bird-Lore* 39 (May–June 1937): 196–201.

"Discussion by Margaret M. Nice of a Nest-Building Male Song Sparrow by William E. Schantz." *The Auk* 54 (April 1937): 191.

Studies in the Life History of the Song Sparrow. I. A Population Study of the Song Sparrow and Other Passerines. Transactions of the Linnaean Society of New York 4 (1937): 1–247. Reprint, New York: Dover, 1964.

1938

"The Biological Significance of Bird Weights." *Bird-Banding* 9 (January 1938): 1–11.

"Die Bedeutung der Temperaturschwellen für die Aktivität des Singammers (*Melospiza melodia*)." *Der Vögelzug* 9 (April 1938): 91–94.

"A Famous Song Sparrow and his Eleven Wives." *Audubon Annual Bulletin, Illinois Audubon Society*, no. 28 (1938): 5–7.

"The Ninth International Ornithological Congress." *Bird-Banding* 9 (October 1938): 190–95.

"Notes on Two Nests of the Eastern Mourning Dove." *The Auk* 55 (January 1938): 95–97.

"Was bestimmt die Zeit des Geangsbeginns am Morgen beim Singammer?" *Der Vögelzug* 9 (July 1938): 184.

1939

"Observations on the Behavior of a Young Cowbird." *Wilson Bulletin* 51 (December 1939): 233–39.

"The Social Kumpan and the Song Sparrow." *The Auk* 56 (July 1939): 255–62.

"'Territorial Song' and Non-Territorial Behavior of Goldfinches in Ohio." *Wilson Bulletin* 51 (June 1939): 123.

The Watcher at the Nest. New York: Macmillan, 1939.

"What Determines the Time of the Song Sparrow's Awakening Song?" *IXme Congrès Ornithologique International Rouen* (1939): 249–55.

1940

"Birds of an Hungarian Lake." *Chicago Naturalist* 3, no. 3 (1940): 79–85.

Editorial. *Wilson Bulletin* 52 (June 1940): 127.

"Golden Orioles." *Audubon Bulletin (Chicago)*, December 1940, 1–5.

"A Spring Trip to Louisiana." *Indiana Audubon Year Book* 17 (1940): 6–13.

Nice, M. M., and Joost Ter Pelkwyk. "'Anting' by the Song Sparrow." *The Auk* 57 (October 1940): 520–22.

1941

"'Courtship Feeding' in Various Birds." *The Auk* 58 (January 1941): 56.

"Observations on the Behavior of a Young Cedar Waxwing." *The Condor* 43 (January–February 1941): 58–64.

"Robins and Cowbird Eggs." *Bird-Banding* 12 (January 1941): 33–34.

"The Role of Territory in Bird-Life." *American Midland Naturalist* 26 (November 1941): 441–87.

"Spring and Winter Hawk Censuses from Illinois to Oklahoma." *The Auk* 58 (July 1941): 403–5.

Nice, M. M., and L. B. Nice. "Christmas Census from Norman, Oklahoma." *Bird-Lore* 43 (February 1941): 43.

Nice, M. M., and Joost Ter Pelkwyk. "Enemy Recognition by the Song Sparrow." *The Auk* 58 (April 1941): 195–214.

1943

Studies in the Life History of the Song Sparrow. II. The Behavior of the Song Sparrow and Other Passerines. Transactions of the Linnaean Society of New York 6 (1943): 1–328. Reprint, New York: Dover, 1964.

1944

"Fall on Interpont." *Chicago Naturalist* 7, no. 3 (1944): 50–55.

"In Search of the Reed Bunting." *Chicago Naturalist* 7, no. 1 (1944): 6–10.

"New Bird Species Recorded for Oklahoma since 1931." *Proceedings of the Oklahoma Academy of Science* 24 (1944): 14–16.

"The Robins of Interpont." *Audubon Bulletin*, no. 50 (June 1944): 1–5.

"Spring Comes in January." *Audubon Bulletin*, no. 49 (March 1944): 1–5.

1945

"Adventures at a Feeding Shelf." *Chicago Naturalist* 8, no. 1 (1945): 8–12.

"Cowbirds Anting." *The Auk* 62 (April 1945): 302–3.

"How Many Times Does a Song Sparrow Sing One Song?" *The Auk* 62 (April 1945): 302.

1946

"Jan Joost ter Pelkwyk, Naturalist." *Chicago Naturalist* 9, no. 2 (1946): 26–35.

"Seven Baby Birds in Altenberg." *Chicago Naturalist* 8, no. 4 (1945–1946): 66–74.

"Weights of Resident and Winter Visitant Song Sparrows in Central Ohio." *The Condor* 48 (January–February 1946): 41–42.

1948

"Desert and Mountain in Southern Arizona." *Audubon Bulletin*, September 1948, 1–7.

"Song Sparrows at Wintergreen Lake." *Jack-Pine Warbler* 26 (October 1948): 143–51.

Nice, M. M., and Ruth H. Thomas. "A Nesting of the Carolina Wren." *Wilson Bulletin* 60 (September 1948): 139–58.

1949

"California Spring." *Audubon Bulletin*, June 1949, 1–7.

"The Laying Rhythm of Cowbirds." *Wilson Bulletin* 61 (December 1949): 231–34.

"A Plea for the Pencil." *Passenger Pigeon* 11 (1949): 98–101.

"The Question of Sexual Dominance." *Ornithologie als biologische Wissenschaft* (1949): 158–61.

1950

"Development of a Redwing (*Agelaius phoeniceus*). *Wilson Bulletin* 62 (June 1950): 87–93.

"Red-Eyed Vireos in Jackson Park." *Audubon Bulletin*, no. 73 (March 1950): 1–4.

1951

"A First Trip to Florida." *Passenger Pigeon* 13 (1951): 55–61.

Nice, M. M., and Constance Nice. "Potholes and Prairies." *Audubon Bulletin*, December 1951, 6–12.

1952

"Some Letters of Althea Sherman." *Iowa Bird Life* 22 (December 1952): 51–55.

Allen, Robert W., and M. M. Nice. "Study of the Breeding Biology of the Purple Martin (*Progne subis*). *American Midland Naturalist* 47 (May 1952): 606–65.

Nice, M. M., and Constance Nice. "Riding Mountain and Delta Marsh." *Passenger Pigeon*, Summer 1952.

1953

"A Baby Sora Rail." *Audubon Bulletin*, no. 84 (December 1953): 1–2.

"The Earliest Mention of Territory." *The Condor* 55 (November–December 1953): 316–17.

"On Loving Vultures." *Florida Naturalist* 26 (January 1953).

"The Question of Ten-Day Incubation Periods." *Wilson Bulletin* 65 (June 1953): 81–93.

"Some Experiences in Imprinting Ducklings." *The Condor* 55 (January–February 1953): 33–37.

1954

"Incubation Periods throughout the Ages." *Centaurus* 3 (1954): 311–59.

"Problems of Incubation Periods in North American Birds." *The Condor* 56 (July–August 1954): 173–97.

Nice, Constance. With sketches by M. M. Nice. "Bird Babes of Delta Marsh." *Nature* 47 (June–July 1954).

1955

"Blue Jay Anting with Hot Chocolate and Soap Suds." *Wilson Bulletin* 67 (March 1955): 64.

1956

"Four Generations of a Song Sparrow Family." *Jack-Pine Warbler* 34 (June 1956): 57–62.

Nice, M. M., Constance Nice, and Dorothea Ewers. "Comparison of Behavior Development in Snow-Shoe Hares and Red Squirrels." *Journal of Mammalogy* 37 (February 1956): 64–74.

1957

"Nesting Success in Altricial Birds." *The Auk* 74 (July 1957): 305–21.

1962

Development of Behavior in Precocial Birds. Illustrated with line drawings by the author. *Transactions of the Linnaean Society of New York* 8 (1962).

1963

"My Debt to Konrad Lorenz." *Zeitschrift für Tierpsychologie* 20 (1963): 461.

1979

Research Is a Passion with Me. Edited by Doris Huestis Speirs; forward by Konrad Lorenz; original drawings by the author selected from her published works. Toronto: Consolidated Amethyst Communications, 1979.

SELECTED REVIEWS

1923

Nice, M. M., and L. B. Nice. Review of *Experimentelle Untersuchungen über das Gefühlsleben des Kindes im Vergleich mit dem des Erwachsene,* by Helga Eng. *Pedagogical Seminary* 30 (March 1923): 99–101.

1925

Review of *Ruben and Ivy Sên,* by Louise J. Milne. *Sunday Oklahoman* (Oklahoma City, OK), November 15, 1925.

Review of *Wonder Tales from China Seas,* by Frances J. Olcott. *Sunday Oklahoman* (Oklahoma City, OK), December 13, 1925.

1926

Review of *Jungle Days,* by William Beebe. *Sunday Oklahoman* (Oklahoma City, OK), January 17, 1926.

Review of *Gold Tree and Silver Tree: A Book of Plays for Children,* by Katherine D. Morse. *Sunday Oklahoman* (Oklahoma City, OK), January 31, 1926.

Review of *The Wind,* by Dorothy Scarborough. *Sunday Oklahoman* (Oklahoma City, OK), May 23, 1926.

Review of *Parenthood and the Newer Psychology,* by Frank Richardson. *Sunday Oklahoman* (Oklahoma City, OK), September 26, 1926.

Review of *Education and the Good Life,* by Bertrand Russell. *Sunday Oklahoman* (Oklahoma City, OK), October 10, 1926.

Review of *The Biography of a Mind,* by Lorine Pruett. *Sunday Oklahoman* (Oklahoma City, OK), October 14, 1926.

Review of *Told Beneath the Northern Lights,* by R. F. Snell. *Sunday Oklahoman* (Oklahoma City, OK), October 24, 1926.

Review of *Joanna Godden Married,* by Sheila Kaye-Smith. *Sunday Oklahoman* (Oklahoma City, OK), December 19, 1926.

1927

Review of *Delineation of American Scenery and Character*, by John James Audubon. *Sunday Oklahoman* (Oklahoma City, OK), January 23, 1927.

Review of *Wonder Tales from Windmill Lands*, by Frances J. Olcott. *Sunday Oklahoman* (Oklahoma City, OK), January 30, 1927.

Reviews of *La main d'Allah*, by E. Bustros; *Servante*, by H. Duvernois; and *Un soir, à Cordone*, by George Grappe. *Books Abroad, University of Oklahoma* 1 (January 1927): 1.

Reviews of *Bison of Clay*, by Max Begouën; and *A Hind in Richmond Park*, by W. H. Hudson. *Sunday Oklahoman* (Oklahoma City, OK), March 20, 1927.

Reviews of *Athinéa: D'Athènes à Florence*, by Ch. Maurras; *La féérie Cinghalaise*, by Francis de Crosset; and *Orchester von Oben*, by Alfred Polgar. *Books Abroad, University of Oklahoma*, April 1, 1927.

1928

Reviews of *Nuits changeantes*, by H. Vauclerc; *Où le diable perdit ses droits*, by M. de Sablières; and *Koja's Wanderjahre*, by A. T. Sonnleitner. *Books Abroad, University of Oklahoma*, January 2, 1928.

Reviews of *Propos familiers*, by A. M. Bonnafous; *Le péan du noveau monde*, by Beatrice Chanler; *Ton amour et ma solitude*, by J. Leduic; *Le fils de l'étrangère*, by Marie le Mière; *Tels qu'ils furent*, by Edouard Estaunié; and *Heinz Hauser, ein Schulmeisterleben*, by Otto Anthes. *Books Abroad, University of Oklahoma*, April 2, 1928.

Review of *Der Leidende siegende Gott*, by Mary Roettger. *Books Abroad, University of Oklahoma*, July 2, 1928.

Reviews of *Rubé*, by R. de Navery; *Rasse*, by A. Harrar; and *An der Grenze des Jenseits*, by G. Meyrink. *Books Abroad, University of Oklahoma*, October 2, 1928.

1929

Reviews of *Dans l'herbe des trois vallées*, by H. Pourrat; and *Himmelfahrt*, by H. Bahr. *Books Abroad, University of Oklahoma*, April 3, 1929.

Review of *La vie des Chouettes*, by G. Guérin. *Books Abroad, University of Oklahoma*, October 3, 1929.

1930

Reviews of *Estelle et Mikon*, by A. Bailly; *Les gentilshommes de ceinture*, by A. Arnoux; *Le manteau de porphyre*, by A. Cahuet; *L'école des femmes*, by A. Gide; *Soleil de Grasse*, by F. de Miomandre; and *Mensch und Tier*, by H. Poppelbaum. *Books Abroad, University of Oklahoma*, January 4, 1930.

Reviews of *Der schmied Roms*, by Rumpelstilzchen; *Das schlafende Feuer*, by H. E. Busse; and *Sous le signe de la P.G. Lafolie de Guy de Maupassant*, by P. Voivenal and L. Lagriffe. *Books Abroad, University of Oklahoma*, April 4, 1930.

Review of *Êtes-vous fous*, by René Creuel. *Books Abroad, University of Oklahoma*, October 4, 1930.

1931

Review of *Das Glück um Brigitte*, by M. Kronberg. *Books Abroad, University of Oklahoma*, April 5, 1931.

1932

Reviews of *Das sterbende Moor*, by O. Erhart-Dachau; and *Service social à travers le monde*, by R. Sand. *Books Abroad, University of Oklahoma*, January 6, 1932.

1933

Reviews of *Störche*, by Siewert; and *Der Vogel Scharch*, by Heinrich. *The Condor* 35 (March 1933): 82.

Reviews of *Les oiseaux*, by R. de Brimont; *Nos bêtes amicales*, by J. H. Rosny, jeune. *Books Abroad, University of Oklahoma*, April 7, 1933.

Review of *Bijdrage tot de biologie ende ecologie van den spreeuw (*Sturnus vulgaris vulgaris *L.) gedurende zijn voortplantingstijd*, by H. N. Kluijver. *Bird-Banding*, October 4, 1933, 209–11.

1934

Reviews of pamphlets and articles: Swedish banding papers, Danish banding papers, recovery of marked birds in England, ringed birds taken in Bulgaria, and six American papers on birds. *Bird-Banding*, January 5, 1934, 49–54.

Review of *Vögelruf und Vögelsand*, by Hans Franke. *Books Abroad, University of Oklahoma*, January 8, 1934.

Review of *Das sterbende Moor*, by O. Ehrhart-Dachan. *The Condor* 36 (March 1934): 92.

Review of recent literature: migration studies, territory, life-history, ecology, longevity, birds and their food, conservation. *Bird-Banding*, April 5, 1934, 94–101.

Review of Dutch studies on nesting birds. *Wilson Bulletin* 46 (June 1934): 130–32.

Review of recent literature: migration studies, banding stations in foreign countries, bird weights, Longevity, effect of light, territory, cooperative ornithology; *Vogelkinder der Waikariffe* by F. Xaver and Graf Zedwitz. *Bird-Banding* 5 (July 1934): 137–46.

Reviews of banding papers, migration theories, ecology, censuses, longevity, weight, territory, bird behavior, cooperative ornithology, references, and abstracts. *Bird-Banding* 5 (October 1934): 195–204.

1935

Reviews of *Aves*, by E. Stresemann; *Life of the Rook*, by G. K. Yeates; *Quest for Birds*, by W. K. Richmond; *Bird City*, by E. A. McIlhenny; and *Eskimo Year. A Naturalist's Adventure in the far North*, by G. M. Sutton. *Bird-Banding* 6 (January 1935): 37–44.

Review of *A Guide to Bird Song*, by A. A. Saunders. *Bird-Lore* 37 (May 1935): 208.

Reviews of *The Behaviour of Animals*, by E. S. Russell; *Auf stillen Pfaden*, by W. von Sanden; and *The Hawks of North America*, by J. B. May. *Bird-Banding* 6 (July 1935): 107–16.

Review of "The Kumpan in the Bird's World: The Fellow-Member of the Species as Releasing Factors of Social Behavior," by Konrad Lorenz. *Bird-Banding* 6 (1935): 113–114, 146–147.

Review of *Tiger und Mensch*, by B. Berg. *Books Abroad, University of Oklahoma* 9 (Summer 1935): 314–15.

Review of *Wild Birds at Home*, by F. H. Herrick. *Bird-Banding* 6 (December 1935): 140–48.

1936

Reviews of *Fauna of the National Parks of the United States*, by G. M. Wright; *Michigan Waterfowl Management*, by M. D. Pirnie; *The Bird Book*, by N. Blanchan; and *Bird and Animal Paintings and Birds of the States*, by R. B. and C. Horsfall. *Bird-Banding* 7 (January 1, 1936).

Reviews of *Distribution of the Breeding Birds of Ohio*, by L. E. Hicks; *The Juvenal Plumage and Postjuvenal Molt in Several Species of Michigan Sparrows*, by G. M. Sutton; *Bird Portraits in Color*, by T. S. Roberts; *Bird Flight*, by G. Aymar; *Dwellers of the Silences*, by A. Sprunt Jr.; and *Oceanic Birds of South America*, by R. C. Murphy. *Bird-Banding* 7 (April 1936): 88–97.

Reviews of *Birds of America*, edited by T. G. Pearson; *Birds of the Green Belt and the Country around London*, by R. M. Lockley; *How to Know British Birds*, by N. H. Joy; and *Every Garden a Bird Sanctuary*, by E. L. Turner. *Bird-Banding* 7 (July 1936): 130–38.

Review of *Ethics of Egg-Collecting*, by E. Parker; *The American Woodcock*, by O. S. Pettingill Jr.; *Birds in the Wilderness*, by G. M. Sutton; and *Preparation of Scientific and Technical Papers*, by S. F. Trelease and E. S. Yule. *Bird-Banding* 7 (October 1936): 173–84.

Review of *La vie des libellules*, by J. Rostand. *Books Abroad, University of Oklahoma* 10 (Winter 1936): 50.

1937

Reviews of *More Songs of Wild Birds*, by A. R. Brand; *Songs of Wild Birds*, by E. M. Nicholson and L. Koch; *Bird Migration: A Short Account*, by A. I. Thomson; *Green Laurels: The Lives and Achievements of the Great Naturalists*, by D. C. Peattie; and *Deserts on the March*, by P. B. Sears. *Bird-Banding* 8 (January 1937): 35–44.

Reviews of *Adventures in Bird Protection*, by T. G. Pearson; *Vertebrate Animals of Point Lobos Reserve, 1934–35*, by J. Grinnell and J. M. Linsdale; *Cleveland Nature Trails*, by A. B. Williams; and *The Distribution and Habits of Madagascar Birds*, by A. L. Rand. *Bird-Banding* 8 (July 1937): 127–38.

Reviews of *Bird Behavior*, by F. B. Kirkman; *Handbuch der deutschen Vogelkunde*, by G. Niethammer; *Concord River*, by William Brewster; *Crooked Bill: Life of a Quail*, by I. H. Johnston; *The Natural History of Magpies*, by J. Linsdale; *A Survey of Resident Game and Furbearers of Missouri*, by P. Bennitt and O. Nagel; *Rund um den Kranich*, by G. Hoffman; and *Ecological Animal Geography*, by R. Hesse, W. C. Allee, and K. P. Schmidt. *Bird-Banding* 8 (October 1937): 177–89.

1938

Reviews of banding and migration, life history, bird behavior, song, ecology, population problems, and conservation; *Handbook of British Birds*, by H. F. Witherby et al.; *Logbook of Minnesota Bird Life 1917–1937*, by T. R. Roberts; *The Blue-Winged Teal*, by L. J. Bennett; *The Lore of the Lyre Bird*, by P. Ambrose; *Unter Säbelschnäblern und Seeschwalben*, by E. Schuhmacher; and *Bobwhite History*, by M. E. Bogle. *Bird-Banding* 9 (April 1938): 103–15.

Reviews of *A Herd of Red Deer*, by F. F. Darling; *Bird Flocks and the Breeding Cycle*, by F. F. Darling; and *Aus dem Leben der Vögel*, by O. Heinroth. *Bird-Banding* 9 (July 1938): 159–72.

1939
Reviews not listed in this bibliography appear in the *Wilson Bulletin*, September and December 1939; *Bird-Banding*, July–October 1939.

1940
Reviews not listed in this bibliography appear in the *Audubon Bulletin*, 1940; *Wilson Bulletin*, December 1940; *Bird-Banding*, October 1940.

1941
Reviews not listed in this bibliography appear in *Bird-Banding*, January, April, July, and October 1941; *Books Abroad, University of Oklahoma*, Summer 1941; *Wilson Bulletin*, December 1941.

1943
Review of *Ecology and Management of the Mourning Dove*, by H. Elliott McClure. *Wilson Bulletin* 55 (September 1943): 198–200.
Review of *A Guide to Bird Watching*, by Joseph J. Hickey. *Wilson Bulletin* 55 (December 1943): 249–50.

1944
Review of *The Canvasback on a Prairie Marsh*, by H. Albert Hochbaum. *Wilson Bulletin* 56 (September 1944): 183–84.

1945
Review of *The Illustrated Encyclopedia of American Birds*, by Leon A. Hausman. *Chicago Naturalist* 8, no. 1 (1945): 16–17.

BIBLIOGRAPHY

ARCHIVAL COLLECTIONS

Anson Daniel Morse Papers, Amherst College Archives and Special Collections.

Edward S. Thomas Collection, Ohio Historical Society.

Ernst Mayr Collection, Harvard University Archives, Pusey Library.

History of Science Collections, University of Oklahoma Libraries.

Margaret Morse Nice Collection, Western History Collections, University of Oklahoma Libraries.

Margaret Morse Nice Papers, Division of Rare and Manuscript Collections, Cornell University Library.

Margaret Morse Papers, Mount Holyoke College Archives and Special Collections.

BOOKS AND ARTICLES

Ainley, Marianne Gosztonyi. "Field Work and Family: North American Women Ornithologists, 1900–1950." In *Uneasy Careers and Intimate Lives: Women in Science, 1789–1979*, edited by Pnina G. Abir-Am and Dorinda Outram, 60–76. New Brunswick, NJ: Rutgers University Press, 1987.

Allen, Arthur A. "The Red-Winged Blackbird: A Study in the Ecology of a Cat-Tailed Marsh." *Proceedings of the Linnaean Society of New York*, 1914, 14–25, 43–128.

Allen, Garland. *Life Science in the Twentieth Century*. New York: Wiley, 1975. Reprint, Cambridge: Cambridge University Press, 1978.

———. "Naturalists and Experimentalists: The Genotype and the Phenotype." *Studies in the History of Biology* 3 (1979): 179–209.

———. "Teaching and Research: Bibliographic Essays." History of Science Society Annual Meeting, San Diego, CA, November 15–18, 2012.

———. "The Transformation of a Science: Thomas Hunt Morgan and the Emergence of a New American Biology." In *Organization of Knowledge in Modern America, 1860–1920*, edited by Alexandra Oleson and John Voss, 123–210. Baltimore: Johns Hopkins University Press, 1979.

Allen, Joseph Asaph. *A Seven Years' Retrospect: An Address Delivered by the Retiring President at the Eighth Congress of the Union, November 19, 1890*. New York: American Ornithological Union, January 1891.

Anonymous. Review of *Behavior of the Song Sparrow*. *Quarterly Review of Biology* 19, no. 2 (June 1944): 176–77.

Bailey, Florence Merriam. *Handbook of Birds of the Western United States*. Boston: Houghton Mifflin, 1902.

Bain, Alexander. *The Emotions and the Will*. London: John W. Parker, 1859.

———. *The Senses and the Intellect*. London: John W. Parker, 1855.

Barrow, Mark V., Jr. *A Passion for Birds: American Ornithology after Audubon*. Princeton, NJ: Princeton University Press, 1998.

Beyerchen, Alan. "What We Now Know about Nazism and Science." *Social Research* 59 (1992): 615–41.

Birkhead, Tim, Jo Wimpenny, and Bob Montgomerie. *Ten Thousand Birds: Ornithology since Darwin*. Princeton, NJ: Princeton University Press, 2014.

Bix, Amy. "'Chicks Who Fix': Women, Tool Knowledge, and Home Repair, 1920–2007." *Women's Studies Quarterly* 37, nos. 1–2 (Spring–Summer 2009): 38–60.

Blanton, Margaret, and Smiley Blanton. *Speech Training for Children*. New York; Century, 1919.

Boakes, Robert. *From Darwin to Behaviourism: Psychology and the Minds of Animals*. Cambridge: Cambridge University Press, 1984.

Boeree, George. "Psychology: The Beginnings." Accessed December 16, 2017. http://webspace.ship.edu/cgboer/psychbeginnings.html.

Bonta, Marcia Myers. "Margaret Morse Nice: Ethologist of the Song Sparrow." In *Women in the Field: America's Pioneering Women Naturalists*, 222–31. College Station: Texas A&M University Press, 1991.

Braun, Marta. *Picturing Time: The Work of Etienne-Jules Marey (1830–1904)*. Chicago: University of Chicago Press, 1992.

Browne, Janet. *Charles Darwin: The Power of Place*. Vol. 2 of *Charles Darwin: A Biography*. London: Jonathan Cape, 2002.

Burkhardt, Richard W., Jr. *Patterns of Behavior: Konrad Lorenz, Niko Tinbergen, and the Founding of Ethology*. Chicago: University of Chicago Press, 2005.

Burkitt, J. P. "A Study of the Robin by Means of Marked Birds." *British Birds* 17 (1924): 294–303.

———. "A Study of the Robin by Means of Marked Birds (Second Paper)." *British Birds* 18 (1925): 97–103.

Burnham, James. *Struggle for the World*. New York: John Day, 1947.

Butts, W. K. "A Study of the Chickadee and White-Breasted Nuthatch by Means of Marked Individuals." *Bird-Banding* 1 (1930): 149–68.

Chapman, Frank M., and Chester A. Reed. *Color Key to North American Birds*. New York: A. M. Eddy de Albion, 1903.

Chomsky, Noam. *Language and Problems of Knowledge: The Managua Lectures*. Cambridge, MA: MIT Press, 1988.

Clark, Hubert L. *Birds of Amherst and Vicinity*. Amherst, MA: J. E. Williams, 1887. Reprint, 2nd rev. ed., 1906.

[Conklin, Edwin G.]. "The Future of America: A Biological Forecast." *Harper's Magazine* 156 (April 1928): 529–39.

Cooter, Roger, and Stephen Pumfrey. "Separate Spheres and Public Places: Reflections on the History of Science Popularization and Science in Popular Culture." *History of Science* 32 (1994): 237–67.

Curie, Eve. *Madame Curie: A Biography.* Garden City, NY: Doubleday, Doran, 1938.

Dahlberg, Ann Elizabeth. "'Strong Sympathy and Fellowship': Margaret Morse Nice's Alternative Scientific Framework." BA thesis, Harvard University, 1995.

Darwin, Charles. "A Biographical Sketch of an Infant." *Mind* 2 (1877): 285–94.

———. *The Descent of Man, and Selection in Relation to Sex.* London: John Murray, 1871.

———. *The Expression of the Emotions in Man and Animals.* London: John Murray, 1872.

———. "Letter of Mr. Charles Darwin." In *Papers on Infant Development,* edited by Emily Talbot, 6–8. Boston: American Social Science Association, January 1882.

———. "The Mental Development of a Child." *Psychological Review,* October 1896, 115–31.

———. *On the Origin of Species by Means of Natural Selection.* London: John Murray, 1859.

Daston, Lorraine J. "British Responses to Psycho-Physiology, 1860–1900." *Isis* 69 (June 1978): 192–208.

Deichmann, Ute. *Biologen unter Hitler: Vertreibung, Karrieren, Forschungsförderung.* Frankfurt: Campus, 1992. Translated by Thomas Dunlap as *Biologists under Hitler* (Cambridge, MA: Harvard University Press, 1996).

Delacour, Jean. Review of *A Population Study of the Song Sparrow,* by Margaret Morse Nice. *L'Oiseau* 7 (1937): 655–56.

Dunlap, Julie. *Birds in the Bushes: A Story about Margaret Morse Nice.* Minneapolis: Carolrhoda Books, 1996.

"Eadweard Muybridge Biography." Biography.com. Updated April 7, 2017. www.biography.com/people/eadweard-muybridge-9419513.

Errington, Paul. Review of *Studies in the Life History of the Song Sparrow. I. A Population Study,* by Margaret Morse Nice. *Wilson Bulletin* 49 (December 1937): 308.

Evans, William. "On the Periods Occupied by Birds in the Incubation of Their Eggs." *Ibis* 33 (January 1891): 52–93.

Farber, Paul L. *Discovering Birds: The Emergence of Ornithology as a Scientific Discipline, 1760–1850.* Dordrecht, Netherlands: D. Reidel, 1982.

———. "The Transformation of Natural History in the Nineteenth Century." *Journal of the History of Biology* 15 (Spring 1982): 145–52.

Friedman, Herbert. Review of *Behavior of the Song Sparrow. Wilson Bulletin* 55, no. 4 (December 1943): 250–52.

Gentry, Thomas G. *Life-Histories of the Birds of Eastern Pennsylvania.* 2 vols. Philadelphia: Self-published, 1876–1877.

———. *Nests and Eggs of Birds of the United States.* Philadelphia: J. A. Wagenseller, 1882.

Gibbons, Felton, and Deborah Strom. *Neighbors to the Birds: A History of Birdwatching in America.* New York: Norton, 1988.

G. M. A. Review of *Studies in the Life History of the Song Sparrow. The Auk* 54, no. 4 (1937): 553–54.

Grant, John B. *Our Common Birds and How to Know Them.* Ann Arbor: University of Michigan Library, 1891.

Grinnell, Joseph. "Editorial Notes and News." *The Condor* 26 (May–June 1924): 115.

Haffer, Jürgen. *Ornithology, Evolution, and Philosophy: The Life and Science of Ernst Mayr, 1904–2005.* Berlin: Springer, 2008.

Haraway, Donna J. *Primate Visions: Gender, Race, and Nature in the World of Modern Science.* New York: Routledge, 1989.

Harvey, Joy. *"Almost a Man of Genius": Clemence Royer, Feminism, and Nineteenth-Century Science.* New Brunswick, NJ: Rutgers University Press, 1997.

———. "Darwin's 'Angels': The Women Correspondents of Charles Darwin." *Intellectual History Review* 19, no. 2 (2009): 197–210.

Harwood, Jonathan. "German Science and Technology under National Socialism." *Perspectives on Science* 5 (1997): 128–51.

Heinroth, Oskar. "Die Beziehungen zwischen Vogelgewicht, Eigewicht, Gelegegewicht und Brutdaur." *Journal für Ornithologie* 70 (1922): 172–285.

Heinroth, Oskar, and Kathe Heinroth. "Verhalten der Felsentaube (Haustaube) *Columbia livia.*" *Zeitschrift für Tierpsychologie* 6 (January–February 1949): 153–201.

Heinroth, Oskar, and Magdalena Heinroth. *Die Vögel Mitteleuropas.* 4 vols. Berlin: Bermühler, 1924–1933.

Herrick, Francis. *The Home Life of Wild Birds: A New Method of the Study and Photography of Birds.* New York: G. P. Putnam, 1905.

———. "Life and Behavior of the Cuckoo." *Journal of Experimental* Zoology 9 (September 1910): 169–233.

Hickey, Joseph J. Review of *Behavior of the Song Sparrow. The Auk* 61 (January 1944): 153–54.

Hicks, Lawrence. Review of *Studies in the Life History of the Song Sparrow I. Bird-Banding* 8, no. 3 (1937): 137–38.

Hodge, Clifton F. *Nature Study and Life.* Boston: Ginn, 1902.

Howard, Henry Eliot. *The British Warblers: A History with Problems of Their Lives.* London: R. H. Porter, 1907–1914.

———. *Territory in Bird Life.* London: John Murray, 1920.

Hrdy, Sarah Blaffer. *The Woman That Never Evolved.* Cambridge, MA: Harvard University Press, 1999.

Hutchinson, G. Evelyn. *An Introduction to Population Ecology.* New Haven, CT: Yale University Press, 1978.

Huxley, Julian. "The Courtship Habits of the Great Crested Grebe." *Proceedings of the Zoological Society of London* 84 (September 1914): 491–562.

Jackson, Jerome A. *George Miksch Sutton: Artist, Scientist, and Teacher.* Norman: University of Oklahoma Press, 2007.

Jonstonus, Johannes. *An History of the Wonderful Things of Nature.* London: John Streeter, 1657.

Kastner, Joseph. *A World of Watchers: An Informal History of the American Passion for Birds.* New York: Alfred A. Knopf, 1986.

Keller, Evelyn Fox. *A Feeling for the Organism.* San Francisco: W. H. Freeman, 1983.

———. *Reflections on Gender and Science.* New Haven, CT: Yale University Press, 1985.

Kevles, Daniel. *In the Name of Genetics and the Uses of Human Heredity.* New York: Alfred A. Knopf, 1985.

Kluijver, H. N. "Bijdrage tot de biologie en de ecologie van den spreeuw (*Sturnus vulgaris vulgaris* L.) gedurende zijn voorplantingstijd." PhD diss., Wageningen University. Wageningen, Netherlands: H. Veenman and Zonen, 1933.

Kohler, Robert E. *Landscapes and Labscapes: Exploring the Lab-Field Border in Biology.* Chicago: University of Chicago Press, 2002.

Kohlstedt, Sally Gregory. *Teaching Children Science: Hands-On Nature Study in North America, 1890–1930.* Chicago: University of Chicago Press, 2010.

Kolfalk, Harriet. *No Woman Tenderfoot: Florence Merriam Bailey, Pioneer Naturalist.* College Station: Texas A&M University Press, 2000.

Korzybski, Alfred. "General Semantics: Toward a New General System of Evaluation and Predictability in Solving Human Problems." In *Alfred Korzybski: Collected Writings, 1920–1950.* Englewood, NJ: Institute of General Semantics. www.gestalt.org/semantic.htm.

———. *Science and Sanity: An Introduction to Non-Aristotelian Systems and General Semantics.* Lancaster, PA: Science Press, 1933.

Kull, Kalevi. *Jakob von Uexküll's Theories of Life.* Albany: State University of New York Press, 2008.

Lehrman, Daniel S. "A Critique of Konrad Lorenz's Theory of Instinctive Behavior." *Quarterly Review of Biology* 28 (December 1953): 337–63.

Leopold, Aldo. Review of *Studies in the Life History of the Song Sparrow, Vol. I. A Population Study of the Song Sparrow. Canadian Field-Naturalist* 51 (November 1937): 126.

Levin, Miriam. *Defining Women's Scientific Enterprise: Mount Holyoke Faculty and the Rise of American Science.* Lebanon, NH: University Press of New England, 2005.

Levy, David. *The University of Oklahoma: A History.* Vol. 1, *1890–1917.* Norman: University of Oklahoma Press, 2005.

Lorenz, Konrad. "Der Kumpan in der Umwelt des Vogels: Der Artgenosse als auslösendes Moment sozialer Verhaltensweisen." *Journal für Ornithologie* 83 (1935): 137–215, 289–413.

———. "Die Angeborenen Formen möglicher Erfahrung" [The inborn forms of possible experience]. *Zeitschrift für Tierpsychologie* 5 (1943): 235–409.

———. "Durch Domestikation verursachte Störungen arteigenen Verhaltens" [Domestication-caused disruptions of species-specific behavior]. *Zeitschrift für angewandte Psychologie und Charakterkunde* 59 (1940): 2–81.

Lutkehaus, Nancy C. *Margaret Mead: The Making of an American Icon*. Princeton, NJ: Princeton University Press: 2008.

Macrakis, Kristie. *Surviving the Swastika: Scientific Research in Nazi Germany*. New York: Oxford University Press, 1993.

Maienschein, Jane, Ronald Rainger, and Keith R. Benson. "Were American Morphologists in Revolt?" *Journal of the History of Biology* 14, no. 1 (1981): 83–87.

Mayr, Ernst. "Bernard Altum and the Territory Theory." *Proceedings of the Linnaean Society of New York* 35–36 (April 1935): 24–38.

Mayr, Ernst, and Ernst Schüz, eds. *Ornithologie als biologische Wissenschaft. 28 Beitrage als Festschrift zum 60 Geburtstag von Erwin Stresemann*. Heidelberg: C. Winter, 1949.

McGavran, Helen. *Mice in the Freezer, Owls on the Porch: The Lives of Naturalists Frederick and Frances Hamerstrom*. Madison: University of Wisconsin Press, 2002.

Merchant, Carolyn. "George Bird Grinnell's Audubon Society: Bridging the Gender Divide in Conservation." *Environmental History* 15 (January 2010): 3–30.

Mill, John Stuart. *A System of Logic*. London: Longman, 1843.

Mitman, Gregg. *Reel Nature: America's Romance with Wildlife on Film*. Cambridge, MA: Harvard University Press, 1999.

Mitman, Gregg, and Richard W. Burkhardt Jr. "Struggling for Identity: The Study of Animal Behavior in America, 1930–1945." In *The Expansion of American Biology*, edited by Keith R. Benson, Jane Maienschein, and Ronald Rainger, 164–94. New Brunswick, NJ: Rutgers University Press, 1991.

Moore, Kathleen Carter. "The Mental Development of a Child." *Psychological Review* (October 1896): 115–31.

Neeley, Kathryn A. *Mary Somerville: Science, Illumination, and the Female Mind*. Cambridge: Cambridge University Press, 2001.

Nicholson, E. M. *How Birds Live*. London: Williams and Norgate, 1929.

Ogilvie, Marilyn Bailey. "Inbreeding, Eugenics, and Helen Dean King (1869–1955)." *Journal of the History of Biology* 40 (2007): 467–507.

———. *Marie Curie: A Biography*. Westport, CT: Greenwood Press, 2004.

———. *Searching the Stars: The Story of Caroline Herschel*. Gloucestershire, UK: History Press, 2008.

———. *Women in Science: Antiquity through the Nineteenth Century; A Biographical Dictionary with Annotated Bibliography*. Cambridge, MA: MIT Press, 1986.

Ogilvie, Marilyn Bailey, and Clifford J. Choquette. *A Dame Full of Vim and Vigor: A Biography of Alice Middleton Boring; Biologist in China*. Amsterdam: Harwood Academic, 1999.

Ogilvie, Marilyn Bailey, and Joy Harvey, eds. *The Biographical Dictionary of Women in Science: Pioneering Lives from Ancient Times to the Mid-20th Century*. 2 vols. New York: Routledge, 2000.

Osborne, Fairfield. *Our Plundered Planet*. London: Faber and Faber, 1948.

Podolsky, Scott. *Pneumonia before Antibiotics: Therapeutic Evolution and Evaluation in Twentieth-Century America*. Baltimore: Johns Hopkins University Press, 2006.

Popenoe, Paul, and Roswell Johnson. *Applied Eugenics*. New York: Macmillan, 1918.

Preyer, William Thierry. "Dr. Preyer's Observations." In *Papers on Infant Development*, edited by Emily Talbot, 44–48. Boston: American Social Science Association, 1882.

Pycior, Helena M., Nancy G. Slack, and Pnina G. Abir-Am, eds. *Creative Couples in the Sciences.* New Brunswick NJ: Rutgers University Press, 1996.

Reed, Chester A. *Land Birds East of the Rockies: Bird Guide, Part 2.* New York: Eddy de Albion, 1905.

———. *Water Birds East of the Rockies: Bird Guide, Part 1.* New York: Eddy de Albion, 1906.

Reingold, Nathan. "Definitions and Speculations: The Professionalisation of Science in America in the Nineteenth Century." In *The Pursuit of Knowledge in the Early American Republic: American Scientific and Learned Societies to the Civil War,* edited by A. Oleson and S. C. Brown, 33–69. Baltimore: Johns Hopkins University Press, 1976.

Rensing, Susan. "Women 'Waking Up' and Moving the Mountain: The Feminist Eugenics of Charlotte Perkins Gilman." *MP: An Online Feminist Journal* 4 (Spring 2013): 96–120.

Rossiter, Margaret W. "The Matilda Effect in Science." *Social Studies of Science* 23, no. 2 (1993): 325–41.

———. *Women Scientists in America: Struggles and Strategies to 1940.* Baltimore: Johns Hopkins University Press, 1982.

Rüting, Torsten. "History and Signficance of Jakob von Uexküll and of His Institute in Hamburg." *Sign Systems Studies* 32, no. ½ (2004): 54–55.

Saunders, Aretas Andrews. *Bird Song.* Albany: New York State Museum, 1929.

Schiebinger, Londa. *Has Feminism Changed Science?* Cambridge, MA: Harvard University Press, 1999.

Schielderup-Ebbe, Thorleif. "Beiträge zur Sozialpsychologie des Haushuhns." *Zeitschrift für Psychologie* 88:225–52.

Scott-Phillips, Thomas C. "Evolutionary Psychology and the Origins of Language." *Journal of Evolutionary Psychology* 8, no. 4 (2010): 289–307.

Selous, Edmund. "An Observational Diary of the Habits of Nightjars (*Caprimulgus europaeus*), Mostly of a Sitting Pair: Notes Taken at Time and on Spot." *Zoologist* 3 (1899): 388–402, 486–505.

Sherman, Althea. *Birds of an Iowa Dooryard.* Ames: Special Collections Department, Iowa State University.

Shinn, Milicent Washburn. *The Biography of a Baby.* Boston: Houghton Mifflin, 1900.

Sih, Andy, Alison Bell, and J. Chadwick Johnson. "Behavioral Syndromes: An Ecological and Evolutionary Overview." *Trends in Ecology and Evolution* 19, no. 7 (2004): 372–78.

Smith, Susan M. "Ducks Fight the Battle of the Sexes in Their Genitals." New Scientist. http://www.newscientist.com/article/dn18316-ducks-fight-the-battle-of-the-sexes-in-their-genitals.html.

———. "Henpecked Males: The General Pattern in Monogamy?" *Journal of Field Ornithology* 51 (1980): 55–64.

Spencer, Herbert. *Principles of Psychology.* London: Longman, 1855. Reprint, 1870.

Strasser, Bruno J. "Collecting Nature: Practices, Styles, and Narratives." *Osiris,* 2nd series 27 (2012): 303–40.

Talbot, Mignon. "*Podokesaurus holyokensis,* a New Dinosaur of the Connecticut Valley." *American Journal of Science* 31 (June 1911): 469–79.

Thackray, Arnold. "Natural Knowledge in Cultural Context: The Manchester Model." *American Historical Review* 79 (1974): 672–709.

Thompson, Barbara S. *My Life.* Eugene, OR: Press of Y2K, 1996.

Tiedemann, Friedrich. *Anatomie und Naturgeschichte der Vögel.* Vol. 1, *Zoologie.* Heidelberg: 1808–1814.

Tinbergen, Nikolaas. "An Objectivist Study of the Innate Behaviour of Animals." *Bibliotheca biotheoretica* 1 (1942): 39–98.

Tinbergen, Nikolaas, and D. J. Kuenen. "Über die auslösenden und richtungsgebenden Reizsituationen der Sperrbewegung von jungen Drosseln (*Turdus m. merula* L. und *T. e. ericetorum* Turton)." *Zeitschrift für Tierpsychologie* 3 (1939): 37–60.

Tolman, Edward Chase. *Purposive Behavior in Animals and Men.* New York: Century, 1932.

Trautman, Milton B. "In Memoriam: Margaret Morse Nice." *The Auk* 94 (July 1977): 430–44.

Tuchman, Arleen Marcia. "Institutions and Disciplines: Recent Work in the History of German Science." *Journal of Modern History* 69 (1997): 298–319.

Uexküll, Jakob von, and Georg Kriszat. *Streifzüge durch die Umwelten von Tieren und Menschen: Ein Bilderbuch unsichtbarer Welten.* Berlin: J. Springer, 1934.

Van Tyne, Josselyn. Review of *Behavior of the Song Sparrow. American Naturalist* 78, no. 774 (January–February 1944): 83–84.

Vogt, William. *Road to Survival.* New York: William Sloane Associates, 1948.

Welker, Robert H. "Miller, Olive Thorne." In *Notable American Women,* edited by Edward T. James, 543–45. Cambridge, MA: Belknap Press of Harvard University Press, 1971.

Williams, Laidlaw. Review of *Behavior of the Song Sparrow. Bird-Banding* 15, no. 1 (January 1944): 41–43.

Wright, Mabel Osgood. *Birdcraft: A Field Book of Two Hundred Song, Game, and Water Birds.* New York: Macmillan, 1897.

———. *The Friendship of Nature: A New England Chronicle of Birds and Flowers.* Edited by Daniel J. Philippon. Baltimore: Johns Hopkins University Press, 1999.

INDEX